ACTIVATED
for MINISTRY

HOW TO RELEASE GOD-GIVEN
IDENTITY & DESTINY IN THE
BELIEVER'S LIFE

KJELL-ROAR JOHANSEN

ACTIVATED FOR MINISTRY

All Scripture quotations, unless otherwise indicated, are taken from the Holy Bible, New International Version®, NIV® Copyright © 1973, 1978, 1984, 2011 by Biblica, Inc.™ Used by permission of Zondervan. All rights reserved worldwide.

Scripture quotations marked ESV are from The ESV® Bible (The Holy Bible, English Standard Version®), copyright © 2001 by Crossway, a publishing ministry of Good News Publishers. They are used by permission. All rights reserved.

Scripture quotations marked NLT are taken from the Holy Bible, New Living Translation, copyright © 1996, 2004, 2015 by Tyndale House Foundation. Used by permission of Tyndale House Publishers, a Division of Tyndale House Ministries, Carol Stream, Illinois 60188. All rights reserved.

Scripture quotations marked NASB taken from the NEW AMERICAN STANDARD BIBLE®, Copyright © 1960, 1962, 1963, 1968, 1971, 1972, 1973, 1975, 1977, 1995 by The Lockman Foundation. Used by permission.

Scripture quotations marked "MSG" or "The Message" are taken from The Message. Copyright 1993, 1994, 1995, 1996, 2000, 2001, 2002. Used by permission of NavPress Publishing Group.

Scripture quotations marked "BSB" are taken from The Holy Bible, Berean Study Bible, BSB. Copyright ©2016, 2018 by Bible Hub. Used by Permission. All Rights Reserved Worldwide.

Scripture and/or notes quoted by permission. Quotations designated (NET) are from the NET Bible® copyright ©1996-2016 by Biblical Studies Press, L.L.C. All rights reserved.

Details in some stories have been omitted or changed to protect the identities of the persons involved.

"Let us honour the blood of Jesus Christ every moment of our lives, and we will be sweet in our souls."
William J. Seymour, the Azusa Street Revival

Copyright © 2023 by Kjell-Roar Johansen

Copyright © Illustrations by Kjell-Roar Johansen

All rights reserved. Printed in the United Kingdom.

Published in the United Kingdom by Kratos Publishers. Last updated November 2023.

Author's website: www.activatedforministry.co.uk

Genre: Non-fiction, Christian Faith, Discipleship & Fivefold Ministry

ISBN: 979-8-3663-7151-3

For Harald Dysjeland,
a Methodist minister whose godly example and remarkable Bible teaching
made a deep and lasting impact on my life.

As my pastor, he was an apostle who believed in me and encouraged me
to explore God's calling to ministry.

So Christ himself gave the apostles, the prophets, the evangelists, the pastors and teachers, to equip his people for works of service, so that the body of Christ may be built up until we all reach unity in the faith and in the knowledge of the Son of God and become mature, attaining to the whole measure of the fullness of Christ.

Ephesians 4:11-13 NIV

Endorsements

I can highly recommend this book to you. In fact, it is 10 books of revelation and truth put into one book.

God has taken KR through the fire, and these truths and mysteries have been revealed to him by the Lord. I love his heart and the time it has taken him to put these precious insights into this book.

May the Lord bless you as you read it.

Richest blessings,

Pastor Ian McCormack (aka The Jellyfishman)
www.aglimpseofeternity.org

I would definitely recommend this book to you. I have a passion for the 'fivefold ministry', and I have loved reading not only KR's thoughts and revelations on the subject, but I have also enjoyed the fact that I know that his wisdom on this subject has come from many years of serving the Lord and being tested in the fire.

KR has a style of writing that is easy to read and which draws you willingly into the hugely valuable truths in this book.

Pastor Pip Earl, His House
www.hishouse.online

Acknowledgements

Life consists of small but significant moments and wondrously unfolds within the community of family, friends and neighbours. Most definitely, workplace, school and church are significant contributors to a fulfilling and purpose-driven existence. In the process of writing this book, there are people I want to acknowledge:

My wife, and best companion, Jane, you are by far the bravest and most remarkable woman I know. Your vulnerability is impressive, your resilience is fierce, and your love for people is unrivalled.

My two daughters, Anja and Lina, whose honesty and creativity I think the world of. You always put up with my crazy stunts and terrible dad jokes. I am proud to be your father.

Adesola Olagundoye, my dear friend and publisher of this book. Thank you for all your valuable feedback and support on my journey as an author. In a post-pandemic era, our ongoing conversation about life and ministry has been a real lifeline to me.

Sam Rogers, a huge thank you for your brilliant editing and proofreading skills. Your insightful commentaries about the book's topics were very much appreciated.

Ian McCormack, for being a great role model as an apostolic father in the Body of Christ, both to the UK and internationally. You are infectious in your passion for the Kingdom and love for people.

My precious network of friends and leaders of HTB - Holy Trinity Brompton - and His House, London. These two incredible churches keep me accountable weekly and inspire me in my walk with the Lord.

All my friends and churches in Norway and Sweden, dear people who have been an important part of my life and ministry.

Contents:

Endorsements 5

Acknowledgements 6

Contents 7

Introduction by the author 9

Prophetic vision & calling 13

Chapter 1 Prophetic purpose 15

Chapter 2 Prophetic process 31

Chapter 3 Prophetic perseverance 61

Chapter 4 Prophetic patterns 87

Chapter 5 Prophetic privileges 103

Chapter 6 Prophetic perspective 141

Chapter 7 Prophetic principles 159

Chapter 8 Prophetic presence 183

Chapter 9 Prophetic power tools 215

Chapter 10 Prophetic pathfinders 233

Chapter 11 Prophetic partners 271

Chapter 12 Prophetic power prayers 287

FIVEFOLD - MINISTRY
5

Introduction

I have written this book out of the Father's desire for us, his children, to flourish in the callings and gifts he has blessed us with. From the beginning of Creation, God devised and perfected a plan: *"For he chose us in him before the creation of the world to be holy and blameless in his sight. In love he predestined us for adoption to sonship through Jesus Christ, in accordance with his pleasure and will— to the praise of his glorious grace, which he has freely given us in the One he loves."* (Eph. 1:4-6 NIV). Our heavenly Father wanted us to experience his saving grace, so we could follow Christ faithfully. Being predestined to glory, he called us to reflect his purposes on earth, to truly know him and to love him. When we become disciples of Jesus Christ, we lead by example as ministers of God's grace. This is why I feel the urge to teach about the fivefold offices or the ministry gifts. God gave the gifts to his [1]church for the equipping of the saints. The apostolic and prophetic offices seem instrumental in releasing identity and destiny into all of God's children. In the book, I use a lot of time and effort to clarify the function of these two specific ministry gifts in relation to the rest of the fivefold offices. While exploring the various topics, I hope you will be blessed by some empowering truths about Spirit-filled ministry.

My goal is to present my insights in a biblical and relevant way. I mainly use the terminology *apostolic* and *prophetic* to describe the main functions of these offices, in keeping with New Testament revelation. I try to show how believers can respond to God's calling and get activated for ministry in his kingdom.

A ministry gift is not fashioned as a means to an end in itself but as a divine tool to equip and mature believers. The spiritual gifts were given by Christ to his Church, which is his earthly Body, the House of his glorious presence. The church is far more than a brick-and-mortar facility; it's distinctly defined as an organic and dynamic formation: It's an assembly of God's elected people—representing Christ and his delegated authority in the spiritual dimension. Before anything else, we are called to minister the gospel of reconciliation between God and mankind. God wants the whole Body of Christ to be built up as a holy priesthood. The concept that we will

---

[1] **Church:** Church is *ecclesia* in the Greek New Testament texts. The translation should be assembly, or *congregation*. The eminent British Bible translator and linguist, William Tyndale (1494-1536), was martyred, as he refused to change congregation into 'church'. Church is commonly used today.

live to see an overcoming and reigning Church emerging on the earth before Christ returns is of great importance. What Paul prophesied was not meant to be a lofty idea—it was set forth as a reachable goal (see Eph. 4:13-15). We cannot organise or implement such a great enterprise through human endeavours or accomplishments. We utterly depend on God's grace in the process of being built into a house of living stones, a habitation for the Lord by the Spirit.

"As you come to him, a living stone rejected by men but in the sight of God chosen and precious, you yourselves like living stones are being built up as a spiritual house, to be a holy priesthood, to offer spiritual sacrifices acceptable to God." (1 Pet. 2:4-5 ESV).

"Consequently, you are no longer foreigners and strangers, but fellow citizens with God's people and also members of his household, built on the foundation of the apostles and prophets, with Christ Jesus himself as the chief cornerstone. In him the whole building is joined together and rises to become a holy temple in the Lord. And in him you too are being built together to become a dwelling in which God lives by his Spirit." (Eph. 2:19-22 NIV).

We are all called to minister the gospel of reconciliation between God and mankind.

We want to picture the full breadth, length, height and depth of Christ's love for his bride, the Church (see Eph. 3:18). As his children, we are relationally united and connected through Christ's matchless and sacrificial love. This kind of unity cannot be manufactured artificially. Because we were sealed with the precious Holy Spirit, it's exclusively the gospel that unifies us (see Eph. 1:13). Doctrines matter, however, subjective experiences must never be elevated over knowing the truth. I believe that what we lack in theological understanding can be obtained by love developed in us by the Holy Spirit. Revelation is supposed to deepen our relationship with the Lord, and faith is best displayed when expressed through our love for our King and each other. Before anything else, God invites us to be intimately rooted and grounded in his awesome love—mere head knowledge is not enough. I consider the Bible to be our main authoritative source, yet I believe in a friendship with its Author. Case in point: Any Bible teaching that fills us with theoretical ideas without amplifying our love for our beloved Saviour can't be wholesome. Although we experience it on the inside, we can't quantify or weigh Christ's marvellous love! I believe God will release his glory as never seen before through our union with him and as a community. The Father reveals, redeems and restores us, and he is intensely passionate and personal about it. To the world, he reveals himself by making us into the image of his beloved Son—to be his sacred dwelling place (see John 14:23, Rom. 8:29, Eph. 2:22). We are his Building, Body, Bride and Battle force (see Ephesians 1-6). How he longs for us to become a shining beacon of hope to the nations! (See Isa. 49:6).

Before anything else, we are called to be intimately rooted and grounded in God's love—mere head knowledge is not enough.

Once again, people will recognise Christ's disciples because of the way they love (see John 13:34-35). Laid-down lovers will bridge the gap between a loving, merciful Creator and a lost and hurting humanity. A powerful demonstration of the gospel is living surrendered God-infused lives, compelled by his truth and love. It's a new lifestyle where we share the bread of heaven, so people can taste and see that the Lord is good! (See Psalm 34:8). By faithfully declaring the gospel, we are unleashing its revolutionising power: God's kindness leads people to repentance (see Rom. 1:16, 2:4). God's ways are inherently supernatural and defy human reasoning. His ways are always good and completely righteous (see also Isa. 55:8-9). He manifests his resplendent glory through incomprehensible mercy (see Eph. 2:4-5).

I think that we will soon see the greatest shift in Christendom since the days of the Book of Acts. A roaring tsunami wave of revival, reformation and transformation is building up with a tremendous force and is about to hit the earth. God has shown me this repeatedly, and many prophetic voices all over the world have the same impression clearly imprinted on their hearts. This extraordinary move of God will be refreshing, restoring and awe-inspiring. It will put a healthy fear of the Lord back into the Church again. God will suddenly come to his temple in holiness and power (see Mal. 3:1). There is also a harvest of souls coming to the Church, which the Lord will add to both existing and future churches (see Acts 2:47). We are on the verge of this new era, inching closer day by day. We sorely need preparedness for the coming outpouring of his Spirit, lest the churches become passive or incapacitated. We risk missing the great opportunities that lie ahead of us unless we seek the Lord of Hosts for a mighty baptism of his fire and love. Being activated for ministry has never been more important than now.

While you work your way through this book, I encourage you to pray, ponder and be sensitive to the Holy Spirit. During the twelve chapters, I cover a lot of ground and recommend you take notes or highlight the parts that resonate with you. I pray you will be blessed and grow in the things of the Lord with a deeper understanding, determination and purpose than before.

—KR Johansen

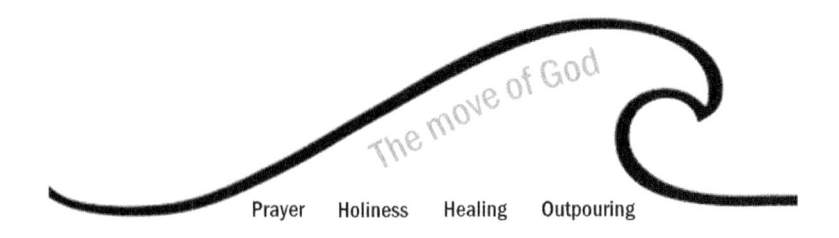

The move of God

Prayer   Holiness   Healing   Outpouring

The prophetic vision that brought our family to the United Kingdom:
During 2013-14, I received a vision from the Lord. I saw the map of Great Britain in a bird's eye view, and my attention was drawn to the Southeast part of England, mainly to Greater London. I saw a large, kneeling figure of a man. He had his back to Europe, with his face towards the West. It was before Brexit happened. Suddenly this kneeling giant was transformed into a golden lion. My impression was that this represents the Body of Christ in the United Kingdom. The Lord will send a great outpouring caused by fervent prayer. I sensed that this unparalleled move of God would affect British society and even influence the Royal Family. As a result of the prophetic vision—and other signs, we felt God's calling to move to London, UK, as soon as possible. After two years of prayer and preparation, we arrived in 2016. Prior to this, we had received several prophecies about how the Lord would call us to the nations. Like Paul, I don't want to disobey the vision from heaven (see Acts 26:19).

The lion is a symbol of the great mother nation of England, but it also represents the Lion of the tribe of Judah, our Lord Jesus. What once made this nation so great is its rich history and Christian heritage. Many of the greatest revivalists came from England and made their mark on numerous nations. In spite of its flaws, The British empire was at the core of the industrial revolution and at the forefront of abolishing the slave-trade worldwide. The English nation created outstanding legislation, built on Magna Carta, with excellence other countries envied and wanted to imitate.

In my vision, the Lion faced westward because this prophetic symbolism connects the United States with what happens in Britain. These two great nations have been interrelated for a very long time, both spiritually and culturally. I felt that what God is about to do would strongly impact North America. I can sense a weighty apostolic mandate resting over the UK: The mighty roar of the Lion of Judah will soon be released with a strength and force we haven't seen up to this point in time! The Lord is about to answer prayers going back several centuries and honour the covenant promises to his beloved and holy people. Let us passionately pray that all God's plans and purposes will be fulfilled without delay and culminate in the much-anticipated spiritual awakening and reformation. Father, raise up your sons and daughters!

"He will roar like a lion, and they will follow the Lord; when he roars, his children will come trembling from the west."

(Hos. 11:10 NET).

"And Jehovah will roar from Zion, and utter his voice from Jerusalem; and the heavens and the earth shall shake: but Jehovah will be a refuge unto his people, and a stronghold to the children of Israel."

(Joel 3:16 ASV).

CHAPTER 1 - PROPHETIC PURPOSE

Prophesy to the bones!

The hand of the Lord was upon me, and he brought me out in the Spirit of the Lord and set me down in the middle of the valley; it was full of bones. And he led me around among them, and behold, there were very many on the surface of the valley, and behold, they were very dry. And he said to me, "Son of man, can these bones live?" And I answered, "O Lord God, you know." Then he said to me, "Prophesy over these bones, and say to them, O dry bones, hear the word of the Lord. Thus says the Lord God to these bones: Behold, I will cause breath to enter you, and you shall live. And I will lay sinews upon you, and will cause flesh to come upon you, and cover you with skin, and put breath in you, and you shall live, and you shall know that I am the Lord." So I prophesied as I was commanded. And as I prophesied, there was a sound, and behold, a rattling, and the bones came together, bone to its bone. And I looked, and behold, there were sinews on them, and flesh had come upon them, and skin had covered them. But there was no breath in them. Then he said to me, "Prophesy to the breath; prophesy, son of man, and say to the breath, Thus says the Lord God: Come from the four winds, O breath, and breathe on these slain, that they may live." So I prophesied as he commanded me, and the breath came into them, and they lived and stood on their feet, an exceedingly great army. Then he said to me, "Son of man, these bones are the whole house of Israel. Behold, they say, 'Our bones are dried up, and our hope is lost; we are indeed cut off.' Therefore prophesy, and say to them, Thus says the Lord God: Behold, I will open your graves and raise you from your graves, O my people. And I will bring you into the land of Israel. And you shall know that I am the Lord, when I open your graves, and raise you from your graves, O my people. And I will put my Spirit within you, and you shall live, and I will place you in your own land. Then you shall know that I am the Lord; I have spoken, and I will do it, declares the Lord." (Ezek. 37:1-14 ESV).

God's plan is always to redeem, restore and remake. He wants to unleash what he originally intended for his creation. Our part is to cooperate and co-build with God, and that is exactly what we do when we prophesy: We listen to him and declare what he is saying. Everywhere we encounter spiritual dryness, God can give us a different perspective to see what he sees and activate the life he desires. Sometimes our lack of perspective seems to come from our lack of compassion for others. It is, therefore, vital to receive the Father's love for us. We will gain the correct prophetic perspective once we passionately pursue God's heart and his loving ways. How awesome it is to partner with the Father and declare how he sees us as his sons and daughters! God's powerful promises always contain purpose, and when we proclaim them, they begin a process of fulfilment. All exist at the sound of his voice. His Word never returns void but always accomplishes what he planned (see Isa. 55:8-11, Heb. 1:3, 11:3).

We are called to cooperate and co-build with God, and that's exactly what we do when we prophesy.

By nature, a prophetic message pulls us close to the Father's tender heart. Creation instinctively longs to get in touch with its awesome Creator. Being Christ's chosen representatives in this world, our fundamental prophetic task is to restore hope to individuals, groups and nations. The Lord resurrects hopes, dreams and destinies by rescuing us from the tombs of despondency and despair. Rising from the rubble of broken lives are the lost, hurt and disillusioned generations—raised to royalty in Christ. *"He raises up the poor from the dust; he lifts the needy from the ash heap to make them sit with princes and inherit a seat of honour. For the pillars of the earth are the LORD's, and on them he has set the world."* (1 Sam. 2:8 ESV). Prophecy powerfully activates our God-given abilities, breathing his life back into us, breaking off death and hopelessness. God is the life-giver, and without returning to him, there is no future or way forward. If we respond and receive his grace, he gives us a new and loving heart, filled with his Holy Spirit. When the Lord resurrects and restores us, he remodels us and positions us in the land of promise for us to possess it. He equips us with his saving grace to carry out his Kingdom's assignments and to access our inheritance in heavenly places (see Eph. 1:3).

When we share prophetic words, it's important to be prompted by God's Spirit without being swept away by emotional impulses. Charismatic Christians at times think they prophesy when they share some random words or figments of their own imagination because they haven't been well tutored in the prophetic by seasoned believers. They lack discernment, as their leaders have allowed them to serve quite superficially. I think it's because these church environments very often encourage contribution more than content (see Jer. 23:25-26, 28-29, 1 Pet. 4:11, 2 Pet. 1:21). How do we prophesy? We prophesy out of faith, built on Scriptural knowledge and revelation while paying undivided attention to God's Holy Spirit. So, we prophesy by faith and not by fantasy (see Mark 11:23, Rom. 12:6). God has often reminded me of a Bible verse or certain keywords related to a verse, in order to share his heart through prophecy, either in a small group or in a larger church gathering. I have also prophesied to individuals. I usually start to pray and bless people. If and when God gives me an impression through a word or a picture, I share it. I pray into it to see if God will show me more. It's astounding how a few but accurate words can unleash power leading to a Holy Spirit encounter. I try not to add to it or embellish it, and I speak plainly without exaggeration. I know that my additions or good intentions will not bring the Lord any glory. Oftentimes the individual or group will attest to the word and confirm it. Make sure to always prophesy out of a place of love by showing the Father's heart to others (see 1 Cor. 13:1-4). How incredible it is when God moves powerfully through prophecy, and people are profoundly touched.

As Christ's representatives, one of the most important prophetic tasks is to restore hope to individuals, groups and nations.

God is even more determined than you and me to reach his goals! He inspires others with hope by demonstrating his Word to us. When he blesses us, he lifts us up and favours us so people can observe his glory. We preach the gospel to our surroundings and display the full gospel concomitantly by showing proof of transformed lives. *"Once we, too, were foolish and disobedient. We were misled and became slaves to many lusts and pleasures. Our lives were full of evil and envy, and we hated each other. But—when God our Saviour revealed his kindness and love, he saved us, not because of the righteous things we had done, but because of his mercy. He washed away our sins, giving us a new birth and new life through the Holy Spirit. He generously poured out the Spirit upon us through Jesus Christ our Saviour."* (Tit. 3:3-6 NLT). What can be more sublime than being redeemed by Christ's precious sacrifice and fully restored to fellowship with our heavenly Father? By his Holy Spirit, we become love letters from him, habitations of prayer and praise, and the doorway to the House of God, which far exceeds a physical structure (see Gen. 28:17). In fact, we are the encounter with God that people are waiting for. We are the River of God that they are stepping into—the crisp air of heaven's breeze blowing into their jaded lives. When we radiate God's presence, people unknowingly enter the sacred zone of his glory. The beauty of holiness is observed and felt by others when our lives emanate love, wisdom and wholeness—the frequency and fragrance of Heaven, an incense pleasing to God and attractive to those who are being saved (2 Cor. 2:15-16 and Eph. 5:1-2).

We are the encounter with God that people are waiting for.

A vision of the River
Some time ago, I had a vivid vision during a prayer meeting. I saw a white riverbank teeming with people from all cultures and backgrounds and knew they represented the Church. They were all praising God for the River of his presence. The scene was buzzing with singing, clapping and dancing. They sang and shouted, "We praise you for the River! Hallelujah!" Despite the activity, they did all but one thing; nobody was actually plunging into the river! I was startled by it but realised that we, all too often, are merely spectators. Going through the motions, we gather but pass up the glorious invite to get inundated with God's presence and love. We forget to *contend* for breakthroughs in our meetings, as we have become insipid and unresponsive. If we are too afraid to 'get wet' and dive into his presence, we miss out on the fullness he represents. Replacing encounters with trivial entertainment is tragic. Some are moved by God during praise and worship, but others are quickened when the Holy Spirit makes a Bible verse come to life. In Ezekiel chapter 47, the angel measured the distance from the riverbank to be 1,000 cubits into the stream.

In the Bible, measurements represent inheritance, potential and what God allows. The curious prophet wasn't urged to be a plain *observer* but instructed to step into the river as an eager *explorer!* So are also we. Each time the angel measured, it was at a distance of 1,000 cubits. The number 1,000, in Hebrew אֶלֶף *elef*, constitutes the number of fullness and abundance. After the first 1,000 cubits, the water reached the ankles, representing walking in freedom. After another 1,000 cubits, the water reached the knees, representing effective prayer. After the third 1,000 cubits, the water swiftly reached the hips, representing the ability to be fruitful and to birth new life. Then, after the fourth 1,000 cubits, the stream of water reached up to the head, and one could no longer stand due to the river's depth and had to swim. The last and final stage represents total surrender and complete trust. The Father wants the Head alone, Christ, our Lord, to be visible. We find all four stages in the New Testament: *"until we all attain to [1]the unity of the faith, and of [2]the knowledge of the Son of God, to [3]a mature man, to [4]the measure of the stature which belongs to the fullness of Christ."* (Eph. 4:13 NASB). God's invitation is that we encounter Christ more and more until we wholly depend on his Spirit.

On another occasion, I had a different picture: God showed me a believer standing by the river with a wooden measuring rod, trying to measure the depth. The river was unplumbed, and the rod was immediately swallowed up. The interpretation is direct and simple. It's about God's fathomless love, the unsearchable mind of his Spirit, according to Eph. 3:20: *"... him who is able to do immeasurably more than all we ask or imagine, according to his power that is at work within us."* We also read: *"But it was to us that God revealed these things by his Spirit. For his Spirit searches out everything and shows us God's deep secrets."* (1 Cor. 2:10 NLT). Human endeavours fail to discern God's mind. We need his presence more than anything else on earth.

King David rejoiced in the Presence: *"You make known to me the path of life; in your presence there is fullness of joy; at your right hand are pleasures forevermore."* (Psalm 16:11 ESV). By entering his presence, all our needs can be satisfied. Jesus is the Gate to the Father and intimacy with him: *"I am the Road, also the Truth, also the Life. No one gets to the Father apart from me. If you really knew me, you would know my Father as well. From now on, you do know him. You've even seen him!"* (John 14:6 MSG). Before we enter Heaven, it's our daily privilege to enter his holy presence through this blessed Way. Jesus is the only way to God, the narrow road leading to life. After receiving salvation, we safely abide in him by immersing ourselves in his holy words, with prayer and thankfulness (see Matt. 7:13-14, John 15:7, Col. 3:16).

Running the race
My wife recently had an intriguing vision about running the race. She noticed a relay race, with each runner having a set distance to run before passing on the baton to the next runner in the team. Each runner must hand off the baton to their successor

within a defined zone, usually marked by triangles on the track. The second runner stands by on a predetermined spot and starts running when the first runner thumps a visual mark on the track. The runner has to use this kind of *flying start* in order to achieve a graceful transition, an action that must take place within the *change-over zone*. She observed how the incoming runner shouted to his teammate to get his immediate attention. The waiting runner was warming up, dressed in a matching outfit—jumping and stretching—yet he was totally unaware of his teammate. Being distracted, he didn't hear the wake-up call. He had no real sense of urgency and was unaware of the red alert. His lack of focus threatened to jeopardise the whole race! Let us stay awake and vigilant: It's a team effort where every member plays a pivotal role. In a change of seasons, we must be up and running and ready for the hand-off marking the next part of the race. Earlier generations are passing their torch of legacy to us. Don't remain stuck in the last season: The Lord says: "Move on! Get ready for the next phase."

In the [2]wilderness of Sinai, the Israelites failed to make the transition into the future the Lord wanted them to occupy. In the critical takeover zone, they disqualified themselves with their worry and unbelief. As a result, they fell behind and perished because they disobeyed his commands. Their distrust and defiance destroyed them. God later raised up their children as loyal champions of the faith. Guided by Joshua, it was the descendants that victoriously advanced towards their final destiny and destination. Interestingly, in Hebrew, our Saviour's name is identical to Joshua's. As [3]Joshua led Israel into their promised land, so also Jesus leads us into our inheritance.

Don't remain stuck in the last season: God says, 'Move on! Get ready for the next phase.'

---

[2] **My comment:** Also called the desert of Sin. By the grace of God, let us move out of the desert of our own sin and rebellion! An eleven days' journey took Israel 40 years because of their disobedience.

[3] **Joshua** - English version of Yeshua יֵשׁוּעַ, a shorter form of Yehoshua. Yoshia is another variant. Source: https://torahportions.ffoz.org/disciples/matthew/jesus-jeshua-joshua-yeshua-yeh.html

Sometimes the Lord gives a repeated invitation with the same words as before. He eagerly wants us to grasp the revelation of what he is about to do. When God tells us that the Promised Land lies ahead of us and that the last season's manna is about to cease, we must press on and cross over the border if we are to eat the food of the land. We live by the daily, fresh and divine bread of Heaven and not by the stale and uninviting bread of religious principles. The living Word of God is the true bread (see Matt. 4:4, 6:9-13). Traditions may satisfy the intellect but are never enough for a hungry heart. There is no time for reminiscing about the past. To win the race, we must abide in God's *now season* and stay devoted to Christ and each other (see John 15:17 and Heb. 12:2).

Sometimes God gives a repeated invitation with the same words as before.

Prophesied potential

The Christian life is about identity. The way we identify with Christ determines how we share in his nature. We must *"wake up to righteousness"* (see 1 Cor. 15:34). It's the literal translation of the first words of this verse. Satan has too long trapped many believers in a state of sin-consciousness, where they experience condemnation and shame. Many imagine they are still sinners, but now with the upgraded status of being a forgiven sinner. That assumption is not correct. We are now considered *righteous* and *holy* by God; we are no longer sinners by standing (see Rom. 4:23-24, 5:1). However, we have the duality of two worlds within us, one holy and one sinful. In retrospect, Paul called himself *"a chief of sinners"* (see 1 Tim. 1:15). Holiness is not denying the fact that all humans have weaknesses or struggle with sin. In fact, we don't trust in our own righteousness; we discard it as *"filthy rags"* (see Isa. 64:6). As overcomers, we rather choose to cling to the righteousness the Lord provided through Jesus' precious blood on the cross. Hallelujah! Both our self-righteousness and sin-consciousness were sorted by him. Hence living in obedience to the gospel is unthinkable without the power of the cross.

Seeing ourselves as dead to sin and alive to righteousness because of the cross is the ultimate game-changer. We rose again with Christ, in line with Romans 6. In fact, baptism is a symbolic act provided for us by God, helping us to acknowledge our new status in him. When we physically interact with the water, through baptism, we spiritually connect with the reality of the newness of life! I consider myself dead to sin but fully alive in Christ. I have incorporated my core identity as a born-again Christian. With resurrection life, the Holy Spirit convicts me of righteousness, just as Jesus promised. His grace is greater than my sin. No one, except Christ's Spirit, can make me ardently pursue the Lord more than sin. A grand-scale transformation requires a true miracle of the heart. It's only made possible by the redeeming power of the gospel (see John 3:19-21, Rom. 5:20-21).

Seeing ourselves as dead to sin and alive to righteousness because of the cross is a game-changer.

How can we be established in the things of God if we are not aware of his thoughts towards us? Dwelling on our sinfulness and shortcomings may create a pattern of self-sabotage, which over time undermines our God-given identity and destiny. Believing in the name of Jesus is believing in God's nature. We can't believe in whom he is without believing in who *we* are because of him. One reality depends on the other.

"But as many as received Him, He gave to them authority to be children of God--to those believing in His name." (John 1:12 BSB).

"God, for whom and through whom everything was made, chose to bring many children into glory. And it was only right that he should make Jesus, through his suffering, a perfect leader, fit to bring them into their salvation." (Heb. 2:10 NLT).

To experience true empowerment as God's children, we must first align ourselves with Heaven's realm. Alignment with our assignment will always cause God to pour his grace and power into our lives. When we obey, God acts! When the Lord called individuals in Scripture, the recurring pattern was often responses of protest, fear or unbelief. After Moses was commissioned, he told God a lame excuse: He could not stand before Pharaoh because he was speech impaired—although he was known to be a great orator (see Acts 7:22). Gideon claimed he was insignificant and the least in his house and family, a nobody. However, when God speaks, he doesn't always call the qualified, but he qualifies the called ones! Prophetic declarations of destiny release an impartation of grace to carry out our destiny, but this is always activated through obedience. When we acknowledge God's call, his Spirit releases the power to perform his word. Look at this sensational verse in Luke: *"For no word from God shall be void of power."* (Luke 1:37 ASV). The meaning of this is: *no freshly spoken word of God will ever be without power to perform itself.* What an amazing statement! Virgin Mary got a similar word by faith, and the Holy Spirit found fertile ground in her heart to plant the divine Seed of a miracle. At that specific moment, the Living Word was conceived within her womb (see Gen. 3:15). God tends to speak through the natural realm, and by paying close attention, we discover new layers of truths about his nature as he veils marvellous mysteries within the created world (see Exod. 3:1-5, Psalm 19:1-11, Isa. 45:15, John 1:1-3, 14; 3:3-13). The human species was created for the supernatural, yet too often, we interpret what our eyes see to a limited extent. Instead, we question God's ability and power to do what is *natural* to him.

Prophetic promise I

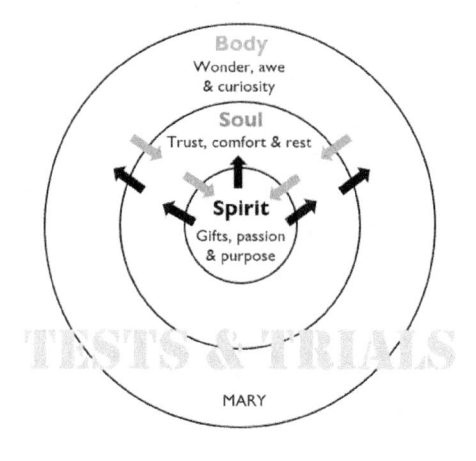

Body
Wonder, awe & curiosity

Soul
Trust, comfort & rest

Spirit
Gifts, passion & purpose

TESTS & TRIALS

MARY

By studying the wonders of nature, you will get an impression of how spectacular he is. He is *super* and *natural* at the same time! One of God's names is Wonder, given that miracles connect to who he is (see Isa. 9:6). His many names reflect variations of his nature. The famous saying "have you lost your marbles" means to lose one's mind. Of course, that rarely happens to us. Besides, it's more common that we *lose the marvels*—we tend to forget how awesome and mighty God's works are. When he reveals to us whom he thinks we are, we tend to react in disbelief because we are second-guessing ourselves. Still, whose report will we believe, God's report or our own? (See Isa. 53:1). Humility in the Kingdom is to approve what the Creator says about us. God's love is not proud nor boastful. It always rejoices in the truth and edifies others (1 Cor. 8:1; 13:6). Not seldom does mere self-deprecation talk down the reality of whom we have become in Christ Jesus through his redemptive work.

We were created for the supernatural, but too often, we interpret the natural to a limited extent. Instead, we question God's ability and power to do what is natural to him.

And Israel was brought very low because of Midian. And the people of Israel cried out for help to the [4]LORD. Now the angel of the LORD came and sat under the terebinth at Ophrah, which belonged to Joash the Abiezrite, while his son Gideon was beating out wheat in the winepress to hide it from the Midianites. And the angel of the LORD appeared to him and said to him, "The LORD is with you, O mighty man of valour." And Gideon said to him, "Please, my lord, if the LORD is with us, why then has all this happened to us? And where are all his wonderful deeds that our fathers recounted to us, saying, 'Did not the LORD bring us up from Egypt?' But now the LORD has forsaken us and given us into the hand of Midian." And the LORD turned to him and said, "Go in this might of yours and save Israel from the hand of Midian; do not I send you?" And he said to him, "Please, Lord, how can I save Israel? Behold, my clan is the weakest in Manasseh, and I am the least in my father's house." And the LORD said to him, "But I will be with you, and you shall strike the Midianites as one man.

---

[4] **YHVH** יְהוָה - the divine name, written as LORD in most translations. It occurs 6,827 times in TANAKH, or the Old Testament. That is far more than any other name used for the Lord. Within Judaism, Adonai or Hashem are the preferred terms used to replace YHWH. Later in the book we will look at its correct pronunciation, Yehovah, as new facts have come to light in recent years.

(Judg. 6:6, 11-16 ESV). Gideon is worth a closer look. We could expect him to leap for joy when God announced he was with him. But no! He certainly wasn't chuffed. The Lord said: *"God is with you, mighty warrior!"* Gideon questioned the message because it went beyond his understanding and felt so surreal. His internal search engine instantly responded: 'no match found'! If it had happened today, Gideon's response to God's call might have sounded like this: 'I have heard all the testimonies about revival. I have been praying, longing and hoping for it, but it didn't come to pass. You have abandoned us, and the enemy is harassing us. Our hopes are dashed.' Gideon's past was full of disheartening events. Grappling with lofty words of hope and a future was very hard. Israel was facing a national emergency daily as bands of raiders looted them, leaving them desperate and destitute. Gideon found himself in these dreadful circumstances when God called him. The angel of the Lord appeared to a rather suspicious Gideon while he was threshing wheat in the family winepress. Perhaps he was hiding, trying to secure the small leftovers of grain from the enemy's relentless blitz attacks? In this specific case, the winepress became a symbol of great transformation. The Lord managed to change a crestfallen Gideon by addressing his core identity. The Lord said, *"I am with you."* Then he said, *"Go in this your might"*. The first stage was: *"You are a mighty man of valour."* The second stage was: *"Now, act as if you are mighty"*. Acting it out required courage and faith. Israel's God said: "Go in your *prophesied* strength." What propelled Gideon to instantly use his gift? The catalyst was the spoken and weighty prophetic words. He had been empowered because *within the prophetic declaration lies the potential*. By hearing and heeding the voice of his living Word, our faith actively responds (see Rom. 10:17).

God transformed Gideon when he addressed his core identity.
Within the prophetic declaration lies the potential.

Despite God's bold declaration, Gideon had to actively engage and act upon the promise, a promise closely connected with his identity. Our devious *enemy* is an *identity thief*. He attempts to hide the truth about who you are in Christ: He aims to steal your identity, kill your testimony and destroy your legacy (see John 10:10). Purpose in your heart not to give in to the nagging voice that says you can't do what the Lord asks you to do and choose to trust in him instead. Shut out the enemy's countless lies and stay in alignment with your assignment. To feel unqualified or unprepared is normal. Once you move forward, you will receive power to perform your mission. *"But you will receive power when the Holy Spirit comes on you; and you will be my witnesses ..."* (Acts 1:8 NIV). *"The Holy Spirit, whom God has given to those who obey him."* (Acts 5:32 NIV). Equipping comes in two stages: **1)** by actively receiving power from the Holy Spirit; and **2)** by promptly responding to release his power. At that very moment, 'mission impossible' becomes possible. The sterling material great heroes are forged from comes from the crucible of crisis.

IDENTITY   TESTIMONY   LEGACY

The enemy is an ID thief: he aims to steal your identity, kill your testimony and destroy your legacy.

We will now take a look at another impressive hero of faith, Jabez. Not much is said about this struggling brother, but enough to embolden us to seek God for our own breakthroughs. All humans have similar choices when meeting adversity in life. Challenging situations can either be perceived as setbacks or divine set-ups! Jabez never blamed God—seeking to fulfil his destiny was his sole focus.

Jabez was more honourable than his brothers, and his mother named him Jabez saying, "Because I bore him with pain." Now Jabez called on the God of Israel, saying, "Oh that You would bless me indeed and enlarge my border, and that Your hand might be with me, and that You would keep me from harm that it may not pain me!" And God granted him what he requested. (1 Chron. 4:9-10 ESV).

Now Jabez called on the God of Israel, saying, "Oh that You would bless me indeed and enlarge my border, and that Your hand might be with me, and that You would keep me from harm that it may not pain me!" And God granted him what he requested. (v. 10 NASB).

Jabez cried out to the God of Israel, "Oh, that you would bless me and enlarge my territory! Let your hand be with me and keep me from harm so that I will be free from pain." And God granted his request. (v. 10 NIV).

Jabez called out to the God of Israel, "If only you would greatly bless me and expand my territory! May your hand be with me! Keep me from harm so I might not endure pain!" God answered his prayer. (v. 10 NET Bible).

Jabez means 'he makes sorrowful' or 'he that causes pain'. He probably spent most of his life trying to escape the meaning of his pitiful name. What agony! In Hebrew, his name is spelt with the four letters Yud-Ayin-Beit-Tzade יעבץ and pronounced *Yaa'vetz*. I am no Hebrew expert, but if we translate the symbolic meaning of each of the letters, we may get the following: *'The right hand of God gives perspective to the house of the righteous'*. And what a different perspective! The story of Jabez shows he had all the odds stacked against him. Despite all of this, the Lord turned his life around. The same principle is seen in Rom. 8:28, which says that *"all things work together for good to those who love God and are called according to His purpose."* Love is used often by God as a covenant expression. Love and trust produce obedience; a direct result of the Holy Spirit's work within us (John 15: 13-14, Phil. 2:13). Jabez, being a member of the prominent tribe of Judah, had a bright future carved out for him. However, Jabez had to contend for his change and maybe prayed for years. His pain wasn't just financial. Much like him, many come from dysfunctional families and have gone through hurt or abuse. But God is the [5]God of the turnaround! How we respond to tough situations in life is a general challenge. I like this [6]quote: 'You cannot tailor-make the situations in life, but you can tailor-make the attitudes to fit those situations.' What do we do when we stand on the precipice of despair? Do we partner with God to get restoration and second chances? Can we exchange a victim mindset for a victor mindset? At times, due to the situations we are facing, we tend to look at ourselves as victims. When that happens, it is quite tempting to go into 'survival mode', where we are sulking and focusing on ourselves. This propensity often comes from a sensory source of perception and can be difficult to escape. Self-

---

[5] **Charlotte Gambill** has written a wonderful book about this, called *Turnaround God*. Published: 24th September 2013 ISBN: 9780849921896 charlottegambill.com
[6] **Zig Ziglar Quotes,** www.ziglar.com

centred and fearful responses might also distract us from seeing the needs of fellow humans. But when we, gently assisted by the Holy Spirit, move towards a mindset of victory, we develop sturdy attitudes of thriving and reviving, receiving abundant life, championing, overcoming and conquering, being empowered by a superior and spiritual perception. Because we are God's children, his grace has granted us access to *"everything that pertains to life and godliness"* (see 2 Pet. 1:3). It lets us prophesy to our circumstances out of sonship and faith (see Mark 11:22-24 and 1 John 5:14).

Using Abraham as an example, Paul wrote: *"God, who calls those things which are not as though they were."* (Rom. 4:17). There are Christians who will interpret the verse as a name-it-and-claim-it passage—they think it puts us in the same category as God. That is taking things too far and isn't supported by Scripture. Indeed, God alone can create something from nothing. We can advance by boldly speaking what he has shown us through revelation, the very moment he activates faith inside us. Abraham faithfully trusted God's promise, softly leaning into the Father's heart. Each time he prayed or talked about it, he partnered with the oat. He was prophesying to his bleak circumstances. At first, he probably felt awkward but incrementally learned to see himself in light of the promise. For the unimaginable to happen, he trusted God. We are in *"Christ, the hope of glory"* (Col. 1:27), and Christ in us cannot be defeated.

It's all a matter of perspective and how we are discerning eternal realities. Christ is the Truth, our new reality. Our golden chance is to be sanctified in the reality of our Saviour, where we clearly see ourselves as forgiven, healed and provided for (John 14:6; 17:17, Rom. 12:2, 1 Cor. 1:30). As a majestic force, faith dreams with God and lets his Holy Spirit imbue our souls' imagination. Subsequently, what you can perceive with your spiritual eyes will manifest in the physical realm. Joel's important prediction about young men having visions and old men having [7]dreams make no sense unless we understand that inspired pictures are part of the language of faith and prophetic expressions (see Jer. 23:18, Joel 2:28, Heb. 11:27). Our source of

---

[7] **My comment:** I got this insight when I did a little study on words: In Hebrew, we have two words that rhyme, Shalom שָׁלוֹם (peace) and Chalom חָלוֹם (dream). The words only differ by one letter, their first letters are Shin and Chet. Chalom begins with Chet, which is connected to חַי *Chay* the force of life. Divinely inspired dreams are full of life and protect lives (see Gen. 20 and Job 33:14-18). When we act upon them, God can bring his Shalom - completeness, prosperity and peace.

spiritual greatness starts in the invisible, it's brewing and brooding in our spirits and minds. Acclaimed inventions saw the light of day through their creators' impressive imagination—they were sketched, engineered and finally manufactured. God, the Creator, unleashed the mighty force of life and spoke into existence what he initially imagined in his unsearchable mind: *"For he spoke, and it came to be; he commanded, and it stood firm"* (Psalm 33:9 ESV). It isn't about tricking our minds, but by faith aligning ourselves with God's sublime throne perspective. Do we really expect to live a blessed life if our thinking bows to the cursed reality of a sinner? A fearful mentality usually leads to defeat and demise, but faith and love are keys to unlocking vitality and strength.

Disappointment, resentment and bitterness prevent many believers from receiving their rightful inheritance and abundant life in Christ Jesus. If not immediately dealt with, the awful poison of unbelief will slowly seep through the unmended cracks of our soul's disillusionment and cause us much harm. Agreeing with these attitudes hardens the heart, distracts us from our calling to live a life of devotion, and crowds out the loving voice of God.

CHAPTER 2 - PROPHETIC PROCESS

Prophetic promises

A promise of greatness is optional until being activated by faith and obedience. The prophetic promise is a declaration and an invitation to partner with God's character. Mary responded in faith, but Gideon reacted in fear. Once God releases a prophetic word of destiny over an individual, a transformation usually begins.

1. The gifts, passion and purpose in our spirit man start to surface.
2. Responses of pain, fear and unbelief in our soul are exposed.
3. Doubt, confusion, or opposition emerge from our soul or the enemy.
4. We are tested and formed by the prophetic word through real-life situations.

And, finally, we see a full purpose and manifestation of the prophetic destiny.

Prophetic promise II

Body
Doubt, confusion & opposition

Soul
Pain, fear & unbelief

Spirit
Gifts, passion & purpose

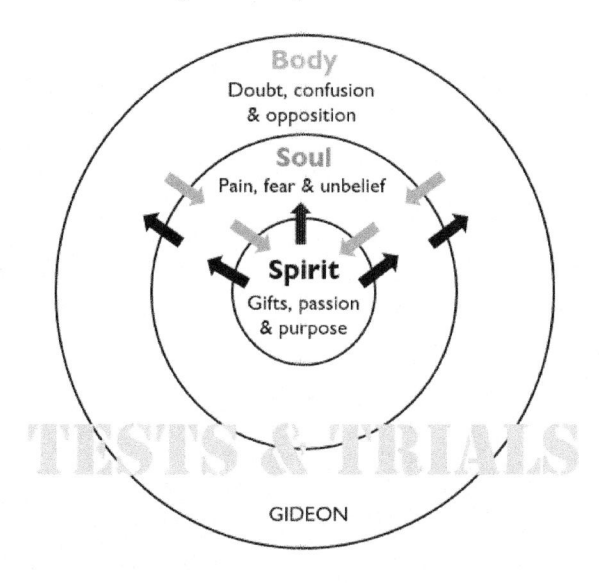

TESTS & TRIALS

GIDEON

The Lord demonstrated this final point in the life of Joseph: *"... until what he had said came to pass, the word of the LORD tested him."* (Psalm 105:19 ESV). Each promise from God can be likened to a seed and its embedded force. Once sown into our hearts and watered and tended to, it germinates, develops roots, sprouts and grows until it bears full-grown fruit (see Mark 4:28). As Christians, we can harness the massive potential the promises represent if we invest in them. We declare the promise, act on the promise and persevere with the promise. The Father, on his side, will move heaven and earth to assist us when we act in concert with his Word. Moses is an excellent example: *"He persevered because he saw him who is invisible."* (see Heb. 11:27). Faith sees, seizes and never ceases. Partaking in the promises positions us to receive divine provision because where the Lord guides, he provides. During this process, he forms Christ within us, and our tests become our testimonies.

Act on the promise
Proclaim Pray & Persevere

We speak the promise, we act on the promise, and we persevere with the promise.

When Gideon heeded the Lord's voice and decided to partner with the promise, something spectacular happened: *"But the Spirit of the LORD clothed Gideon, and he sounded the trumpet, and the Abiezrites were called out to follow him."* (Judg. 6:34 ESV). The Spirit *clothed* him; this is the literal translation. When Gideon moved in the direction God pointed him, a powerful anointing took hold of him and gave him abilities beyond the ordinary. God wants to fill and possess us. Gideon's name means 'the one that cuts down,' or 'destroyer'. His spiritual destiny was to destroy darkness and establish light. When he fulfilled his mission and partnered with the prophetic promise, it was a personal triumph. The Lord created us, and he wants us to be his vessels. It's him and us—we are a team!

The Almighty also asked Gideon to tear down his family's Baal altar and demolish the Asherah pole in his hometown. Idolatry brought the Israelites into bondage and oppression under the Midianites. When Gideon, in the still of the night, tore down those pagan altars, he declared: 'I am taking back my family's bloodline by pleading allegiance to the Lord.' Idolatry is a major spiritual stronghold. It's pervading all the world's different cultures. Our baleful foe effectively exploits idolatry as his main access point to perpetuate his destructive agendas. If we idolise anything in our lives other than God, we have to confront these strongholds. That is how the Everlasting Rock becomes our only stronghold, refuge and place of safety (see Prov. 18:10).

"But when a stronger man attacks and conquers him, he takes away the first man's armour on which the man relied and divides up his plunder." (Luke 11:22 NET Bible). *"The LORD is my rock and my fortress and my deliverer, my God, my rock, in whom I take refuge, my shield, and the horn of my salvation, my stronghold."* (Psalm 18:2 ESV).

God created us, and he wants us to be his vessels. It's him and us—we are a team!

As with Gideon, we often live without a full awareness of our true identity. Could it perhaps be that we attempt to escape the responsibility and effort that living up to our potential might involve? Our developed Western societies try to avoid any discomfort. Scores of people ingest antidepressants to alleviate emotional distress. Sadly, some commit suicide to end their misery indefinitely. At some point, we have to *feel* the pain to deal with its cause. Numbing out unpleasant feelings also cancels out the good ones. By seeking God, we can enter a state where we, enabled by grace, outbrave angst, pain and shame. The Holy Spirit is an amazing Helper; he yearns to assist us in this process of change (see Rom. 8:26-27). Most people are unaware of the abundant life and hope God longs to give us, to deliver us from affliction. The gospel releases God's ever-flowing grace to each one of us, salvation in Jesus' mighty name. Wretched sparrows and restless swallows are coming to perch in our Father's presence. The tiny, hopeless and weary ones find shelter in the holy place: *"Even the sparrow has found a home, and the swallow a nest for herself, where she may have her young—a place near your altar, LORD Almighty, my King and my God. Blessed are those who dwell in your house; they are ever praising you."* (Psalm 84:3-4 NIV).

By seeking God, we can enter into a position where we are enabled by grace to confront fear, pain and shame.

The fearful Gideon first had to get rid of his family's idolatry by rededicating his household to the Lord. From that point onwards, God promoted him to address his nation's emblematic issues. He embarked on a sizeable rescue mission to save Israel from the enemy's hands and went from obscurity to fame, from a private citizen to a public figure. God is able to entrust us with greater purposes, but only after we are willing to assume responsibility for our home situation. For that reason, Gideon initiated his personal house cleaning. Profound significance and purpose emerged from Gideon's response to God's directive. The purpose of our gifts manifests once we commit to the right values, vision, and mission. We fulfil God's calling by taking responsibility and have no alternate route to find true contentment. Becoming the best version of ourselves involves discomfort and pain, but the rewards are lasting and eternal. Don't forget that maintaining personal consistency and integrity will actively push you and me forward to advance God's plan. So, let us bid farewell to La-la land and engage in combat with our faithful Kingdom comrades. Amidst life's chaos and struggles, God wants us to enjoy happiness, blessings and affection.

WARFARE vs FUNFAIR

A call to prominence brings suffering and warfare because *opposition* is the training ground for all God's people. Suffering and glory go hand in hand, adversity breeds greatness. We are more than we think we are. Our human capacity is much larger than we usually realise, but it often stays unused due to disregard or discouragement. Therefore, we have to be pushed, stretched and challenged. God offended Gideon's mind. At the same time, he kindled the fire in his heart! What followed was a destiny-defining moment. He finally accepted his assignment by facing his victimised state of mind. That took a lot of courage to do. Refusing to do so would have been a huge loss for him. Not responding to God's call would have ended in defeat. A short-term lack of composure inevitably results in self-inflicted moral damage. In the long run, it affects our surroundings. Letting things slide is a hotbed for evil to take over, but daily dedication and discipline is a recipe for success: *"And let us not grow weary of doing good, for in due season we will reap, if we do not give up."* (Gal. 6:9 NET).

We must abandon the expedient stuff we have clasped onto at the expense of future gain. Shouldn't we try to pursue meaningful and lasting things? God is challenging us to become better than we are and to set things straight for future generations. To sacrifice what we could become for what we currently are is inadvisable. By wishing to be presentable and nice Christians, we settle for less. Our mission is to become world changers. We should be a well-watered garden in a sun-scorched land, and we become this thriving oasis by surrendering to Christ (see Isa. 58:11). In battle, selfish efforts are foolish; we need community. Living as Christians is 'mission impossible'. Thankfully, *"all things are possible with God"* (see Matt. 19:26, Luke 1:37).

A call to prominence brings suffering and warfare because *opposition* is the training ground for all God's people.

Ancient Israel understood the correlation between individual responsibility and justice in society as a whole. They believed their deliverers to be champions sent by God. The godly among them recognised the anointing the Lord had placed on their defenders. Supporting these chosen and anointed leaders, over time, was profitable for them, as they knew they preserved the future and the national identity of God's people. Self-interest was a sacrilege, a sign of contempt for God's covenant. Phineas, a paragon of a zealous priest, slayed a fornicating fellow Israelite and his mistress. The Lord hailed his resolute move as an act of worship. Phineas' deed abated God's judgement against Israel because it released his mercy on them (see Num. 25:7-13). When put to the test, authentic leaders will always rise up with courage and wisdom. Although he was unfledged and shy, young David defeated the defiant Goliath with a smooth pebble during national distress (see 1 Sam. 17). Neither quick-wittedness nor his sling-wielding, nimble fingers gave him the victory. Trusting in the Lord's name was the secret to his victory. The Bible is replete with skirmishes where heroes of faith rose with uncanny distinctiveness from their fellow men.

Partnership with the prophetic
Whenever a prophetic word is released, it initiates a process. Without exception, it starts the trajectory of transformation. However, it may take some time from the get-go until we notice a full manifestation of the promise. *"For still the vision awaits its appointed time; it hastens to the end—it will not lie. If it seems slow, wait for it; it will surely come; it will not delay."* (Hab. 2:3 ESV). A word from God can be released years before it comes to fruition. God is a master of timing. In the meantime, it may

seem like nothing is going on, yet God often adds more and more confirming words during such a drawn-out period. Jesus compared the process with farming: *"The kingdom of God is as if a man should scatter seed on the ground. He sleeps and rises night and day, and the seed sprouts and grows; he knows not how. The earth produces by itself, first the blade, then the ear, then the full grain in the ear. But when the grain is ripe, at once he puts in the sickle, because the harvest has come."* (Mark 4:26-29 ESV). The passage reveals the truth about waiting periods. When the seed is put into the ground, it isn't visible but concealed. There is a lot going on in a seemingly tranquil season. For instance, [8]a giant bamboo will grow its roots for three years. That's quite a long time! After being rooted, it will shoot up several metres within a few weeks. Ask yourself if you are growing your roots. Be conscious of how a bamboo season may lie around the corner with sudden breakthrough, increase and acceleration! The palm tree's roots take years to develop. Remember that there is no shortcut to permanent change or success. God is decidedly thorough in all that he does. Directly after a hurricane's landfall, one can notice how trees with established roots, such as tropical palm trees, stay quite unharmed and perky while the surrounding areas look like a tumultuous warzone—full of debris and twisted metal. *"The righteous will flourish like a palm tree, they will grow like a cedar of Lebanon."* (Psalm 92:12 NLT).

God is a master of timing.

Let us make sure we never lose sight of the life-changing process initiated by the eternal Word of God. The following passage describes it beautifully: *"For as the rain and the snow come down from heaven and do not return there but water the earth, making it bring forth and sprout, giving seed to the sower and bread to the eater, so shall my word be that goes out from my mouth; it shall not return to me empty, but it shall accomplish that which I purpose, and shall succeed in the thing for which I sent it."* (Isa. 55:10-11 ESV). Preceding any major breakthrough, God prepares hearts and situations to make certain that the event he planned will be as effective and long-lasting as possible. God is the ultimate strategist! We should carefully align with his heart and take ownership of his many promises by constantly reminding ourselves

---

[8] **Giant bamboo** - *Dendrocalamus giganteus,* commonly known as giant bamboo, is a giant tropical and subtropical, dense-clumping species native to Southeast Asia. It is one of the largest bamboo species in the world. Source: en.wikipedia.org

of what he showed us. Being focused and determined in our partnership with the prophetic makes room for the Holy Spirit to fully perform God's Word. Most of the time, we partner with the Lord through persistent prayer. Knowing that our enemy will contest the prophetic promise and try to contradict it through numerous circumstances, telling us it cannot happen, we have to learn to stand our ground. In the biblical Rosetta Stone of parables, the Parable of the Sower, Jesus said that the responsive hearers are those who ponder the Word and never let go of the promise: *"As for that in the good soil, they are those who, hearing the word, hold it fast in an honest and good heart, and bear fruit with patience."* (Luke 8:15 ESV). The ones by the wayside proudly refused the Word, those on rocky ground were stuck in a haze of fear and confusion, and those among thorns got distracted by idolatry. But how do we hold the word of promise fast? To keep it unaffected by external factors, we voice it through prayer and proclamation. What you received a prophecy about, or prayed for, might not happen overnight or transpire as you imagined it. Don't get discouraged! The Almighty will powerfully intervene, sometimes with a sudden and swift change. Until then, stand your ground and own your zone!

For some decades, a plethora of prophecies have been released about a worldwide awakening. It is set to be the greatest outpouring of the Spirit in history, giving rise to a remarkable shift and a transformation. I believe a season of convergence is upon us, when a lot of promises will merge into a momentum. We will see a revival that carries the DNA of all earlier moves of God. The Lord, in his mercy, prepares and equips *the kind of believers he needs* for the season ahead. Revival comes with new faces, as God raises up individuals as an answer to prayer. Have you ever heard the term [9]'A nameless and faceless generation'? It's an expression used to describe the many end-time believers the Lord is raising up. It seems like a spiritual concept, but we must view it in the context of how God works. All cute comments aside: Why do we expect it to be a nameless and faceless generation? Are we threatened by the possibility of the Lord raising up people we might disapprove of? Or, even worse,

---

[9] **Nameless and faceless:** The concept is spiritual when it points to how we do not seek glory and fame for ourselves. Building own brands or large ministries are the opposite. God often uses those the world looks down on, and soon we will see a generation of men and women moving together like one man and one army. They won't flaunt themselves, but in unity lift up the only Name that deserves eternal praise and adoration, Jesus, the name above all names!

someone we know? We were, in fact, all created by God with a name and a face, and I am convinced that we are called to reflect his nature as individuals. In Hebrew, the word for face is *panim*—meaning faces. It relates to the different facial expressions we have as humans, but it seems to go far beyond this explanation. Emotions, or our inner man, is פְּנִים *pnim*, a slight variation of פָּנִים *panim*. Let me add that biblical Hebrew has all kinds of word plays, not obvious to English readers. The patriarch Jacob, after fighting with the angel, declared that he had seen *"the faces of God"*, in Hebrew *'panim El panim'*. At Penuel, Jacob had a face-to-face encounter with the Lord (see Gen. 32:30, Exod. 33:11). The angels galore who encircle God's throne, are they bristling with eyes because they were created to endlessly gaze on his glory? (See Ezek. 10:12, Rev. 4:8). And are they crying out *"Holy, holy, holy"* because they constantly encounter the innumerable expressions of the Holy One? Could his faces somehow be mirrored in the myriads of redeemed humans? The thought is awe-inspiring and mind-blowing. Of course, we really don't know if it is so, but it is not implausible since we were created in the image and likeness of the triune God. Do we dare to think of our reality as a multifaceted or multidimensional construct? To believe that we carry a part of the Lord's substance and essence is wonderful and incredible due to the fact that we are surrounded by humans in so many shapes and forms (see Gen. 1:26-27). A part of redemption is to unlock our divine potential for the Lord's glory to shine through us. This glory usually manifests through our faces:

"For God, who said, "Let light shine out of darkness," made his light shine in our hearts to give us the light of the knowledge of God's glory displayed in the face of Christ." (2 Cor. 4:6 NIV). [10]The Sanhedrin saw the face of Stephen—the first martyr—and his face shone like the face of an angel (Acts 6:15, 2 Cor. 4:6-7).

All earlier men and women of faith were known in Heaven. Many were hidden for years until God made them the centre of public attention. They transitioned from

---

[10] **The Sanhedrin** was a Jewish council of seventy-one members. They were patterned after the seventy elders that God established through Moses. In the gospels they are called, "the council of the elders." In Judea, they were under Roman authority and could not carry out capital punishment. This is why we find them sending Jesus to Pilate after they had condemned him to death. They acknowledged to Pilate that they did not have the authority to execute anyone.
When Jerusalem was destroyed in A.D. 70 the Sanhedrin ceased to exist.
Source: www.blueletterbible.org › faq › don_stewart_1313

obscurity to notability. The Lord exclusively begets sons and kings and knows us all by name. *"He determines the number of the stars and calls them each by name."* (Psalm 147:4). The Scripture describes the angels, God's messengers, as stars, and the righteous are also depicted as 'stars' in his eyes (see Job 38:7, Dan. 12:3, Rev. 1:20; 12:4). Our heavenly Father definitely finds great contentment in promoting and favouring his chosen ones as answers to prayer. Each new move of the Lord came with new faces. The awesome Creator of the sun, moon and stars and billions of galaxies affectionately longs to bestow on us his delightful presence because he most intensely dislikes uniformity and anonymity. We noticed how the Lord enveloped Gideon with his mighty Spirit. Whenever Gideon moved forward, so also did God! The Father is pleased to put us on display as long as we remain surrendered to his purposes. By this, we prove to be hidden with Christ in God (see Col. 3:3). Jesus said: *"He who has seen me has seen the Father."* (John 14:9). In the same way, God called us to glorify him and not seek fame or make a name for ourselves.

Every new move of God also came with new faces. The Lord affectionately longs to bestow on us his delightful presence because he most intensely dislikes conformity and anonymity.

During the Iron Curtain, the esteemed Richard Wurmbrand, a Romanian priest of Jewish descent, suffered persecution for his faith. While incarcerated, he witnessed to an inmate, although this was expressly prohibited. On hearing the gospel, the fellow jailbird asked what Christ was like. Richard replied: "Oh, he is just like me." Instantly, the impressed inmate responded: "Is he like you? Then I really want to know him!" Many of the accounts in the four gospels can be interpreted in the light of Jesus being God and not a man. For instance, we are tempted to oversimplify the narrative and link the miracles to his deity and his kindness to his humanity. We might arrive at the conclusion that operating the way Jesus did is beyond human reach. If this is so, why did Jesus send out his disciples to preach and do miracles? Having Jesus as our example, I believe in a dimension of the Spirit where we are called to enter as servants of the living God. As the Son of Man, Jesus fully relied on the Holy Spirit, and as the Son of God, all the great works he did undoubtedly reflected the Father. Of course, Jesus in the flesh was God, united with the Father, but he was also a human allowing the Most High to shine through him with all his attributes (see John 1:1-3, 14-18). In the capacity of being a sinless man, he carried a limitless anointing, a fact confirmed by all the remarkable miracles he performed. Let me further stress that Jesus did not empty himself of his deity, he poured himself into humanity! He still continued to be God, even when he bore the wrath of the Father on the cross (see Phil. 2:5-11). The inner circle of his disciples beheld his glory on [11]the Mount of Transfiguration (see Luke 9:28-36, 2 Pet. 1:16-18). Because he was God, he didn't need to be born again. He had no personal sin. With this in mind, it's clear that we aren't equal to our blessed Lord Jesus, let alone little 'gods'. Still, you and I are sons and joint heirs with Christ and called to minister with the same Holy Spirit. When people meet us, they should encounter the Father's love through us because we are his witnesses (see Luke 24:44-49, John 15:26-27, Acts 1:8). God, in his sovereignty, decides whether he wants to move through us with preaching, prophecy, healing or acts of kindness. Jesus set the standard, so we could follow in his footsteps. In reality, imitating Jesus is imitating the Father. We display his heart to those around us, even in our suffering and persecution (see Eph. 5:1, 1 Pet. 2:21).

Jesus did not empty himself of his deity, he poured himself into humanity!

As the Body of Christ emerges globally, the old era with just a few famous preachers will soon be over. In the coming awakening of God, the nations will be flooded with preachers, all moving in fivefold ministry. It's bound to happen in order for the great end-time harvest to come in. God can prepare adverse circumstances for believers, as often seen in the biblical record. In choosing to do so, he sets the dark backdrop for a major reformation. Black velvet makes the diamonds shine brighter, like stars in the night. The setback can be a setup! Jesus used a lot of agricultural references in his storytelling. The parable about the wheat and tares illustrates this principle perfectly (see Matt. 13:24-30). God gave me a picture where I saw the roots of the wheat entangled by the roots of the tares. As the wheat developed, its roots were strengthened and getting thicker, causing the roots of the tares to lose their grip. Pressure and persecution bring about purity and strength. God can use inspiration to move you forward, but desperation might prove to be even more effective. Holy discontentment with the status quo and a growing urge to pray are prophetic signals

---

[11] **Mount Hermon** (2814 metres or 9,232 feet high) "a high mountain" (Matthew 17:1).

about how God is at work. Being stuck in a tight spot, misunderstood and rejected, are situations he uses to help his people to succeed against all odds. To progress in the Lord, moving onwards and upwards, is often caused by a hunger for what he has in store for those who love him (see 1 Cor. 2:9, Eph. 2:10). Without pain, no gain. With no need, no desire to succeed. This was true for Israel before the Exodus from Egypt and is often true for us as well.

Pressure and persecution bring purity and strength.

While in captivity, great despair led to Israel's outcry. After centuries, the Lord sent the people Moses or מֹשֶׁה *Moshe* as a deliverer (see Exod. 3:7-8). Was God's tarrying a cruel game he enjoyed playing? Not in the least! The interval was a phase in a timely and well-coordinated campaign to prepare his people for a dramatic shift in history.

The prophetic and the Father's heart

The prophetic always points us towards the Father's heart for us, giving us purpose and direction in our walk with him. We understand the essence of the prophetic by recognising God's own nature. God is a good Father and is not to be compared with some dysfunctional earthly father. He wants to heal us from any misconceptions we have of him and to develop trust in his goodness. *"He heals the broken-hearted and binds up their wounds."* (Psalm 147:3). It's vital to receive the Father's love for us on a regular basis. His love affirms our true identity. We look for people's approval in order to tell ourselves that we matter and compensate for our lack of worth through performance-driven behaviour. But we are human beings, not human doings! As God's children, we need to see that we have been totally accepted by the Father, in Jesus, his Beloved One. Lord Jesus didn't die on the cross to make you valuable; he died because you were already priceless to him! The Great Shepherd gave up his breath to redeem you back to the Father. His intentions are redemptive without fail.

Words like redeem, recover and restore precisely express the Father's lavish heart. It's the sole reason why Jesus came *"to seek and to save the lost"* (see Luke 19:10). Do you welcome the Father's love just for you? A believer is a *receiver* and also a *perceiver*. When you perceive him, you receive from him. We are called to gaze at Jesus, *"the author and finisher of our faith"* (see Heb. 12:2). When the Israelites looked to [12]the copper serpent in the desert, they were healed from the poisonous snakes (see Num. 21:6-9). It symbolises the destructive venom of sin and how we all get saved, healed and delivered when we behold the wooden and wonderful cross (see John 3:14-16). Jesus offers complete healing. The Bible says: *"For God so loved the world ..."* The word *so* refers to *in this way*; it points to the previous example concerning the copper snake on the pole erected by God's servant Moses. I love Eric Gilmour's beautiful quote: 'The greatest message about God is not to behave, but to behold.'

Remember that Jesus didn't die on the cross to make you valuable; he died because you were already precious to him!

Can we live like the cross to some extent was unnecessary? I believe so, although it's not done with deliberate intent. I think some of us tend to relate more easily to sickness, disability, addiction and lack than being in Christ. Negativity is something we humans gravitate towards; it's our natural course of action. But some Christians seem to build their identity around a particular condition and, in a perverted sense, pride themselves on being sick, wounded or incomplete. It gives people a reason to sympathise with such victims of life. Is it sensible to act like victimhood is a virtue when it's not? As an avid reader of the Bible, I conclude that all victims died on the cross with Jesus; there are only victors left! It's time for us to leave the pity party. Of course, we desire to help those who are *real victims* and don't waste our resources.

True followers of Jesus understand how to walk in their new identity because of the cross. Once we gain the same perspective as the Lord has, it will liberate us. I am not looking down on the fact that some of us need full healing for both body and soul. We absolutely do. Whether you want to contend for your healing or not, you can rest safely in God's loving embrace. Fight each battle you face without ever losing hope, and stay faithful until the end (see Heb. 3:14, 6:11-12). Hold on to what you have and let no one seize your crown (Rev. 3:11). With that being said, grumbling about hardship, sickness and lack is anything but helpful, and it's not in line with

---

[12] **Snake on the pole:** It is likely that the Greeks got their symbol, often used in modern medicine, called the rod of Asclepius, from Moses. Hebrew culture trickled down to all great cultures of the world, in the shape of stories or myths. Thus, pagan knockoffs were based on the original revelation.

the Father's purposes for you and me. Wouldn't it be far better to direct our gaze to God's goodness, encouraging each other by stirring hope and building faith? If we remain buried in the quagmire of self-imposed limitations, we will slowly suffocate. Let us rather lend each other a helping hand as we move towards completeness. We should abandon a fatalistic mindset in whatever way, shape or form it has taken. Advancing in faith is not living in denial. Instead, we choose to honestly confess our state of affairs and make it a matter of prayer, not one of despair: *"For I know the plans I have for you,"* declares the LORD, *"plans to prosper you and not to harm you, plans to give you hope and a future."* (Jer. 29:11 NIV).

True followers of Jesus understand how to walk in their new identity because of the cross.

Living superficially is to depend on the physical realm more than the unseen realm of God's kingdom. Over time, it results in unbelief, making us vulnerable to religious spirits—which are truly wicked spirits of deception—causing us to have a hard time receiving the good gifts from the Lord. God only has good and perfect gifts for us, as *"the Father of lights"* (see James 1:17). He wants to give the Holy Spirit to those who ask him for it (see Luke 11:13). God called us to be his sons under grace, not slaves under sin. We got the Spirit of sonship and not the spirit of slavery (see Rom. 8:15). A son knows that he is an heir and acknowledges the bliss of privileges as well as the burden of responsibilities. He expects good things to happen as a part of his identity as a son. We believe in his promises to us because we are sons, not beggars. That said, good things for a child of God may be diametrically opposed to a non-believer's life goals. Worldly desires revolve around momentary contentment of no lasting or eternal value. In contrast, a child of God willingly accepts discipline and correction as proof of the Father's affirmative love. God loves us too much to allow us to continue with sinful behaviour. He wants us to partake in his holiness.

"Since we respected our earthly fathers who disciplined us, shouldn't we submit even more to the discipline of the Father of our spirits, and live forever? For our earthly fathers disciplined us for a few years, doing the best they knew how. But God's discipline is always good for us, so that we might share in his holiness." (Heb. 12:9-10 NLT).

Suffering is a part of our calling as well; it deepens our relationship with God and proves authentic faith. *"For you have been given not only the privilege of trusting in Christ but also the privilege of suffering for him."* (Phil. 1:29 NLT). The Lord's courageous people of promise know that suffering brings him glory, it benefits our growth. By placing our trust in Jesus Christ alone and not in temporary things, we hold him more precious than fleeting pleasures and treasures of this world.

Sickness, suffering and breakthrough

A belief where we integrate our doubts, fears or defeats could prove problematic for us. Worship directs our attention to the God of Glory. Isn't it more benign to focus on God's promises as we pray for healing and wholeness? (See Heb. 12:11-13, James 1:2-7). To process the mystery of pain and suffering is indeed challenging, in particular, the difficult question: 'Why doesn't everybody get healed?' (See Deut. 29:29, Job. 2:1-11, 2 Cor. 12:6-7, Heb. 11:32-40). At times, we face tough dilemmas regarding sickness: It's not uncommon that believers who once got healed relapse. Questions then arise: Was their healing genuine? Did they fail to trust God? I think an accusatory approach to their situation is mistaken. To assert that they lacked faith is to oversimplify and is nothing less than sad and disrespectful. Christians battling a severe and chronic disease know how cumbersome that can be. They deserve our deep empathy. As I see it, we are fighting against darkness and might get hurt several times. The ongoing spiritual war explains the rationale. No soldier is perfect or fully experienced, and this fallen world forces us to deal with pain and loss. Our faith is terribly lightweight and immature if we gauge spirituality through the lens of being in perfect health or never suffering from adverse life events. The Bible contains quite a few enigmas; think about this riddle: Elisha got the double portion he asked God for but contracted a deadly illness anyway. Years after his passing, they threw a dead man into his sepulchre. The unfortunate fellow touched the deceased prophet's skeletal remains and was miraculously resuscitated (see 2 Kings 13:14, 20-21).

God is unfailingly in control but sometimes seems to have a higher purpose for you and me. We can leave our questions at God's altar and believe the Sovereign Lord loves us, whether we receive our healing or not while eagerly awaiting the day of resurrection. In light of all this, should we accept a handful and sporadic healings as the irreversible norm defining our churches? After all, healing is the children's bread;

we share in it through covenant (see Mark 7:24-30). Signs and wonders were meant to follow us. It is as a part of God confirming his Word (see Mark 16:20, Acts 4:29-30). Cultivating a deeper relationship with the Father by asking him to move in an unrestricted fashion in our lives is very important. The miraculous is augmented in an atmosphere of extravagant worship. Are we willing to authorise the Holy Spirit to flow without limiting his activities? He manifests wherever God's Word is held in high esteem because he responds to our hunger (see Acts 12:24). We must linger in his presence and should never expect God to be squeezed into a mediocre service with a few worship songs and a brief sermon. The Spirit is not gentlemanlike; he is no junior-sized Holy Spirit! Moving with unpredictable and violent force, he brings a full-scale *invasion* of the Kingdom. God can't be rushed, pushed or scheduled, but he may gloriously ambush us with his presence! Sadly, some churches have lost the sense of wonder and reverence for him, a chilly attitude divesting their members of life-changing encounters with the Holy One. If our standards are below average, we will expect less and rarely experience the glory of God. The rife sins of not praying, complacent attitudes and lukewarm hearts endanger many churches (see Luke 18:1-8, James 4: 4, Rev. 2:5, 3:1-2).

I admire those who endure hardship and sickness, regardless of their own agony and trauma. They keep on fighting, always expecting more from God for themselves and others. Unrelenting God-chasers fuel their passion for God, despite their painful ordeals. When others are 'throwing in the towel', they pursue the Lord even more fervently. I think of them as forerunners of the coming move of God, where we will witness exceptional manifestations of the Spirit. God is ramping up the pace of the race now. We are entering a new era where the Body of Christ on earth will rush forward by the mighty power of the Holy Spirit in many and untold ways. The Lord recently reminded me of a scene from the movie 'Forrest Gump', released in 1994. Forrest needed an incentive to start practising his unique abilities. The poor boy was stigmatised and bullied. When his friend, Jenny, shouted: "Run, Forrest, run!" he started to do the unthinkable. As he began to run, the leg braces fell off; his disability left him. He ran like a tempest, and his tormentors were unable to keep up. He even outran their bicycles! It depicts the state of the Body of Christ until now. For far too long, we have been ridiculed by the world, treated with contempt and marginalised. Not dwelling on the past, we have to trust the prophets when they cry out: "Run,

Church, run!" Now is the time to put off weight and run the race of grace! As we repent and seek the Lord, a part of it is to receive a fresh perspective on who we really are. We were built to run! *"Even youths will become weak and tired, and young men will fall in exhaustion. But those who trust in the LORD will find new strength. They will soar high on wings like eagles. They will run and not grow weary. They will walk and not faint."* (Isa. 40:30-31 NLT). It's time for us to unplug from the matrix of sin, ignorance, human traditions, religious systems and false expectations which previously held us back from experiencing our capacity. The game is afoot! Prepare and get ready; everything is about to change drastically. The next phase marks a great shift in history, a renaissance, where the [13]Church will be perceived in a fresh and unconventional way. Elijah, the zealous prophet of fire, unexpectedly outran king Ahab's speediest chariot after his smashing success at Mount Carmel (see 1 Kings 18:46). A revived and prophetic people will advance in the swift power of the Spirit!

Now is the time to put off weight and run the race of grace!

I am convinced that the Lord has realms of extreme mercy and goodness yet to be explored by those who seek his face. Godsent revival usually manifests if Christians unite in love and hunger for more of the Holy Spirit, engaging together as one man. When a hub is created for the Lord, he shows up. Functioning churches should be characterised by consistent biblical teaching, relentless prayer and Holy Spirit fire. There is a desperate need for more congregations to transition into apostolic revival

---

[13] **The Church:** Another term for the Body of Christ on earth, born-again and serving in God's Spirit. These are the people whose heart the Lord controls, who resist the satanic systems of this world. Lamentably, institutionalised Christianity has been corrupted and infiltrated by the same worldly systems and can't be relied on. *"We know that we are children of God, and that the whole world is under the control of the evil one."* (1 John 5:19).

centres. These will be led by mature leaders that are risk-takers who invest in their members. This is how I believe churches are supposed to operate. We want believers thoroughly equipped and released for Kingdom ministry, who impact church and society profoundly. Antioch was such a location. This great church had a dynamic fivefold leadership. It was the city where the disciples first were called *Christians* (see Acts 11:20-21, 26; 13:1-12). Concerning revival and outpouring, we want people to encounter Jesus through the gospel. The early revivalists laboured in prayer—they begged God to intervene mercifully. These men and women of great character and stature were devoted servants of the Lord who preached repentance perpetually. Sin was addressed at once, and the Blood was offered as a remedy for sinners and saints. Salvations, signs and wonders followed because of intimacy with the Lord and each other (see Acts 2:42-47). We cannot bypass God's order of events. How reckless to think that we can achieve similar results by leaving out the Holy Spirit through our shortcuts. We must abandon weak human efforts to somehow assist God. Some of today's so-called 'revivals' are orchestrated carnal undertakings with a methodology at odds with the gospel, like theatrics, sensationalism and emotional manipulation.

Historical records reveal that even some of the most powerful revivals were finally infiltrated as Satan hijacked them. He relentlessly attempted to distort these events with excesses and bizarre demonic manifestations because he was determined to destroy and discredit them. The reformer revivalists of old ran into these kinds of counterfeits on a regular basis and therefore warned against them. John Wesley said: 'At the first, revival is true and pure, but after a few weeks, watch for counterfeits.' Are we able to distinguish the [14]hypes from the real deal? We must be vigilant as watchmen on the walls and as God's messengers. Let us pray for the grace to keep the moves from God on track (see Psalm 127:1, Isa. 62:6, Ezek. 33:17, Acts 20:28).

In a wider sense, we can skilfully apply the principles of God's kingdom to influence our surrounding culture of family, friends, the local community and workplaces, et cetera. These attitudes of the heart are central to what Jesus taught in the Beatitudes: Gentleness, humility, mercy, purity and perseverance—virtues of true God-lovers

---

[14] **My comment:** *"Now faith is the assurance of things hoped for, the conviction of things not seen."* (Heb. 11:1 ESV). The verb used in this verse is hoped for, not *hyped*—the difference is huge.

(see Matt. 5:3-12). We effectively overcome evil by doing good. Any effort to spread a Kingdom culture of love and honour through servanthood is extremely effective (see Rom. 12:21). Don't despise the small beginnings. What you carry into everyday settings is precious. Let Christ shine through you! At this very hour, the Lord raises up heroes to conquer territories the enemy previously occupied. The new Kingdom adventurers are committed followers of Jesus, powerfully armed with his Word! We stand on the shoulders of brave men and women from the past: Our responsibility is to make sure to preserve and sustain the breakthroughs and triumphs from earlier moves of God. What better legacy can we leave than raising up the next generation as champions of faith? Now is the time for the ambassadors of God's kingdom to emerge, with an indomitable spirit, for the glory of his Name. Undoubtedly, earlier revivals brought countless blessings to the culture by causing reformation through acts of reconciliation and restorative power. We want the same for our day and age.

The reformer revivalists took their calling seriously and showed proof of fivefold visionary leadership. Good leaders impact today's generation, but great leaders train others to impact future generations. The same prophetic pattern is seen in the Bible. Let us dream big dreams with God and allow him to widen our horizons. We should resist the urge to adopt a shallow social media culture where leaders seek praise from their tribe of sycophantic followers instead of loyally building the House of God. Positive affirmation is all well and good, but a constant craving for public attention and admiration is unhealthy. My main gripe is leaders who behave in a narcissistic and worldly manner. On top of that, to pastor a church is a momentous assignment. That kind of responsibility should by far outweigh the pursuit of popularity.

The Scripture doesn't start out with salvation; it begins with Creation. That is why the gospel should be proclaimed *"to all creation"* (see Mark 16:15). The gospel of Christ is the central revelation, the main piece of God's restoration process. God, in his dealings with humankind, seems to appear firstly as Creator, secondly as Lord, and thirdly as Saviour. All his purposes are redemptive. The Father wants all people to repent. Having a glimpse into the future judgements, as described in the Book of Revelation, we see how God continually tries to turn people back to him. Sadly, we mostly notice: *"... but they did not repent"*. To repent is to change direction, to turn or return, in Hebrew תְּשׁוּבָה *teshuvah*. Also, it means to change our mindset, in Greek μετάνοια *metanoia*. By actively receiving God's grace, we stop thinking and acting foolishly. Instead, we start doing the right thing and stay the course. Jesus declared: *"The kingdom of God is at hand. Repent and believe the gospel."* (Mark 1:15). *"At hand"* means near and accessible. The gospel of the Kingdom is hidden in prophetic passages about Israel and Messiah and demonstrated by the presence of God. When boldly preached, the gospel brings transformation because people accept its truth. The Jews were admonished to listen to the prophet Moses spoke about. The apostles confirmed this person to be Jesus or Yeshua (see Deut. 18:15-18, Acts 3:22-23). When the Kingdom is released, demons are expelled, the sick are healed, the dead are raised, sinners are made holy, and relationships and finances are restored. God's goodness leads to repentance (see Rom. 2:4). By showing God's heart, we direct people towards the Father to connect their hearts to him. What is more gratifying than this? Repentance is sometimes viewed as an austere command issued by the Lord. What I have seen transcends this limited view: I see repentance as the stunning result of the Holy Spirit's influence on the heart (see Jer. 17:14). When people open up to a gospel preached with love—yielding to its message—God miraculously turns their hearts to him. Jesus said: *"No one can come to me unless the Father who sent me draws him"* (John. 6:44 ESV). Experiencing the Father's love and admitting our sin may coincide at the same time. Repentance is cooperation with the Holy Spirit—it's our response when we hear the truth. If we reciprocate God's love, he will transform and touch us. He gently draws us with cords of love (see Hos. 11:4).

The gospel, by divine decree, is to be declared [15]*"first to the Jew, then to the Gentile"* (see Rom. 1:16). Let us actively befriend both Jews and other groups in the context of [16]building rapport through God's love.

Core Kingdom dynamics are distinctly outlined in the Parable of the Lost Son (Luke 15:11-32). Jesus communicated by using stories in a brilliant and efficient way. His creative genius was demonstrated through an ability to invent tales on the spot, to

---

[15] **Salvation:** To say that Jews don't need the gospel, is heresy. We all need Yeshua as our Saviour! Why else did Paul have an urge to reach his own nation? See also Rom. 9:1-5; 10:12-13; 11:28-32.

[16] **Build rapport:** Rapport is a harmonious relationship between people who have established mutual trust. Building rapport is how humans connect, identify shared feelings, and establish two-way communication. Rapport develops out of meaningful conversations and a willingness to embrace different points of view. Source: www.masterclass.com/articles/how-to-build-rapport

highlight pressing matters. In a culture saturated with religious talk and tradition, he used unconventional style and evocative imagery. Through unique storytelling, he delivered his essential messages wrapped in relatable metaphors. Although some topics were controversial, he always kept the full attention of his audience. Some of the expressions were clearly aimed at the religious leaders of his day. The broad use of [17]parables, as we see it in the four gospels, wasn't Jesus' brainchild but a tradition found within Second Temple rabbinic Judaism. This parable is both beautiful and mesmerising. It contains anecdotal pieces of wisdom and moral lessons, as expected from all great stories. It has been referred to as 'The Parable of the Prodigal Son'. An alternative title could have been 'the waiting father'. The narrative accentuates basic truths about sonship and repentance. It is also a dire warning about how dangerous hypocrisy is. To unjustly judge others remains a temptation for all believers.

We know the famous tale, but some of the nuances of the story could easily escape our notice. As Christians, most of us are fairly acquainted with the order of events: The younger son asked for his share of the estate, probably in cash. This troubled kid then left home, went abroad and squandered his wealth on loose living. When he became depleted of resources, he debased himself even more by tending to the pigs of a foreigner. To Jews, pigs are considered detestable and unclean [18]non-kosher animals. When a famine hit and ravaged the land, he worked for a pittance. He ate whatever the herd of swine gobbled. Behaving like a party animal, the wayward and rebellious child ended up with the animals (see Eccl. 3:18-19). In his dishevelled state, he finally came to his senses. After regaining his sanity, he concocted a bold plan: The first phase was returning to his father's house. At least the food at home would be decent. If he succeeded with his little ploy, he could end up being hired as a servant and get a roof over his head again. He carefully rehearsed his brief speech of apology before he returned to his homeland. I think he made that decision out of sheer convenience. We may also deduce from his vile behaviour that he didn't regret his many indiscretions. His relatives likely knew the misfortune he had suffered so

---

[17] **My comment:** For further study, I recommend Brad H. Young's extremely well-researched book: *The Parables: Jewish Tradition and Christian Interpretation*

[18] **Non-kosher:** Having a physical or moral blemish to make impure according to dietary or ceremonial laws. Source: www.vocabulary.com/dictionary/nonkosher My comments: Apparently, pork was popular among the Roman occupants and a business opportunity for some Gentiles. As such, it explains the herd of pigs held by Greek settlers in the land of the Gerasenes (Luke 8:26-37).

far. Of course, the disturbing reports relayed to his family and community would have dishonoured his father considerably. In ancient times, honour was a central value in the Middle East, and still is. On his return, his father rushed to meet with him, hugged him and kissed him! He chased down his weary son before the agitated villagers could. Thus, the son escaped public ridicule and humiliation, customary in the dominant culture. The father's unselfish action of mercy and love must have overwhelmed the woeful son because he was instantly overcome with remorse. He confessed his terrible mistake with sincere self-reproach and sorrow but left out the clause: *"Make me like one of your hired servants."* Unexpectedly, he had an epiphany and a sudden change of heart the very moment his father embraced him and loved on him. Because he chose to align with the truth and admit that he was unworthy of being his father's son, no time was wasted. The father told his servants to array him in the best robe, put a ring on his finger and put sandals on his feet. Besides, he even ordered the fattened calf to be prepared for the impromptu homecoming party he threw for his son.

We don't know if this dad had posted lookouts to notify him if his son was seen in the vicinity. Regardless, with intense longing, he nervously looked for his son each day. By the same token, our heavenly Father yearns and longs for fellowship with each one of us. The parable tells us how the gospel provides more than forgiveness, as it offers full restoration for repentant sinners. It's grace upon grace, as well as life plus abundant life (see Psalm 23:5, John 1:16; 10:10). The stylish robe, the sandals and the ring in verse 22 are unmistakable symbols of our elevated status in God's Kingdom. They signify how the Father reinstates us with authority, sonship and royal dignity. God pours his favour and tribute upon us, withholding no good thing for his dear children—those who abide in his Beloved Son (Psalm 84:11 and Col. 1:12-14). Do you feel adrift and isolated? God made Jesus the Mercy Seat. Run to him, and he will welcome you with his unceasing grace (see [19]Rom 3:25, Heb. 4:16).

---

[19] **Mercy Seat:** Greek ἱλαστήριον *hilasterion*. The lid on the Ark of the covenant where the covering angels' wings stretched forth towards each other, where blood from the atoning sacrifice was sprinkled. In Hebrew כַּפֹּרֶת *kapporeth* Exod. 25:17-22, Lev. 16:2 etc. From *kapar* - to cover.

[20]Just as I am, I would be lost
But mercy and grace my freedom bought
And now to glory in Your cross
Oh Lamb of God I come, I come

Once he heard the reports about his brother's return, [21]the elder son's reaction was merciless. Upon noticing joyfulness, music and dance, he got terribly angry. Surely, he refused to join in on the festivities due to a long and festering resentment against his rude and disloyal brother. He accused his father of receiving his youngest son so extravagantly—even slaughtering the fattened calf for him! Playing the victim, he chided his father for being unfair. He argued that despite his many years of service, he wasn't given anything to celebrate with, not even a young goat. His father reacted with sadness and surprise and told him he could party whenever he wanted because he was worth the splurge. After all, he was a legitimate son and heir. He didn't need to plead or grovel for anything. Daft as it might sound: With a fragmented soul severely scarred by sin, the youngest son applied for the position of a servant but was instead restored to sonship. His envious and forlorn brother perceived himself more as a servant than a son, which is an outright tragedy. The bigger discussion is: Which of the two siblings showed signs of being alienated? Who was, in actual fact, the lost, love-starved and lonely soul? Sonship can't be experienced through a self-righteous mindset, and its countless benefits don't depend on a flawless performance but on unconditional love and a real sense of belonging and identity. The Lord pursues us

---

[20] **Just as I am** Songwriters: Ricky Jackson / Ran Jackson / William B (p.d.) Bradbury / Charlotte (p.d.) Elliott Just as I Am lyrics © Black Eye Music, Integrity's Hosanna! Music, Be Essential Songs

[21] **The elder son:** In the parable, the elder son might point to the Pharisees and the Scribes, and their rather legalistic interpretation of the Torah, as well as their contempt for Jesus receiving sinners and extending grace to them. Jesus repeatedly criticised their many traditions and practises. He called them hypocrites, as they believed God's Word, but lacked love and mercy. Do we love like Jesus did?

with his goodness and loving-kindness (see Psalm 23:6). Unaware of their cheerless condition, many Christians strive for God's approval through church attendance, giving, serving and behaving in a good or presumably godly way. Because they feel undervalued, they overcompensate and conclude that their strong sense of duty will somehow compel God to owe them a favour. To be crystal clear: The Father's grace is completely unearned, undeserved and unmerited. In his eyes, we can't increase or decrease in value the same way stocks or shares do on the stock exchange. God don't assess us through our duties or accomplishments; to him, we are more than servants.

The Father's grace is completely unearned, undeserved and unmerited.

God's children enjoy his boundless flow of grace and the bliss of redemption. Our Father doesn't love us despite our weaknesses but because of them! He is drawn to the underdogs and the misfits; the broken ones are beautiful to him. Vulnerability invokes his presence. It's time to break free from that foul orphan spirit which has choked the Body of Christ for so long. You are a son and heir, a royal king and priest, given a seat of honour in the heavenly places in Christ! *"As He is, so are we in this world!"* (see 1 John 4:17). We fight the good fight from an elevated place of victory, from heaven towards earth. The first Adam was of the earth; the last Adam, Christ, is from Heaven (see 1 Cor. 15:47). Our position as believers of the New Covenant is more glorious than what Adam enjoyed. We represent the resurrected, glorified Christ and share in his celestial nature. This will be increasingly understood as the coming great awakening gets closer, with the Holy Spirit poured out upon all flesh. We are approaching a turning point where the sons of God will be revealed (see Joel 2:28, Rom. 8:19, Col. 3:4). God's majestic government will manifest through sons who humbly carry Kingdom glory in earthen vessels (2 Cor. 4:5-10).

Our enemy hates sonship. Even Yeshua, the Messiah, was attacked at the core of his identity. *And when Jesus was baptised, immediately he went up from the water, and behold, the heavens were opened to him, and he saw the Spirit of God descending like a dove and coming to rest on him; and behold, a voice from heaven said, "This is my beloved Son, with whom I am well pleased."* (Matt. 3:16-17 ESV). After the baptism of John, the Father announced from Heaven the true identity of Jesus as his beloved son. Following his baptism and the infilling of the Holy Spirit, the Holy Spirit led

Jesus into the remote desert in confrontation with the devil (see also Lev. 16:3-22, *Azazel*). Keep in mind how God allows for a prophetic word to be tested as he did with Joseph. In the furnace of affliction, we learn how to become overcomers. The devil questions who we are, and he tries to sow his dragon seeds of doubt because he is determined to rob us of our potential. If we yield to his temptations, our authority over him will be quickly neutralised, a fact very well known to him. Provokingly, he queried Jesus, *"If you are the Son of God ... "* With worldly-wise savviness, he tried to divert Jesus from his royal assignment as the Son of God. Questioning God's will, he tempted the Messiah to perform as a miracle worker for selfish gain by turning rocks into bread. Jesus' response was first-rate: Undistracted, he announced that his food outmatched temporary cuisine. He fed off the promises of God twenty-four-seven because his premium sustenance was God's perfect will.

God always allows for a prophetic word to be tested.

What the enemy didn't remind Jesus of was the expression *"beloved son"*. The devil's strategy was to cleverly omit the word *beloved*, the defining word of the unique and intimate relationship Jesus shared with the Father. But his scheme failed miserably: Jesus was self-aware of who he was, namely, *"a beloved son of God"*. God's banner over us is love: *"He has brought me to the house of wine, and his banner over me is love."* (Song of Songs 2:4 BSB). Sonship is also connected to governance—to rule and reign over his creation and to rule in life. *"For if, because of one man's trespass, death reigned through that one man, much more will those who receive the abundance of grace and the free gift of righteousness reign in life through the one man Jesus Christ."* (Rom. 5:17 ESV).

BELOVED

Adam's assignment was remarkably similar to Jesus' mission in subduing the earth and defeating the hordes of wickedness. If we fail to remember that we are sons and heirs—beloved children of God—the enemy is quick to gain access to steal, kill and destroy. That is why sonship is at the centre of God's heart. We demonstrate our sonship in two ways: Through a close covenant relationship with the Father and as representatives of his life and authority. To receive God's all-embracing love for us intentionally, on a day-to-day basis, is crucial. Prayer, worship and praise build our relationship with him and protect what he entrusted us. *"Then the LORD God placed the man in [22]the Garden of Eden to cultivate it and guard it."* (Gen. 2:15).

We build and cultivate, but we also watch over and protect our relationship with God, our Creator. Failing to guard it is like having an orchard without boundaries or walls, without protection for the fruit we produce. *"A person without self-control is like a city with broken-down walls."* (Prov. 25:28 NLT). *"Continue steadfastly in prayer, being watchful in it with thanksgiving."* (Col. 4:2 ESV). Fatherlessness is an issue because most of our Western societies lack fathers. As claimed by statistics, in cases where the offender didn't know their father or the father left at a tender age, they commonly resort to crime. We find a skyrocketing increase among those with a criminal rap sheet. To have consistent and loving fathers are consequential—their contribution to our lives is vital. They build safe havens and snug spaces where sons and daughters can develop into doting fathers and mothers.

A testimony – the power of prophetic declarations

My next story is a testimony about how God uses prophetic declarations to bring transformation. Some years ago, I felt the Father's heart for a particular woman at church. The whole thing started just after we had begun a conversation. I told her: "You're a warrior!" I continued to address the core of her identity as a daughter of God—prophesying and affirming her with the Father's love. She started to weep, deeply impacted by the Holy Spirit. She told me her biological father didn't support her emotionally but failed to express affection for her. Furthermore, she also dealt with difficult relationships where she regularly felt accused or inadequate. That I, as a grown man, affirmed her was an empowering experience. She received a lot of emotional healing during the 15-20 minutes I ministered to her. Prophecy isn't confined to the forecast of future events. When we communicate what the Father

---

[22] **Gan-Eden** גַּן־עֵדֶן: The word used for garden actually means an enclosed garden, implying a secluded temple area with a barrier. *Gan* means "*garden* as enclosure" *Eden* means "fruitful, well-watered". If this was a garden-sanctuary, Adam was given a priestly duty to look after it (see Gen. 2:15 and Num. 3:6-7). For further study see: www.ritmeyer.com/2017/02/07/the-genesis-sanctuary/

says about a person or an event in the here and now, it is prophecy. She later told me how she felt she got activated on the inside. All of a sudden, it brought life to her potential. It was like hitting the switch on an internal dormant system. When she encountered the Father's love, she garnered new confidence and fear had to flee. It was a redefining moment in her walk with the Lord and changed her perspective on God and herself. In the coming weeks and months, she felt terrific and unbeatable, according to the scripture: *"No weapon formed against you shall prosper, and you will refute every tongue that accuses you. This is the heritage of the servants of the LORD, and their vindication is from Me," declares the LORD.* (Isa. 54:17 BSB).

To receive God's all-embracing love for us intentionally, on a day-to-day basis, is crucial.

When people don't feel cared for or lack fathers, they tend to quit church. It is, therefore, heavily on the Father's heart to heal and restore relationships. As God is pouring out his Spirit, he will address the issue of fatherlessness at a deep level. *"He will turn the hearts of the parents to their children, and the hearts of the children to their parents; or else I will come and strike the land with total destruction."* (Mal. 4:6 NIV). Most translations use *fathers*. In this eleventh hour, the Lord has planned to eradicate the orphan spirit through fathers who will nourish believers emotionally and spiritually. God's mercy through the release of true fathers will *"triumph over judgement"* (James 2:13). According to what the Holy Spirit revealed to me, he will soon visit his Church and [23]heal four generations of fathers simultaneously. That kind of restoration signifies that the Lord can reverse the curse and break cycles of fear, rejection and addictions. The Bible explains that God visits sins on children until the third or fourth generation, but he maintains his חֶסֶד *chesed*—or covenant love, to a thousand generations (see Exod. 34:7, Num. 14:18). I can still recall how fearful I was as a new believer. I struggled to see God as the loving Father he is. He had to take me on a long journey of healing before I recognised my intrinsic value. No matter where I am or how I feel, I am always surrounded by his unfailing love.

---

[23] **My comment:** The pagan and evil Jezebel married king Ahab and undermined his masculinity through witchcraft. *The spirit of Elijah* is the solution because it pushes back false prophets and connects people's heart to the Father, resulting in true purpose and restoration. The Lord heals the fatherless, as the attacks on men's God-given role and the family are ended by the Prophetic Spirit.

I am very fond of this [24]song:

> Father, father me
> I need Your love
> I need Your love
>
> Father, father me
> I feel so alone
> Longing for a home
>
> I need comfort, I need shelter
> I need healing for my soul
> Take this fear that I surrender
> Take me in, take me home
> Father me
>
> Father
> Father me
> Call me by name
> Call me by name
>
> Father, father me
> Take me to Your home
> Adopt me as Your own
>
> I need comfort, I need shelter
> I need healing for my soul
> Take this pain that I surrender
> Take me in, take me home

---

[24] **Father, father me:** Lyrics written by the Canadian worship leader Brian Doerksen, copyright © 1994 Father's House Publishing/All That Janz/East Broadway Music. All rights reserved. International copyright secured.

We are called to reflect the Father. Men, who are fathers, need to receive the Father's love by laying hold of healing and wholeness. In order to become good fathers, we have to be fathered ourselves. *"Even if you had ten thousand guardians in Christ, you do not have many fathers, for in Christ Jesus I became your father through the gospel."* (1 Cor. 4:15 NIV). In fact, the apostle Paul was unmarried and childless, yet he understood the significance of fatherhood. [25]'The Church has a greater need for spiritual fathers than for CEOs!' The cry for fathers to disciple and strengthen the Body of Christ is actualising the urgent need for genuine apostles. Paul's care for all the congregations he supervised epitomised a father's approach. He addressed the leaders of the church at Ephesus this way:

"Pay careful attention to yourselves and to all the flock, in which the Holy Spirit has made you overseers, to care for the church of God, which he obtained with his own blood. I know that after my departure fierce wolves will come in among you, not sparing the flock; and from among your own selves will arise men speaking twisted things, to draw away the disciples after them. Therefore, be alert, remembering that for three years I did not cease night or day to admonish every one with tears. And now I commend you to God and to the word of his grace, which is able to build you up and to give you the inheritance among all those who are sanctified. I coveted no one's silver or gold or apparel. You yourselves know that these hands ministered to my necessities and to those who were with me. In all things I have shown you that by working hard in this way we must help the weak and remember the words of the Lord Jesus, how he himself said, 'It is more blessed to give than to receive.' (Acts 20:28-35 ESV).

The cry for fathers to disciple and strengthen the Body of Christ is actualising the urgent need for genuine apostles. Paul's care for all the congregations he supervised epitomised a father's approach.

Paul lovingly watched over the churches he had planted, as with a flock: He warned and taught them in their homes and publicly. Time and again, he didn't burden them financially but took care of himself and his team. He protected and provided as a caring father would do through his apostolic ideal. We often refer to miracles as

---

[25] **Quote** from pastor John A. Holt.

a sign of apostleship, but what about fatherly attributes? (See 1 Cor. 4:15, 2 Cor. 12:12). Maybe that seems unimpressive and quite ordinary, but apostolic fathers demonstrate the Father's heart. Will they ignore your shortcomings? No, but they will help you to grow in the discipline of the Lord. If we only look for blessings from our leaders without receiving correction or guidance, how do we expect to progress steadily and consistently in the faith? When Christians live in compromise, they expect their leaders to give them grace by defending their bad decisions. It puzzles me. The same people don't hesitate to spurn constructive advice. Perhaps those who are out of line don't need any more space or grace but to be gently put in their place.

Successful discipleship is a combination of tough love and tender loving care. Please consider these two questions: 1. Do you honestly want to be mentored by seasoned leaders? 2. Are you committed enough to take responsibility for your emotional and spiritual progress? The truth is, if we are unwilling to welcome corrections, we will fail. Some believers ask favoured leaders to mentor them but do it slothfully and indecisively. A minority follows through with what they have been advised because personal reform comes at a price. On the threshing floor of our hearts, God, in his love, vigorously seeks to winnow out the chaff, so the pure wheat of eternal value may remain (see Luke 3:16-17). We have to let go of our cynical and unsanctified attitudes, soulish dross and fruitless self-justification. *"Therefore go out from their midst, and be separate from them, says the Lord, and touch no unclean thing; then I will welcome you, and I will be a father to you, and you shall be sons and daughters to me, says the Lord Almighty." Since we have these promises, beloved, let us cleanse ourselves from every defilement of body and spirit, bringing holiness to completion in the fear of God.* (2 Cor 6:17-18; 7:1 ESV). *Then Jesus told his disciples, "If anyone would come after me, let him deny himself and take up his cross and follow me."* (Matt. 16:24 ESV). Spiritual parenthood intends to disciple and discipline sons and daughters to live upright and sanctified lives, inspiring and leading them by example. Without a doubt, any mature fivefold minister can function as a spiritual parent or a mentor. *"A disciple is not above his teacher, but everyone when he is fully trained will be like his teacher."* (Luke 6:40 ESV). The next illustration shows all the different stages of discipleship. By the way, the principles also work for supervisors and managers that want to develop their employees:

4 STAGES OF DICIPLESHIP

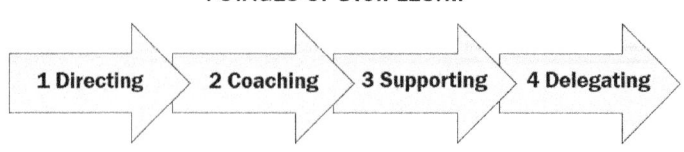

1 Directing → 2 Coaching → 3 Supporting → 4 Delegating

Teaching, rebuking, correcting and training 2 Tim 3:16

We will address spiritual authority more closely in chapter 10. We will also discuss the debated topic of apostolic covering. A heads-up: I don't insist on defending the concept, but I hope you will find my thoughts intriguing.

FIVEFOLD MINISTRY 5

Without a doubt, any mature fivefold minister can function as a spiritual parent or a mentor.

CHAPTER 3 - PROPHETIC PERSEVERANCE

Pursuit of truth

The Lord desires to bless and renew us by giving us a spiritual upgrade by improving our perception of him. An upgrade is an impartation of his nature. It's not difficult for God to do it, but it requires our cooperation with his Spirit. The Bible speaks of an enlightened path for those who stay close to God. *"But the path of the righteous is like the light of dawn, which shines brighter and brighter until full day."* (Prov. 4:18 ESV). If we listen to God and obey him, he helps us to be transformed *"from glory to glory"* (see 2 Cor. 3:17-18). His grace is transitional and progressive. It takes us from a previous season of glory and launches us into a new season with more of his glory. Obedience brings us to the next plateau of faith. We tend to slip back into the same old habits when we instead could move onwards and upwards. However, we should fix our gaze on Jesus and a Kingdom lifestyle, fully aware that our loyalty to him will be put to the test. When we confront sinfulness, compromise or darkness, we face the same dilemma: To resist or retreat—comparable to the fight or flight response. As Christians, God calls us to defeat all kinds of adversity and opposition without being bested by it. I have translated an old [26]Norwegian folktale, and I hope it will cheer you up. While we read this quaint little tale together, let us contemplate the importance of renewing our minds.

"The pig that was unhappy with his way of life."

Once upon a time, there was this pig that was unhappy with his way of life. For that reason, he decided to go to the Magistrates' Court, as he wanted to ask the judge for a new way of life. He would try his luck just like everyone else and see what the judge could offer him.

"What is your complaint?" the judge asked. "Oh, I am so disgruntled with my way of life, Sir!" the pig answered. "The horse munches oats, and the cow gets flour with water, and they both live in dry stables and cowsheds, whilst I only get pods and

---

[26] **My comment:** Asbjørnsen and Moe's Folktales, original title "Grisen og levemåten hans."

mirky water. During the daytime, I wade through soggy mud, and at night-time, I wallow in dirty, wet straws. Could you please tell me what justice there is in this, Your Honour?" he enquired. Well, the judge admitted that the pig had proven his point. He examined his books and gave him a verdict for a new way of life. "It is not fair that you should have a harsher regimen," he said. "From now on, you will eat wheat and pulses and sleep on silk sheets."

Well, the pig showed such gratitude and delight over this that he forgot whether it was night or day! On his way home, he chatted and grunted, "Wheat and pulses and sleeping on silk sheets! Wheat and pulses and sleeping on silk sheets! Wheat and pulses and sleeping on silk sheets!" After a bit, the road took a slight bend, passing through some woods where the fox was listening from one of the clearings nearby. The fox at once set out to play his cheeky little trick. With a soft and subtle voice, the fox began to whisper, "Pods and scraps and lying in muck!" To begin with, the pig didn't pay much attention to the noise. It kept on rehearsing, "Wheat and pulses and sleeping on silk sheets!" But still, the ceaseless chatter vexed him greatly: "Pods and scraps and laying in muck! Pods and scraps and laying in muck! Pods and scraps and laying in muck!" Finally, the pig gave in, and before he realised it, he repeated the exact same words. When he returned to the farm, all the animals began to ask him how his appearance in court went. "Did you get a verdict for a new way of life?" they asked him. "All right, all right", the pig replied: "Pods and scraps and lying in muck! Pods and scraps and lying in muck!" **The End.**

The pig knew he had options to live a fuller and happier life. On hearing the gospel for the first time or perusing the Bible, many of us get revved up and hopeful. We acknowledge that we come from a broken background due to a fallen world and the problems we have to struggle with, but we discover there is more to life than living in survival mode. Deep down inside, we anxiously long for our Maker's recognition and unknowingly seek to get our God-given dignity restored to us. When applied to life, God's promises come with rehabilitation to spirit, soul and body: Forgiveness for the spirit, sanctification for the soul and healing for the body. We are sons under grace and no longer slaves under sin. We are kings and priests, joint heirs with Christ and covenant people belonging to God's household. Our lives should, therefore, exhibit a higher standard because we represent the King of kings. Partnering with God's promises sets us on a pathway of radical change. His unmerited favour helps us rise above our challenges and become like Christ in our thinking and conduct.

Partnering with God's promises sets us on the path of radical change.

The pig went to the Magistrates' Court to get a verdict for a new way of life, which he was graciously granted. Our heavenly Father did the same through his covenant with Abraham. He fulfilled his oath in Christ through the cross and the resurrection. We are no longer under a curse but heirs of the promises and destined for blessing (see Gal. 3:7-9, 13). The Lord's final verdict was written in blood, signed for through Christ's redemptive sacrifice. Every believer embarks on a pilgrimage of change to gradually receive more of Christ's abundant life. Transitioning from one mentality to another requires effort, as old habits die hard. If we don't put our minds to it, we will resume our old habits (see Rom. 12:2, Phil. 2:12-13). Praise God that his Holy Spirit is always determined to coach us in the process of change! Let us abide in Christ and depend on his grace (see John 15:7). As time goes by, we learn to adopt the Father's perception of us, and we do it by constantly immersing ourselves in biblical truths about identity. Confessing God's Word, repeating his great promises aloud, is a tenable approach in laying hold of a superior spiritual reality: Christ in us, the Hope of glory, the new creation and the new self (see Col. 1:27, 3:9-10).

If we abide in Christ and depend on his grace, God's Spirit is always determined to coach us in the process of change.

The Word of God is not a compilation of dead formulas but contains living truths, able to impart his nature into every area of our lives. Jesus said his words are *"Spirit and life"* (see John. 6:63 and 2 Pet. 1:3-4). Renewing our minds isn't self-centred but about following Jesus wholeheartedly. Please forgive my little detour: God told Israel to speak his Word daily, remember the promises, and practically obey him. The Lord wanted Joshua to keep his mind focused and not lose track of his assignment (see Deut. 11:18-19, Jos. 1:8). We forego this biblical principle if we use confessions to force God's hand by commanding copious blessings to materialise. That is a view closely connected to New Age ideologies, like the law of attraction. Today, it's scary to see how churches shamelessly promote erroneous doctrines where they use faith, positive confessions and donations to hoard material wealth. This might as well be witchcraft disguised as charismatic spirituality, yet many get hooked on it. Are our motives on the same wavelength as the Father's plans for us? Do we confess God's Word with a pure and undistracted heart by choice?

When we set out to renew our minds, we enter into a savage battleground because our old nemesis wars against us. Satan tries to stop transformation from happening. In this process, we need perseverance while we contend for a permanent change of perspective. The fable's sweet but unsuspecting pig was at first elated by the blissful promise of a revamped and revived lifestyle. Enthused, he repeatedly talked about his new destiny on his way back to the farm. But the mischievous fox strategically interfered by whispering a different message along the way. Initially, the pig ignored the distracting voice, but because the fox persisted with its clever ruse, the gullible pig quickly succumbed to the compelling message. Simply put, the pig lost his focus and got duped by that lie from the fox.

When we sincerely renew our minds, we enter into a savage battleground. Our nemesis wars against us to stop every transformation from happening.

Most believers set out on their journey with great optimism, trusting the Father to be a caring and supportive God. Sadly, many lose heart after fiery trials and various disappointments. Our sworn enemy is a thief and murderer who only wants to steal, kill and destroy. He knows our history with God amounts to a powerful testimony and a valuable asset to be reckoned with. The devil has been around for thousands of years and is determined to wear us out. His calculated strategy is to entice us through compromise by brainwashing us to settle for a distorted reality. In terms of biblical doctrine, let us examine this claim: 'Christ purchased full forgiveness for our sins on the cross, but we are all still sinners.' The above statement acknowledges forgiveness but denies our right standing with God. It is partly true but has a wrong conclusion. If you are born-again, you will suffer from condemnation because this view prevents you from having bold faith. In the same way, to believe sickness to be a godsend whose sole purpose is to make you humbler is a misconception. I am not a proponent of measuring abundant life by material possessions or good health, which is a warped approach to this subject (see Luke 12:15). Neither do I think that misery is a proof of godliness (see Prov. 30:7-9). What truly matters is loving God with our eyes fixed on the eternal price. That said, our souls' enemy tries to inject his sneaky lies by twisting the truth to appeal to human reasoning (see Matt. 16:23).

Let us delve into the analogy with the fox and see what the Bible teaches: *"Catch the foxes for us, the little foxes that spoil the vineyards, for our vineyards are in blossom."* (Song 2:15 ESV). Foxes depict sinful attitudes and thoughts that need to be nipped in the bud to prevent trouble further down the line. False prophets are compared to foxes, so too are persecutors (see Ezek. 13:4, Luke 13:32). On the whole, foxes are considered vermin because they make much mischief. The notorious London foxes are everywhere: They traipse the streets and rummage through the rubbish bins at night. They scale walls and fences with catlike ease and navigate the rooftops. Their screams make your blood curdle. The pig in the folktale had but one fox stalking him. That situation pales in comparison with today's jarring voices of countless 'foxes', striving to distract us and destroy our divine calling. The spirit of this age wants to hypnotise us into a mindset where we regard ungodly lifestyles as tolerable. We suffer a bombardment of propaganda messages conveying that wallowing in the muck of immorality and depravity is not only commendable but normal. Many are scared of leaving such a depraved way of life because they fear what it entails: Those who rebel against the set norms are often ridiculed among their peers and in society at large. The next step is called [27] the spiral of silence, a phase where people's opinions retreat into silence in the face of perceived social animosity when they no longer hear people they meet or in the media voicing opinions similar to their own.

---

[27] **According to author Rupert Darwall:** "the idea of the spiral of silence was developed by West Germany's foremost pollster who, wait for it, worked in Joseph Goebbels' Ministry of Public Enlightenment and Propaganda." www.conservativewoman.co.uk/kathy-gyngell-interview-rupert-darwall-sinister-forces-behind-green-agenda/

The spirit of this age wants to hypnotise us into a mindset where we regard ungodly lifestyles as tolerable.

A rigged but clever system of worldly beliefs causes people to self-censor and censor each other. Basically, it's the mechanism of control, much like a crab tank syndrome: You don't need a lid on a crab tank. Why is that so? The other crabs will swiftly pull down the crabs that try to get out! Let me add: Concerning some topics, a healthy dialogue is almost impossible. In today's climate, we have crossed a threshold where dangerous ideologies have destroyed common sense. At times, if a debate arises, even fellow Christians will immediately attempt to correct you with misguided rhetoric, as they also fall under the spell of public disinformation. By design, the adversary makes use of a secular system to bewitch those he can sway (see 2 Cor. 11:3-4; 14-15, Gal. 3:1, Rev. 18:3). Today's mainstream media is the main engine of this gigantic [28]propaganda machinery. It's a vehicle driven by philosophies that regularly collide with traditional and biblical values. Ideological bigotry is inescapable because a few mega-corporations exclusively own and control most of the media outlets. These institutions seem hell-bent on mental uniformity, as they want to outlaw dissent.

Not only that, keenly supported by social media giants, they shut down the voice of truth and censor ideas they find unpleasant. This behaviour confirms the following quote by Philip Moeller: 'The truth is never dangerous. Except when told.' After 'fact-checking' you and others, they will mislabel your content as 'false' by blocking it and thus limiting its reach. Their adverse weapon is the calculated use of digital algorithms, with which they control the main flow of information and our view of reality. Their efforts are flagrant violations of one of our fundamental human rights, the right to freedom of expression. As I see it, journalists should feel an obligation to report events and viewpoints in an accurate and unbiased manner and then let the public decide for themselves what to think. The media outlets spin the narratives

---

[28] **Propaganda**: Today we see widespread use of deceptive propaganda techniques, mainly communicated through the mass media, official bodies and academia. Indoctrination is rampant and facts are being systematically suppressed, distorted or derided. Lately, tech giants have interfered by censoring users of social media platforms in a very unsettling way by deliberately colluding with powerful entities, at the expense of civil liberties. In Revelation, the word *pharmakeia* points to drugs and witchcraft. As a concept, it is likely to include cutting-edge technologies, to manipulate minds and control individuals and populations (see Rev. 18:23, 19:21).

their bosses dictate. They operate as thought police and want to gag people with opinions other than their own. If we analyse the general news coverage from the big media corporations, we regularly see synchronised efforts to present the same views on certain events and topics, using similar buzzwords, as if they were reading from the same script. If you dare to dispute their reports, they will try to discredit you, despite your rational objections. These media outlets have joined forces with the groups that collude against humanity, with an unhinged obsession to enslave us all. Legacy media is a part of the insidious establishment. Their power brokers hide in plain sight or secretly plot behind the scenes. [29]Prophecy expert, Paul McGuire, an author of many books, explains these actors' methods: 'Highly advanced, modern technologies also exist in the realm of scientific mind control, persuasion and creating groupthink for controlling the masses. Political campaigns, public opinion and wars have always been manipulated through the mass media's use of advertising techniques, propaganda, social engineering and the science of mind control.' Media power is about controlling narratives, often through mass hypnosis. Smokescreens, red herrings and false flags are tooled by the media to fool and control us. In a raging and ongoing spiritual war, the invisible battle for our minds, we must firmly stand our ground. We can stay abreast of the developments without being psychologically manipulated or mortified. Yet, finding truthful reports has never been trickier than now.

The moral dilemmas we come across aren't new, but also portrayed in John Bunyan's classic allegorical novel [30]'Pilgrim's progress'. It's historically considered the first British novel. For many decades, this book was widespread and only second best after the Bible by sold copies. It's a treasured, brilliant masterpiece. It has influenced countless literature lovers, including a long list of celebrated authors and preachers. Pilgrim embarks on his risky journey of faith, leaving the world behind and heading for Mount Zion, the Celestial City. In the epic saga, Pilgrim and his faithful friend Faithful face fierce opposition in the public sphere. As the plot thickens, the two

---

[29] **Source:** paulmcguire.us/nwv031218.html
[30] *The Pilgrim's Progress from This World, to That Which Is to Come* is a 1678 Christian allegory written by John Bunyan. It's regarded as one of the most significant works of religious, theological fiction in English literature. It has been translated into more than 200 languages and has never been out of print. In addition to *The Pilgrim's Progress,* Bunyan wrote nearly sixty titles, many of them expanded sermons. Bunyan came from the village of Elstow, near Bedford. Source: en.wikipedia.org

pious pilgrims arrive at Vanity Fair, asking to buy the precious commodity of truth. The mob treats them horribly, jeering and hurling abuse. The taunted companions get arrested and interrogated for refusing to buy the market's merchandise. Accursed worldly stuff is dangerous for a true child of God (see Jos. 7:10-26). Kingdom virtues are diametrically opposed to the worldly and degenerate Babylonian system. With his prophetic insight, Paul predicted the fate of all true believers: *"Indeed, all who desire to live a godly life in Christ Jesus will be persecuted."* (2 Tim. 3:12 ESV).

When you challenge the *Tyranny of Tolerance* in today's pop culture, you risk being denounced by the media demagogues as a bigot or a hater. A post-Christian society attacks truth from all sides. Truth is both booed and tabooed. Lies are perpetuated with the unsavoury intent to disregard scientific facts or rewrite history. Influential and moneyed cabals fund coordinated and vicious propaganda campaigns against those who support pro-life, [31]biological sex and marriage between man and woman, as these are the traditional views. [32]Nefarious groups have for decades sought to deconstruct the Christian family values in society and legalise the killing of sacred life in the mother's womb, as well as criminalise individuals who protest against this atrocity and other violations of God's ordinances. The latest savage onslaught is the chemical and physical mutilation of children, championed by a militant transgender lobby. This grotesque attack on identity is a matter very few people dare to protest. Are these political issues? No, they are, in fact, moral and spiritual issues. Abortion is by far the worst. This Holocaust of the womb yearly accounts for 73 million deaths worldwide (see Psalm 106:37-38, Jer. 32:35). I oppose the system behind this vile industry, but without pointing fingers at those who have had abortions and now regret it. The Lord, in his infinite mercy, will pardon any sin for those who lament their transgressions and turn to him. Shouldn't our legislative bodies uphold life and not defend or applaud a barbaric culture of death? Capitalising on fear, these actors

---

[31] **My comment:** Biological genders are scientific facts. There are only two: man and woman. The current push for so-called trans-rights is eroding the concept "woman". To create a new social order, they use doctored reports and wilfully altered language. Where are the feminists today?

[32] **Nefarious groups:** The cloak-and-dagger *Illuminati's* operations and networks. With carefully crafted narratives, these global elite families hide their sinister activities while keeping the population divided. It's not silly conspiracy drivel, but we talk about very real people who partake in satanism and dark arts. They are behind the Luciferian agenda, leading up to the New World Order, or the beast system. See Fritz Springmeier and his books, where he provides detailed information about this.

abuse governmental systems and create grim scenarios. By thinking the end justifies the means, they let no crisis go to waste to further their plans (see Psalm 2, 1 Cor. 2:6-8, Eph. 6:12, 1 John 5:19). Miscellaneous, egregious [33]subversion strategies have been implemented with the intent to distract, disrupt, destabilise, demoralise and destroy nations that once professed a solid faith in God. By driving a hard bargain, the global elites overplayed their hand for millions to see: 2020 marks the dismal year where these shady architects seized the pandemic as a fertile opportunity to initiate unwarranted worldwide chaos and change many laws. Was the crisis a dress rehearsal for a slew of other pre-planned events? The usual pandemic protocols were ignored. Unscientific and draconian measures, like harmful lockdowns and mask mandates were imposed, and basic unalienable rights were abruptly rescinded. In many places, [34]the remedy was far worse than the sickness itself, a fact vastly understated. Mass media [35]covered up this debacle, acting as arbiters of truth. In post-war times, many countries' governments were guilty of insane and unmatched overreach.

When [36]a crisis becomes a pretext for curtailing civil or human rights, I conclude it is A) orchestrated or B) weaponised to fit the elite's interests. Ordinary people don't get how guileful actors operate. In retrospect, it's easy to see how the virus scenario was politicised and propagandised, causing great damage to the public. It generated distrust in politicians and their favoured panel of medical expertise. The officially sanctioned programme was mitigation through mass inoculation, but people died while queuing for these jabs. Antibody therapies and other remedies, like the highly efficacious drug Ivermectin, were not in the picture. Facts about natural immunity for those who have had the disease were withheld or lied about. The sordid alliance of Big pharma, Big government, Big media and Big tech reared its ugly hydra heads. The unscrupulous push for vaccine mandates and passports was unsolicited and

---

[33] **Subversion** (from the Latin word subvertere, 'overthrow') refers to a process by which the values and principles of a system in place are contradicted or reversed, in an attempt to transform the established social order and its structures of power, authority, hierarchy, and social norms. Source: en.wikipedia.org

[34] See also: www.pandata.org/protocol-for-reopening-society/

[35] **My comment:** A cover-up is usually *a covert op. The media and big tech institutions frequently collaborate with and are assets for secret agencies like the CIA. The implications are grave because people systematically receive propaganda and not honest reporting. *a covert operation*

[36] **Hegelian dialectic:** Also known as problem–reaction–solution (PRS) To create the chaos and then offer a way to restore order. See also: dictionary.com/browse/hegelian-dialectic

illegal, and the real death toll was far lower than they claimed. This underhanded ploy was manoeuvred as a [37]Trojan horse to suppress the workforce, centralise power and help oligarchs to accumulate enormous wealth. It put into motion a huge financial restructuring programme, the Great Reset, that seeks a presumed 'equal outcome'. If applied, technocratic governance will curb financial freedom and other natural rights for ordinary citizens. Together with green policies like 'Climate Change' and 'Global Warming', the purpose of these efforts is, by many believed, not to involve sustainable living but social engineering to boost coercive control. The self-styled green protagonists smoothly gloss over the undemocratic aspects of their avowed philanthropic environmentalism. On the geopolitical scene, the establishment, via its varied operations and networks, follow the playbook for its [38]Neo-Feudal utopia—the emerging beast system. Before our very eyes, we see it manifests. Events like these are distinct prophetic pointers to the upcoming endgame before Christ's return. Nervous Christian leaders slate this dark narrative as they reject disturbing political speculation and conspiracies. Well, maybe they suffer from tunnel vision.

I think there is currently a danger for believers to simplify or complicate situations requiring prophetic discernment. Our Lord seriously warned us, through the Book of Revelation, of the coming deception, lawlessness and its iron-fisted system. There is a staggering number of churches that don't teach this book. To them, it's heavily controversial. Do we interpret significant cosmic events through the prophetic lens? Ignorance isn't always bliss. On the contrary, those who read *"the revelation from Jesus Christ"* will be blessed (see Rev. 1:1-3). Friends, it is time to wake up from our naïve slumber and burst the gigantic fantasy bubble many of us live in. What lies ahead is the dystopian society of a future authoritarian World State. The train has already left the station, and the world is getting increasingly more [39]Orwellian as we speak. The polarisation of society shows that our foe is working fast and relentlessly.

---

[37] **Trojan horse** - In British English 2. a trap intended to undermine an enemy. **Source:** collinsdictionary.com **My comment:** See also Rev. 6:2 The white horse of false peace precedes destruction. It's much like the peace offering the Greeks presented to Troy; the big wooden horse carrying hostile soldiers inside. A crisis that crashes economies but profits billionaires is just that.

[38] **Neo-feudalism** - This system is a repeat of the kind of society that existed in Mediaeval times, characterised by lesser social mobility and greater concentrations of power to a privileged few.

[39] **"Orwellian"** is an adjective describing a situation, idea, or societal condition that George Orwell identified as being destructive to the welfare of a free and open society. Source: en.wikipedia.org

Basic rights, like freedom of conscience, freedom of speech and freedom of religion, are under siege. The same goes for the right to own private property, freely assemble and engage in protests. The military-industrial complex or National Security State and their misuse of surveillance technology is booming, justified by purported safety concerns and the 'war on terror'. Should we allow peer pressure or manufactured social agendas to silence us? As citizens, we are wise if we act and use our voices and our votes. It's critical to take our stand now when policies threaten our civil liberties. If we fail to fight back, our freedoms may be lost once and for all. Nonetheless, we should never conflate freedom of speech and spiritual freedom. As God's children, we already have his permission to share the gospel publicly.

The tenets of Western society were built upon solid Judeo-Christian values, but these central pillars are heavily assaulted: *"When the foundations are being destroyed, what can the righteous do?"* (Psalm 11:3 NIV). When essential moral values steadily erode, families and communities disintegrate. An antidote to spiritual and moral decline is an authentic community. These are the sanctified believers—the praying House of God—built on the foundation of the apostles and prophets, having Christ Jesus as the chief Cornerstone (see Isa. 56:7, Eph. 2:20). In the heat of the discussion, we must always call to mind that God's love trumps all political ideologies. By taking the high ground, we address the root causes in prayer. We must voice our concerns without vilifying our opponents. We consciously attack the hidden forces behind activists through targeted spiritual warfare. In reality, we destroy their disjointed ideas with articulated truth, taking thoughts and attitudes captive—displaying the mind of Christ (see 2 Cor. 10:4-5). I can add that biblical conservative organisations fighting the battle legally on our behalf require our prayers and financial support. Today, we see a worldwide uprising as a burgeoning grassroots movement emerges: Millions of people support critical thinking, honest debates and free speech. These peace-loving citizens say good riddance to many decades of crumbling policies and sweeping systemic corruption enacted by governments responsible for colluding with massive corporate interests. Awakening to the truth, people are tired of being spoon-fed what to think, what to speak and what to do. We have a golden moment as believers to share the immutable gospel with them by anchoring their strengths and struggles in a spiritual reality. While we fight travesties of justice, as Christians, the gospel's redemptive power should make us aim for righteousness above and beyond civil rights. No public policy can reform the heart. The Holy Spirit is the one who creates inward change. At times, it's helpful to identify as believers and downplay some of our political views because of a changed reality. It's admirable if we are upstanding citizens and patriots, but that should never eclipse our calling to proclaim the gospel first. We can impact the surrounding culture with an excellent lifestyle by rising up in the prophetic and unifying Spirit of Truth. By doing that, we manifest unbroken and unrelenting love—pointing people to Christ alone. How do we engage with an increasingly hostile environment? As stated in the Book of Acts, Stephen became the first martyr as he wouldn't budge an inch in the face of persecution. Nehemiah, Daniel, Esther and other great models from the Bible were all godly persons who categorically refused to give in to the forces of wickedness. Knowing their cultural setting, they spoke the truth in love and stood by their faith. We can imitate them. When we do this, we blaze a trail for coming generations. All important truths are manifestly surrounded by controversies. Why is this so? The answer is simple: The devil opposes the truth. He hates it and has built a matrix of deception. If the truth is publicly contested or made light of, God's people will struggle to achieve reformative change for future generations. Research shows that it just takes two decades to indoctrinate a generation with atheistic ideologies, such as Neo-Marxism. We must beseech the Lord to raise up righteous people in politics or other key areas of influence. The next verse describes the moral decline of society: *"Justice is turned back, and righteousness stands far away; for truth has stumbled in the public squares, and uprightness cannot enter."* (Isa 59:14 ESV). The truth stirs controversy or causes people to get upset and riled up. There is always a price to pay for speaking the truth, but the eternal reward is greater. *"Behold, you delight in truth in the inward being, and you teach me wisdom in the secret heart."* (Psalm 51:6 ESV). If we live with integrity, perhaps our words of truth will be used by God to bring the lost back to him:

"But refuse foolish and ignorant speculations, knowing that they produce quarrels. The Lord's bondservant must not be quarrelsome, but be kind to all, able to teach, patient when wronged, with gentleness correcting those who are in opposition, if perhaps God may grant them repentance leading to the knowledge of the truth and they may come to their senses and escape from the snare of the devil, having been held captive by him to do his will." (2 Tim. 2:23-26 NASB).

Be gentle but always courageous! Confidently proclaim the truth in love and share the unadulterated gospel. Together, as God's people, we are raising up the archway of truth, where righteousness can enter, so his kingdom can be demonstrated.

Having an *awareness* of our true *identity* is what the renewing of our minds is genuinely about. Knowing the good, the acceptable, and the perfect will of God is essential (see Rom. 12:2). Jesus Christ is *"the Way, the Truth and the Life"* (see John 14:6). Christ is our Life, an expression of the perfect will of God. It may take tenacity to change our mindset and to fully realise what we have in him. Let us look closer at this verse: *"I have been crucified with Christ. It is no longer I who live, but Christ who lives in me. And the life I now live in the flesh I live by faith in the Son of God, who loved and gave himself for me."* (Gal. 2:20 ESV). Paul's great revelation of the cross encompassed both past and present realities. If and when we are tempted by sin, we can easily quote this verse, but it is more demanding to act on. If a truth isn't yet our felt reality, we should cry out to God for help to resist (see Matt. 26:41, John 8:31-32). It's powerful when the penny finally drops, and we reckon ourselves as already crucified, empowered by this amazing truth. I died with Christ: My old nature died; it was removed by the cross (see Rom. 6:6, Gal. 6:14). Still, we must implement this reality daily by faith. We are on the journey of unlearning the ways of the world by putting aside the habits coming from our former fallen state. We consider ourselves dead because we died to sin and were raised in righteousness. Thus, we became fully alive in Christ! Awaking to righteousness is a key component of living with integrity (see 1 Cor. 15:34). After a while, we will enter into a realm of rest—once we learn to depend on the Lord—while we make holiness a daily habit (see Heb. 4:1-11).

Christ is our Life, an expression of the perfect will of God. It may take tenacity to change our mindset and to fully realise what we have in him.

Our Saviour's cross is considered offensive within Rabbinic Judaism. The historical, awful atrocities against the Jewish people, done in the name of Christianity, partly explain why. Secondly, we have the pervasive antisemitic replacement theology and, lastly, the traditional rabbinic rejection of Jesus as the Jewish Messiah. In Israel, even the symbol of the cross is avoided in many schools, to the extent that plus signs are shunned when teaching maths. Instead, an inverted capital T is being used (⊥). In ancient times, cursed people were hung on trees (see Deut. 21:23, Gal. 3:13). Most Jews don't realise that Yeshua died in our place—we were the accursed ones. He did it for us! The prophet foresaw the reaction from his own people: *"By oppression and judgement he was taken away; and as for his generation, who considered that he was cut off out of the land of the living, stricken for the transgression of my people?"* (Isa. 53:8 ESV). Several rabbis believed in the suffering Messiah, as portrayed in [40]Isaiah chapter 53. The belief was accepted by many Jewish sages up to the 8th century. Today, some of the prophetic passages have been removed from the synagogues' Haftarah readings because they clearly point to Jesus as Israel's Messiah. Are these prophecies so literal and convincing that the spokesmen of Judaism fear their own could turn to the Christian faith? It's a logical explanation as to why they hide them.

Ironically, nothing is more genuinely Jewish than the carpenter from Nazareth, the promised Messiah. Many baffled Jews discover this when they dare to examine the New Testament, despite their rabbis' doomsayer warnings. Very often, Judaism doesn't refer to [41]the Torah itself but to its many *interpretations* and traditions, also known as the oral tradition. The oral Torah was added *after* the destruction of the second Temple. In doing so, the crafty rabbis tried to circumvent God's commands. Like the nuisance of today's liberal theology, the rabbinic traditions often obscure God's Word by creating loopholes or additions to it. Jesus didn't come to abolish the Law or Torah, but to *fulfil* it, and he meant the *written* Word (see Matt. 5:17).

How did Jesus fulfil the Torah?
1. His teaching validated the Scriptures as authentic and binding.
The Living Word confirmed the written Word.
2. As the perfect Man, he obeyed all the commands and exemplified them.
He became an embodiment of the Menorah, the Ark, the Lamb, the Tabernacle, etc.
3. Jesus demonstrated the practical application of the Torah.
He showed the intent behind the commands to be compassion and love.

---

[40] **Rabbi Rashi** (1040-1105 a.d.) didn't consider this chapter to be Messianic, the idea that the suffering servant was Israel, emerged as an alternative explanation. The 17th-century Jewish historian, Raphael Levi, revealed that the rabbis used to read Isaiah 53 in synagogues. But the chapter led to arguments and confusion, hence they decided to remove it from the prophetic synagogue portions.
[41] **Torah:** the word means instruction or teaching and comprises the five books of Moses.

The events and stories from the Old Testament are familiar to most Jews, but only a handful of people have done their own research. Even fewer know Yeshua's Jewish connection. When a messianic Jew read Isaiah chapter 53 to his father, he instantly exclaimed: "This is all about your Jesus!" He was unaware that this paramount text comes from the Bible's most famous prophet. The rabbis who fail to acknowledge Yeshua as the Messiah proves exactly what they contradict. Thus he has to be the promised Messiah! No other Jewish person historically fits the precise prophetic narrative like this disputed Nazarene. The proof is conclusive. However, we know he is a sign to be spoken against (see Luke 2:34). The shape of the cross is enthralling, and it was known as a covenant sign long before the infamous Romans used the wooden tool as a cruel mechanism of torture and execution. In the not-too-distant future, our beloved Jewish friends will readily embrace the cross by acknowledging Yeshua as their Messiah, who has already come: *"... they will look to me, the one they have pierced."* (Zech. 12:10 NET). Against the sceptics' preposterous claims, the New Testament contains a lot of empirical evidence, like eyewitness reports. By applying forensic methods to determine truth, it is not hard to prove that the stories of the gospels were based on the factual history involving tangible events. *"For we did not follow cleverly devised myths when we made known to you the power and coming of our Lord Jesus Christ, but we were eyewitnesses of his majesty."* (2 Pet. 1:16 ESV).

In Gen. 1:1, we find the letters Aleph and Tav, as it reads: *"Beresheet bara Elohim et hashamayim ve'et ha'arets."* בְּרֵאשִׁית בָּרָא אֱלֹהִים אֵת הַשָּׁמַיִם וְאֵת הָאָרֶץ Some scholars argue that the two letters, in the middle of the paragraph (אֵת), represent Christ, the personified Word. *"In the beginning God - Aleph-Tav - created the heavens and the earth."* That may, in fact, be true. The Book of Revelation describes Jesus with the Greek term [42]Alpha and Omega, which equals Aleph-Tav, the first and the last letter of the Hebrew alphabet (see Rev. 21:6, 22:13). The oldest symbols for both letters are the oxhead, for Aleph (𐤀), and the cross (X), for Tav. The ancient pictograph for Tav is two crossed sticks. These letters symbolise 'the strength of the covenant'. The Hebrew alphabet had the X as the covenant sign. Interestingly, the Tabernacle's furniture was laid out in the perfect shape of the cross. In the wilderness, when Israel

---

[42] **Article, Aleph-Tav:** www.oneforisrael.org/bible-based-teaching-from-israel/a-little-word-with-a-big-meaning/ **My comment:** Some scholars think *Bar-reishit* in Gen. 1:1 means the firstborn son.

camped around the Tabernacle, it could be viewed from above in the configuration of a cross! To the north, we had Dan, with the banner of an Eagle, then Asher and Naphtali. To the east, Judah, with the banner of a Lion, then Issachar and Zebulun. To the west, Ephraim, with the banner of an Ox, then Manasseh and Benjamin. To the south, Reuben, with a banner of a Man's head, and then Simeon and Gad. The Tabernacle was situated in the centre, with the tribe of Levi representing God's presence. In the Book of Revelation, we find the four living creatures with similar features, like the banners of the twelve tribes, now facing towards the Throne.

LION
OX
MAN
EAGLE

In the wilderness, when Israel camped around the Tabernacle, it could be viewed from above in the configuration of a cross!

The pattern followed is, as in heaven, so on earth. The symbolism of the cross is fascinating: One beam is vertical—denoting reconciliation from Heaven towards earth, as ordained by the Father, whilst the other beam is horizontal—signifying the impact of reconciliation on a societal level, displayed through the believers. In the same way, we receive forgiveness from the Father; we release forgiveness, all by the grace of God. The cross of Christ became history's greatest plus sign! It now adds forgiveness, healing, deliverance and restoration to mankind. To receive the gospel without becoming a part of it is virtually impossible. Once received, it affects our lives in many ways. Obedience releases a domino effect. The cross is a multiplication sign as well. In John 12:24, Jesus revealed how the single kernel must die in order to multiply and bear fruit. The law of multiplication runs as a principle throughout Scripture. When we die to our own carnal agendas, we get fully awakened to God's purposes and plans. The Kingdom expands because God's grace makes his Spirit flow freely through us. Besides, there is a huge difference between a self-serving and a God-serving life. We have the opportunity to either indulge the flesh or surrender to the Spirit of Christ (see Gal. 5:16-26).

The Christian life starts with *done*, whilst man-made religions concentrate on doing. Grace and works are totally opposite of each other. As we now have seen, through the cross, all of us legally died to sin. We were crucified with Christ—past tense—it did happen. Our old self was finished off. Full stop. Our challenge is to partner with this brand-new reality and act like our old lifestyle was done with. By the Spirit of God, we daily deaden the deeds of the flesh (see Rom. 8:13). When we exercise the life in the Spirit and keep in step with him, the ninefold fruit manifests through us in beautiful ways: *"But the Holy Spirit produces this kind of fruit in our lives: love, joy, peace, patience, kindness, goodness, faithfulness, gentleness, and self-control. There is no law against these things!"* (Gal. 5:22-23 NLT). If we respond to God's Word, it activates his presence in and through us. The fruit of the Spirit is referred to as one *fruit*, singular, not separate fruits. Do you have love? Then you also have patience and self-control. It's a package deal. By allowing the Holy Spirit to express himself through us, it inevitably brings his majestic world into ours! Let us eagerly give in to our spirit's constant yearning to encounter the Father on a daily basis and sustain our longing for him alone.

The fruit of the Spirit is referred to as one *fruit*, singular, not separate fruits. Do you have love? Then you also have patience and self-control.

Regarding the cross: Two vital truths came into effect through Jesus' finished work. One is metaphorically speaking *negative*, and one is *positive*. The *negative* represents what we died to, and the *positive* is what we came alive to. These two concepts reflect different sides of the same reality. Please allow me to elaborate:

1) Do you know you lost your 'right' to act independently because you died with Christ on the cross? Some Christians think that their right to live on their terms still applies. These believers treat the precious gifts of eternal life and forgiveness as convenient contributions to their predominantly self-centred lives. God's forgiveness becomes an excuse for saying things like: "I'm only human." Ignoring the consequences of sin by using faith to shirk our responsibilities is to flout God's holy standards. To repent of sin is to admit we are human, yet also endowed with divine power: We are a new creation in Christ Jesus (see 2 Cor. 5:17). On our conversion, when we were born of God, a new realm of grace opened up to us. It enabled us to imitate Christ and the Father. At that point, we surrendered to God's perfect will. It was a lead-in to a yielded life, where we follow the Father's will: *"For it is God who works in you to will and to act in order to fulfil his good purpose."* (Phil. 2:13 NIV). Even decisions like where to live and where to work are matters we should pray about (see James 4:13-16). Yet most Christians live in the same place, from the cradle to the grave. Do you know that none of us has the right to get offended anymore? Love is not easily aggravated or infuriated, the Bible tells us (see 1 Cor. 13:5). We are wise to remain anchored in God's love by praying in the Holy Spirit (Jude 1:20-21). Offence, anger and resentment cause believers to misrepresent the gospel: It separates close friends and grieves the Spirit of God. It is wiser to choose the perfect way of love. There is no other viable option if we truly want to follow Jesus Christ.

Did you realise that because of the cross, we lost the 'right' to speak our minds? Our non-stop whinging on social media platforms reveals a real lack of composure. Let us exercise sound judgement and abide by the famous saying, 'If you don't have anything nice to say, say nothing at all.' In an increasingly polarised society, we face uncommon and complex challenges. Since the arrival of social networking services, a novel trend has been rising: If we disagree, we retract our support from individuals or coalitions we dislike or actively oppose them. Cancel Culture has arrived because the *Ego* has landed! Many believers, being citizens of a so-called free society, think they can criticise the same way others do. Nothing is further from the truth. Since we turned to Christ for salvation, the cross changed that reality for good. I don't mean we shouldn't try to exert our influence by addressing the more serious issues. We definitely should, but it requires wisdom because we are called to follow in the footsteps of our Saviour. Some think that political power will solve these issues, but unless you understand this minefield and are called to take it on, politics may be the wrong path. As disciples, we were commissioned to go into *"all the world";* hence our skills and leverage will naturally vary. There is no question about it. The Lord wants his representatives everywhere.

To our surprise, it appears like the disciples didn't immediately seek to petition the governing institutions in order to abolish heinous practices like slavery and other social injustices. Initially, they addressed these tough challenges by demonstrating the gospel—often enduring persecution and death in the process—and they left an indelible mark. In the end, all social classes were impacted through effective soul-winning, including high officials. When these leaders' hearts mellowed, it did affect their policies. Over the first 100 years of Christianity, huge swathes of the Middle East had received the true gospel. [43]The impious Roman empire was brought to its knee. Paul was assigned to witness to kings and commanders (see Acts 9:15). The New Testament authors urged the Church to pray for people in government and honour persons of high standing (see 1 Tim. 2:1-4, 1 Pet. 3:13-17). To practically facilitate reconciliation between God and man, our intercession is required. When the Lord touches and transforms our hearts, this will eventually reshape our society on a collective scale. Intercession is oftentimes an underrated spiritual catalyst for righteousness, despite being extremely powerful. Together with the preaching of God's Word, it will cause godly people to rise to authority (see Prov. 28:28, 29:2).

God wants his servants to occupy the territory the devil has stolen. It's time for the slumbering giant to wake up and speak up! Let us not cower in fear but declare the truth with boldness. The Lord can unseat ungodly rulers and dismantle their evil influence in order to further his good plans for our planet (see Psalm 2:1-12, Dan. 2:21, 2 Cor. 10:4-6). Lately, several prophecies have surfaced about how God wants to judge corruption in high places. It seems like God is preparing for an Exodus-like showdown, on a global scale, unlike anything we have ever seen, but it's far too early to be self-congratulatory. Creating seismic shifts in history will require our watchful support of these prophecies and substantial intercession. It will tip the scales in our favour, provided that God is our only hope.

2) Do you know you now have the privilege and the power to live a Christlike life? Christ left a pattern for us all to imitate (see Eph. 5:1-2). Note that in Lev. 11:44 and 1 Pet. 1:16, we read: *"Be holy as I am holy."* The old command still stands. Under the New Covenant's reality, enforcement changed into empowerment! During the Old Covenant, God instructed his people to live separately and abhor the surrounding Gentile nations' despicable practices, a decree that was non-negotiable. Hidden

---

[43] **My comment:** The Romans tolerated numerous different religions, but Christianity was far from a conventional religion. Because of the belief in a resurrected Saviour, they viewed it as a dangerous superstition. Over five million Christians were persecuted and killed by the Roman government for the duration of 250 years. It began with Nero in 54 A.D., and ended with Diocletian in 313 A.D.

within the strict command was a prophetic hint about the Messianic reality. The phrase *"thou shalt", and thou shalt not"*, would soon transition into *"you will be able to"* and *"you will have the power to resist!"* The Holy Spirit gave the Law, or [44]Torah, on Mount Sinai, and he would one day inscribe his laws on the tablets of our hearts (see Ezek. 11:19-20; 36:26-27 and Jer. 31:33). Modern citizens love their tablets and are infatuated with their handheld contraptions, but nobody writes better apps than God for the eternal tablets of the human hearts! The Jewish people got the Torah during the first recorded Pentecost. Christians view the second Pentecost as a main transformative event—when the Father poured out his Spirit upon the 120 praying disciples gathered in the upper room, in Jerusalem, 50 days after Jesus' resurrection (see Luke 24:46-49, Acts 2:1-4). Intoxicated with the new wine, they boldly preached the gospel. God faithfully fulfilled his promise; to empower his own people through his glorious, enabling and indwelling presence. By virtue of imputed righteousness, holiness could be imparted. Imputed righteousness represents how God, the Father, now sees us through Christ's perfect life and credits his righteousness as a gift to us. The next verse brilliantly expresses this truth: *"For by one sacrifice he has made perfect forever those who are being made holy."* (Heb. 10:14). The game-changer is God's glory moving into our core, the human spirit. What can be more beautiful than touched and transformed people, filled and led by the wonderful Holy Ghost?

The cross can be regarded as a crossing, a junction where two crossroads meet. It embodies choice. Nobody is left unchallenged by the straightforward message of the cross (see 1 Cor. 2:2). The cross epitomises either salvation or judgement. Some individuals are surprisingly clever to understand what it represents: It repulses them,

---

[44] **The Torah:** Most rabbis believe in both a written Torah and an oral Torah. The oral Torah is the compilation of writings forming the Talmud. By using their own traditions, the Scribes, the Pharisees and later the rabbis interpreted the written Torah, which are the five books of Moses. At times their interpretation collided with what God commanded Moses, thus their tradition nullified God's Word (see Mark 7:13). Jesus warned against it. *"The teachers of the law and the Pharisees sit in Moses' seat. So, you must be careful to do everything he [Moses] tells you. But do not do what they [the Pharisees/Scribes] do, for they do not practise what they preach."* See Matt. 23:2-3 - according to the Hebrew manuscript of Matthew. See also v. 13. Rabbinical authority must lean on the *written* revelation of the Scripture, and not on different rabbis' alternative interpretations. See also: oneforisrael.org/bible-based-teaching-from-israel/the-twisted-drash-interpretations-of-the-rabbis/

as they instinctively understand it brings death to self. I have noticed how some non-believers find themselves at risk of losing control of their own life by embracing the cross, and they have an acute awareness of it. They are right. Of course, death to self is only one of the effects of the cross. Its stunning beauty is earmarked for those who pierce the sacred veil of salvation. It's mind-boggling how some Christians can treat the cross so flippantly. Salvation by the cross is to surrender to the Lordship of Jesus Christ. 'Cross-marked' is a phrase commonly used within Nordic Christianity—it describes devout and surrendered believers. I think of it as a title of honour for those who willingly follow Christ in the face of being ridiculed and persecuted for his name's sake. There is a reproach to bear when we follow our Lord and Saviour: *"So also Jesus suffered and died outside the city gates to make his people holy by means of his own blood. So let us go out to him, outside the camp, and bear the disgrace he bore."* (Heb. 13:12-13 NLT). On receiving God's salvation and abounding life, our choice is to allow Jesus to assert ownership over us. Beware that those who do not enter the sheepfold through Christ the Lord, the Gate for the sheep, will later on be rendered useless because they are illegitimate thieves and imposters (see John 10:1-10).

Salvation by the cross is, in essence, to accept the Lordship of Jesus Christ.

Why do some Christians imagine that forgiveness is unconditional and lordship is somehow optional? As a result, the teachings like hyper-grace have crept into many churches. It's considered one of the greatest heresies of the 21st century. Let us go over the following verse: *"But there is forgiveness with thee, that thou mayest be feared."* (Psalm 130:4 ASV). *"Whoever conceals their sins does not prosper, but the one who confesses and renounces them finds mercy."* (Prov. 28:13 NIV). The fear of the Lord is cited because: 1) God alone can forgive us, a sobering reminder. 2) Without genuine repentance, forgiveness might be forfeited (see Heb. 6:4-9, 1 John 5:16-18). Absolution of sins is a concept occasionally interpreted quite lopsided by Western churches. Often we ask God to forgive us for our sins but then repeat our blunders many times over. Is seclusiveness a part of the problem, that we hide our secret selves from God and our fellowships? Are we trying to avoid exposure, dismayed by our shame? Do we misconstrue openness as a weakness? Of course, we should resist the devil's temptations but not disregard brotherly help. We are encouraged to confess our sins and weaknesses and pray for each other, to get healed and made whole (see

James 5:16-20). Confession of sins was central to the early Methodist revival. The astute John Wesley connected sanctification to community—he coined the phrase [45]*social holiness*. God's holy people knew they needed to confess their wrongdoings, renounce them and turn away from them. Israel initially sought permanent change, even when they lived under an inferior covenant (see Heb. 8:7-13). If we are honest, we will admit that we live on a moral greyscale—we need God's grace every second of the day. There is also a *grace-scale* where we can enjoy and reflect his goodness.

It's actually possible to confess your *sins* without confessing your *sin*. We see a small distinction between Psalm 32 and Psalm 51. In the first psalm, David confesses his transgressions, but in the latter, he divulges his iniquity—the invisible source of his actions. In Joel 2:13, we read: *"Rend your hearts, not your garments."* Repentance wasn't regarded as an outward exercise but an inward turning away from sin. Israel's duplicity as an idol-worshipping people, on the pretence of serving Yehovah, was exposed by the ancient prophets: *"... they have turned unto me the back, and not the face"* (Jer. 32:33 ASV). Unrequited love grieved the Father's heart immensely! John the Baptist told the sanctimonious Pharisees: *"Produce fruit worthy of repentance!"* (Matt. 3:8). God-fearing behaviour leads to a change from within, but some believers have seared their consciences by repeatedly overstepping the boundaries of grace. They still profess their faith in the crucifixion, but in a misguided way. They don't have a repentant heart because they are desensitised. Below the silent surface lurks the deadly but treacherous undercurrent of false comfort that precedes false peace and false rest (see Jer. 6:14). May the Lord prevent us from entering into such a tragic state! If we refuse to obey God after receiving salvation, it can be devastating to assume forgiveness. Obedience is the fruit of Christ's redemptive love continuously at work in our hearts. In our newfound love, we zealously *desire* to follow his will. His life-giving Spirit inside us inspires us to please our Lord and Saviour.

"... according to the foreknowledge of God the Father by being set apart by the Spirit for obedience and for sprinkling with Jesus Christ's blood. May grace and peace be yours in full measure! (1 Pet. 1:2 NET).

---

[45] **Source:** See the article at seedbed.com - Kevin Watson, the Methodist Band meeting: Confession is for Protestants too!

Those who seek him receive the grace to carry out his Word, and this Bible verse explains it: The blood of Christ is reserved for people who repent and trust in him. In essence, sin is not believing; refusing to repent (see John 16:9). Without a contrite heart, we cannot receive God's forgiveness. This is an incontrovertible fact. See also 1 John 1:7 NIV: *"But if we walk in the light, as he is in the light, we have fellowship with one another, and the blood of Jesus, his Son, purifies us from all sin."* To walk together in holiness and brotherly love is proof of our conversion. Can we rightfully claim to be God's legitimate children without bearing fruit? We rarely hear this kind of preaching from the pulpits. Weak and permissive pastors are afraid of disquieting their listeners. They prefer jolly people over holy people and recklessly risk eternal damnation for those they refuse to caution. Apostasy is dangerous. Is it unloving to sound the alarm? Was it not God, through his faithful servants, and not man, who set forth repentance as a condition to be cleansed by Christ's blood? Faith and repentance are synonymous expressions of receiving everlasting life (see John 17:3, Acts 20:21). By trusting in Jesus, we seek to please him, and his grace helps us change for the better. Let us not receive his precious grace in vain (see Acts 20:21, Tit. 2:11, 2 Cor. 6:1). Truly happy *"are all who fear the Lord, who walk in his ways"* (see Psalm 128:1). When we choose sanctification we get fulfilled and no day is ever uneventful.

The blood of Christ is reserved for people who repent and trust in him.

The cross represents both suffering and transformation. Although vital, the cross was never meant to become our final destination. Let me rephrase that: The primary purpose of our co-crucifixion with Christ was to reconcile us with God, the Father, positioning us to receive overflowing life from him. When we died with Christ, we became dead to sin and alive to God (see Romans 6:1-11). We finally arrived at our destination when we rose again with our Saviour. We were included in his glorious resurrection, and the cross became the transition to a victorious life with the Risen One. Having that in mind, we choose not to dwell on our past missteps but focus on the newness of life—our newfound identity in him. Of course, it's wrong to think of the cross as insignificant or obsolete, as remission of sins cannot be received apart from the cross. God's Holy Spirit always reverts our attention to the cross, over and over again. The bloodstained cross remains forever the epicentre of the gospel. Joshua's exploits in the promised land hint at this reality because he always returned to the prominent [46]Gilgal. When Joshua left the camp at Gilgal and then returned to Gilgal, we see how Israel victoriously fought off their enemies and stayed on track. Whereas in the Book of Judges, which records the period after Joshua, we don't see that pattern anymore. At this point, Israel faced defeat. Gilgal is a foreshadowing of Calvary, where Jesus died and removed our sin, guilt and shame. On the third day, the stone at the tomb was rolled away, testifying how sin was paid for indefinitely.

If we fail to think of Golgotha as our source of victory, we will very quickly derail spiritually and lose pace in our race of grace (see Heb. 12:1-2). In our Christian faith, we don't evidence a morbid curiosity by rehearsing the reality of the cross time and again when we *"proclaim the Lord's death until he comes"* (1 Cor. 11:26 NIV). What we *celebrate* is the *victory* Jesus won on our behalf. It's very important to remind ourselves of what the Crucifixion signifies in our daily walk with the Lord: *"But far be it from me to boast except in the cross of our Lord Jesus Christ, by which the world has been crucified to me, and I to the world."* (Gal. 6:14 ESV).

In our walk with Christ, history's unforgettable moment of redemption is our safe reference point. The forever Blameless Passover Lamb of God obliterated our sin by his sacrifice. We confidently choose to confess the victory won on our behalf by trusting in the cross, as we remind powers and principalities that they were disarmed and conquered once and for all (see Eph. 3:10, Col. 2:15). We no longer mourn in front of the cross—only focusing on sorrow, suffering or shortcomings. By God's mercy, we have now made the transition to the resurrection side of the cross! Our focus shifted from past sinfulness to present righteousness. With grateful adoration, we look to Jesus by humbly clinging to his eternal and saving grace. We don't trust in our own substandard works but in the Saviour alone (1 Cor. 1:30, Eph. 2:9-10). Being heirs to the Kingdom, we access a privileged place of eternal victory. We have crossed over to our blood-bought inheritance, sealed by Jesus' resurrection.

The bloodstained cross remains forever the epicentre of the gospel.

---

[46] **Gilgal -** גִּלְגָּל was where the Israelites encamped immediately after crossing the River Jordan. The Israelites were circumcised there, and it means 'rolled way', as their shame was removed. This act was a rite of passage, a ceremonial event, marking their distinct identity as God's people.

```
    A
    M
GR  A  CE
    Z
    I
    N
    G
```

CHAPTER 4 - PROPHETIC PATTERNS

The power of the testimony

When we browse the text of Hebrews chapters 11 and 12, the author introduces us to a great cloud of witnesses from times past and their powerful testimonies. Chapter 12 portrays Jesus as the ultimate witness because of the heartache and hardship he endured—culminating at the cross, where he shed his holy blood on our behalf. Sermons from Hebrews 11 about the heroes of faith are pretty standard, as well as messages from Hebrews 12 about fixing our eyes on Jesus. Have you noticed the common thread in these two chapters? A witty preacher once said: "Taking a text out of context is conning the text." We can say Amen to that. The Old Testament has different types, shadows and pictures of Jesus, which are prophetic paradigms or patterns (see Luke 24:44). These heroes of faith carry a vast body of revelation about the workings of the Holy Spirit during their lifetime. 1 Pet. 1:11 specifically explains that it was the Spirit of Christ who worked in and through the prophets under the Old Covenant. By studying the accounts of Joseph, Moses, Gideon, Samuel and many others who belong to the cloud of witnesses, we find magnificent characteristics of Christ revealed. Their powerful testimonies are far from outdated but relate closely to our walk with God today.

In the Old Testament, we see different types, shadows, pictures and prophecies of Jesus, which are prophetic paradigms or patterns.

"Therefore, since we are surrounded by such a huge crowd of witnesses to the life of faith, let us strip off every weight that slows us down, especially the sin that so easily trips us up. And let us run with endurance the race God has set before us." We do this by keeping our *"eyes on Jesus, the champion who initiates and perfects our faith. Because of the joy awaiting him, he endured the cross, disregarding its shame. Now he is seated in the place of honour beside God's throne. Think of all the hostility he endured from sinful people; then you won't become weary and give up."* (Heb. 12:1-3 NLT).

Chapter 12 starts with the word *"therefore"*. It refers to the previous chapter and the recorded stories of the heroes of faith. *"Therefore"* basically means: "taking this into consideration". What exactly are we to consider? The clue is the huge crowd or the great cloud of witnesses. We can review and study their stories and testimonies to learn how God intervened and then act on these truths in our own lives. Is it within reach to get an impartation of the same kind of grace and wisdom the heroes of faith received from God? In conquering sin and weaknesses, can we learn from them? Or get sudden breakthroughs? I firmly believe so because I have experienced this first hand. Several years ago, we held meetings in two Pentecostal churches in Norway. We preached at different locations but in the same region. In the morning service, I expounded the Prayer of Jabez (see 1 Chron. 4:9-10). The prayer is not a formula but an incredible testimony. What happened next was thrilling. My wife, Jane, is used to moving in revelatory gifts, like words of knowledge and words of wisdom. She got no concrete words, or images, whereas I got detailed pictures revealed to me by the Holy Spirit. Without realising it, I had entered an unexpected realm of grace. Once the meeting began, I shared what I got. As God's released his presence, many people were touched. At that time, Jane got something to share as well.

Before we left, the church had prepared a meal for us. Some local friends joined us at the table. Once again, I received pictures and words from God. I told the husband of one of the servers that I could see he was getting new lungs. I also felt a burning sensation in my chest. At that very moment, I said out loud that God was healing him. His wife immediately exclaimed: "He has [47]COPD!" Three days later, the pastor of the church wrote us a message that this elderly man had put on his training gear as he wanted to go for a run. Despite protests from his wife, he informed her that he felt absolutely great! When his doctor examined him, he found no trace of this vile chronic disease. It was totally gone. Glory to God!

When I preached about the prayer of Jabez, the Lord extended my 'borders', as with Jabez. The impact of his story drastically surpassed my expectations and galvanised me into a stronger use of spiritual gifts. At that point, the Holy Spirit imparted increased supernatural grace for both revelation and miracles. When the author of Hebrews wrote his grand epistle, I am sure he was fully aware of the potential the testimonies represented to his audience. Are you in need of healing, deliverance,

---

[47] **Chronic obstructive pulmonary disease** (COPD) is a group of progressive lung diseases.

resilience or empowerment? When you study these witnesses' distress, pain and vulnerability, their issues will help you identify and detect the same things in your life. Researching a biblical character with similar struggles as ours, and studying their life story, can be exceedingly rewarding if we pay close attention to how they overcame. Let their stories inspire you to receive the same kind of grace. Jot down the insights you get, then pray into it and ponder it. Discover the tools God is giving you through the process, and then start using your new tools. Explore the power of the testimony! *"For the testimony of Jesus is the spirit of prophecy."* (Rev. 19:10 ESV). Testimonies prophesy about Jesus—they bear his name and nature. Predictions are a small part of prophecy. Prophecy offers prospects for transformation, available through the encounters embedded in the testimonies. Paul verified this powerful principle in these important verses: *"All Scripture is God-breathed and is useful for teaching, rebuking, correcting and training in righteousness, so that the servant of God may be thoroughly equipped for every good work."* (2 Tim. 3:16-17 NIV). When we start to study the promises, we embark on a journey of discovery into the boundless treasure trove of God's loving heart. Miraculous interventions and riches untold are locked up within the prophetic dimension. By faith, we tap into what God did through the blessed and ancient doors of testimonies. Many relive their visitations when they share their own strong encounters with the Lord. These are flashbacks to eternal moments of divine intervention. Graham Cooke, well-known for his incisive and eloquent style, said this: 'A testimony is a victory to be replicated.'

A testimony is a victory to be replicated.

Our Lord never intended the Bible just to be a storybook or a set of rules. God is, of course, the ultimate storyteller. It's history but also *his* story. Stories and promises were handed down to us to proclaim God's faithfulness and unlock potential. If we seek his face, he will provide us with his hidden manna (see Rev. 2:17). The Bible is a manual to discover Immanuel! Jesus, [48]The Living Word, is [49]God's explicit and

---

[48] **Rhema:** Note that in Rom. 10:8 the Greek term ῥῆμα *rhema* is used twice and directly connected to Christ, the active and personified Word of faith. We live by the daily rhema (see Matt. 4:4).

[49] **Logos:** In John 1:1, 14 the Greek λόγος *logos* is interpreted as the defining cosmic principle or plan. John also directly connects *logos* with the Word of God, namely the second person of the Trinity - Jesus - the divine reason behind all Creation (see Gen. 1:1, Rom. 11:36 and Col. 1:15-17).

expressed will, revealed in the flesh; he who descended, resurrected and ascended into undying glory. Preparing the ground for personal encounters is wise. Can we emulate their lives? No, but we can ask God for the grace to love and obey as fiercely as they did by mimicking a yielded and trusting lifestyle. Early Jewish and Christian believers often applied the Old Testament stories as templates of faith, courage and wisdom. By reciting these stories, they aroused hope and expectation. From time to time, they accessed remarkable grace. God can utilise testimonies, or the laying on of hands, to impart grace. Still, I can't imagine how to impart spiritual maturity. We develop individual growth relationally, which takes time and effort. Once we have discovered the biblical road map, it inspires us to get our own unique history with the Lord. Then we might experience heroic levels of faith as well!

God with us   Ἐμμανουήλ | עִמָּנוּאֵל   Immanuel
God's Word

The Bible is a manual to discover Immanuel!

King David was a man who loved God's presence. At his lowest point, at Ziklag, *"David strengthened himself in the Lord"* (1 Sam. 30:6). How did he regain his sturdiness? I envision how David reminded himself about past encounters with the Lord and the prophetic words he once received. Maybe he also contemplated how Joseph, Moses and the other patriarchs persevered through trials. As a result, his spirit was fired up, his soul encouraged, and his body invigorated. By turning despair into dependence on God, he activated his faith. After doing so, he got the courage to pursue his enemies and won a great victory (see 1 Sam. 30:1-30). The nation of Israel was instructed to constantly keep God's testimonies: *"You shall diligently keep the commandments of the Lord your God, and his testimonies and his statutes, which he has commanded you."* (Deut. 6:17 ESV). To keep means to observe and to watch over. A part of the covenant was to remember the Lord's testimonies. Testimonies were intended to be remembered, reviewed and rehearsed because they reminded God's people of the Almighty's historical involvement and the covenant blessings they corporately enjoyed over and over again. As a matter of fact, God inaugurated [50]the biblical feasts as fixed appointments to help Israel to commemorate their most noteworthy testimonies. Testimonies prophesy the very essence of God's nature. They confirm his faithfulness and the reliability of his promises. Besides, they also inspire faith in the same kind of miraculous works because they relay God's unique perspectives. Testimony, in Hebrew עֵדוּת *aydooth,* has a root word with the three letters [51]Ayin-Vav-Dalet; it means 'to return, to repeat and to do again.' Aren't we praying for a repetition when we ask the Father to encounter us? "Lord, do it again!"

The testimonies were to be remembered, reviewed and rehearsed.

Without testimonies, it is difficult to sustain a faith culture. That kind of culture rests on love, honour and faith. The Kingdom is a culture of the heart. A vital part of that heart culture is to nurture a supernatural realm through testimonies, where we share anointed stories of our Lord's mighty acts. When God's people forgot his testimonies, the flow of miraculous acts ceased, and their victories ground to an abrupt halt. You and I need to call to mind constantly who God is if we want to collaborate with him. We are all called to mirror God's generosity. If we withhold testimonies, we might prevent others from being blessed. Being stingy with the seeds of blessings thwarts the harvest. God wants us to regularly plant the seeds of our testimonies in the soil of others' hearts because faith comes by hearing. If you lack testimonies of your own, use other people's testimonies! You will soon get your own library of amazing encounters. We should be ready in season and out of season: Keep both a short and a longer version of your salvation story. Arm yourself with ample supplies of testimonies because it's part of keeping God's testimonies (see 2 Tim. 4:2). Pray for the Holy Spirit to remind you about what God has done in your past and keep written records of it. Be honest and vulnerable when you share, and make your experience relatable. People won't love you less but be comforted by it.

---

[50] **The Feasts** - The three major biblical feasts are: 1) The Feast of Unleavened Bread - פֶּסַח *Pesach*/Passover - coinciding with the barley harvest 2) The Feast of Weeks - שָׁבוּעוֹת Shavuot/Pentecost - coinciding with the wheat harvest 3) The Feast of Booths סוּכּוֹת - Sukkot/Tabernacles - coinciding with the grape harvest. For further study, check out: www.hebrew4christians.com/Holidays/holidays.html *Pesach* also means to spare or protect.
[51] **Ayin-Vav-Dalet:** Letters refer to pictures, Ayin (eyes), Vav (connection), Dalet (doorway). As we watch and listen, we connect a testimony to God's promises and enter into his presence.

Without testimonies, it is difficult to sustain a faith culture. That kind of culture rests on love, honour and faith. The Kingdom is a culture of the heart.

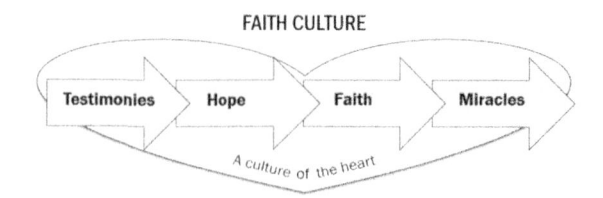

FAITH CULTURE

Testimonies → Hope → Faith → Miracles

A culture of the heart

By releasing stories about God's goodness, we could get a wonderful harvest! If we share real stories about specific diseases being healed, I believe we will see a surge of healings in those specific areas. We all need the different 'crops' of harvest. When we share testimonies in Spirit-led and strategic ways, it will impact the world around us. I want to mention a few obstacles: We want cancer exterminated, mental illnesses eliminated, and poverty eradicated. Above all, we want people to receive the saving grace of Christ! The glorious result of partnering with God, by repeatedly declaring his majestic deeds, is seen in this prophecy: *"The days are coming," declares the Lord, "when the reaper will be overtaken by the ploughman and the planter by the one treading grapes. New wine will drip from the mountains and flow from all the hills, and I will bring my people Israel back from exile. They will rebuild the ruined cities and live in them. They will plant vineyards and drink their wine; they will make gardens and eat their fruit. I will plant Israel in their own land, never again to be uprooted from the land I have given them," says the Lord your God.* (Amos 9:13-15 NIV). This specific passage precisely prophesies about the unusual fertility of Israel's soil during Messiah's reign. It also prophetically indicates a dramatic increase of the miraculous, and an abundance of rich blessings through the outpouring of God's Holy Spirit, a process further accelerated by the active cooperation of his covenant people. We clearly observe breakthrough, increase and acceleration at the same time!

Timothy was instructed to preserve all of Paul's teachings and to follow his example of Christlike living by *"the grace that is in Christ Jesus"* (see 2 Tim. 2:1-2). In another epistle, Paul encouraged the same mindset: *"Whatever you have learned or received or heard from me—or seen in me—put it into practice. And the God of peace will be with you."* (Phil. 4:9 NIV). Encounters and teaching go hand in hand. Let us learn from Christ's faithful servants and study their successful work. In doing so, we can access a principle which is extremely powerful. It's a privilege to mentor others in the areas where we have experienced our own breakthroughs. Sharing your stories can serve as useful tools to inspire others to be victorious in the same way as yourself. We dump dead weight and get rid of sin by gazing on righteousness because Christ is our Righteousness (Heb. 12:2). Christians who display the same mindset model a life-giving ideal, brilliantly conveyed in a memorable verse: *"Awake to soberness righteously, and sin not; for some have no knowledge of God: I speak this to move you to shame.* (1 Cor. 15:34 ASV). The Corinth church was richly blessed with sufficient resources to live godly lives, but Paul discussed some believers' lack of sanctification. The reason for their negligence? Human philosophies muddied their spiritual vision and caused a stunted faith. We all have blind spots, but once pointed out by others, we need to address them. We acknowledge Christ, the Righteous One, as our Advocate with the Father by confessing our sins, not by concealing them (see 1 John 2:1-2). By bringing our sins into the open, we implicitly trust him to forgive, cleanse and restore us. Besides, focusing on *not sinning* may actually reinforce the presence of sin because by doing so, we give it too much recognition (see Rom. 7:14-20). We usually stumble into the pitfalls of self-hatred or self-admiration. Jesus' quite telling anecdote about the Pharisee and the tax collector perfectly shows how to deal with our moral flaws (see Luke 18:9-14). Whereas the timid tax collector confessed his sinfulness, the prideful Pharisee refused to take ownership of his wrongdoings. Only the wise ones among us admit the simple fact that we are all lost without God.

To deal with our behaviour, we first have to address our identity. By focusing on Christ as our solution, we learn to move our attention away from the problem and break its grip. Christ is our Wisdom, our Righteousness and our Sanctification, and these overarching spiritual truths minister life to us (see 1 Cor. 1:30). Habitual sin and addictions can be broken by either repentance or deliverance. If it cannot be crucified, it must be expelled, in Jesus' name. We have to rely on the Holy Spirit for discernment in each case. Renewing our minds is critical if we want an accurate perspective because it helps us to receive divine vitality, healing and deliverance. The liberating force of righteousness is real. It's a *love-identity* that concentrates on the person of Christ rather than on our personal weaknesses. Ask yourself who you really are. If you are a son or daughter of the Most High God, you have the power and authority given to you by Jesus to be victorious (see Luke 10:19, John 1:12, Eph. 1:21-22). It's wise to consider that God created you and me for righteous living and not for sin. If you struggle or encounter shame, you possess the ability and authority the Father gave you to relentlessly bounce back again and again by turning your face towards Jesus. We become victorious through our ongoing resilience.

To deal with our behaviour, we first have to address our identity. By focusing on Christ as our solution, we learn to move our attention away from the problem and break its grip.

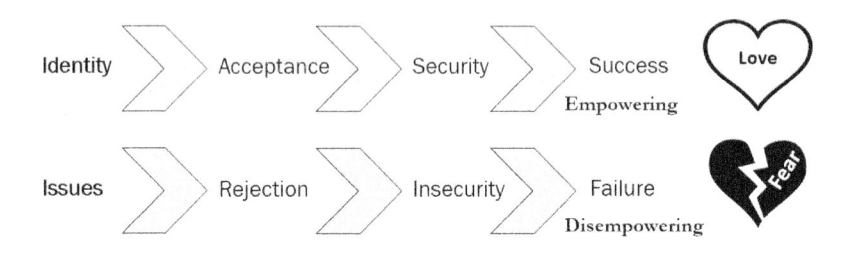

Identity → Acceptance → Security → Success — Love
Empowering

Issues → Rejection → Insecurity → Failure — Fear
Disempowering

As a concept, repentance isn't limited to *what* we are repenting of but also includes *who w*e are turning to. We read: *"... how you turned to God from idols to serve the living and true God."* (1 Thess. 1:9 ESV). This isn't just semantics. We are unable to turn away from idols unless we first turn to our living and loving Father! Once we take responsibility for our mistakes, it's important to receive God's forgiveness and love from a place of safety in him. To believe that you are loved is empowering in itself. All of us are a work in progress. We daily learn to live dependent on the Spirit. The Father trains us in righteousness all the time. The Christian life isn't a quick-fix: In this process, we achieve to put off the old self by putting on the new self. Because of humanity's fallen and broken condition, we have been steeped in a mindset of sin-consciousness and need to be aware of our brand-new mindset of righteousness in Christ Jesus. The first mindset is rooted in fear, but the second mindset is rooted in love. *"There is therefore now no condemnation for those who are in Christ Jesus. For the law of the Spirit of life has set you free in Christ Jesus from the law of sin and death."* (Rom. 8:1-2 ESV). May the Lord help us to comprehend what life-changing relationship we now enjoy with the Father! It's a connection established by Christ's sacrifice, enabled by his precious Holy Spirit: *"Now all of us can come to the Father through the same Holy Spirit because of what Christ has done for us."* (Eph. 2:18 NLT).

To believe that you are loved is empowering in itself.

Similar to the law of gravity, the law of sin and death pulls us downwards to where we are earth-bound and enslaved. Praise God that there is a higher law and a higher realm for every believer to occupy! Like the law of lift, the law of the Spirit of life lifts us up to make us heaven-bound and free. God's fresh wind of the Spirit lifts us upwards into heavenly places. From these heights, we take hold of the throne room perspective, as our God says: *"Come up here, and I will show you what must take place after this."* (Rev. 4:1 ESV). On the high summit of revelation, God gives us bright flashes of hope and a future. Israel's deliverance is a useful illustration. Listen to this grandiose picture: *"You have seen what I did to the Egyptians. You know how I carried you on eagles' wings and brought you to myself."* (Exod. 19:4 NLT). The beautiful destinations for believers are profound personal encounters with a merciful God based on his covenant promises. The Lord didn't want Israel to engage exclusively with a set of principles but invited them to his presence—into his loving embrace. The Father desires a heart-to-heart connection with all of his dear children.

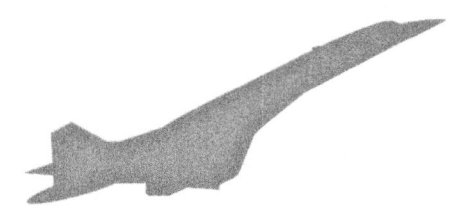

Christ modelled righteousness for us, and Paul, who pursued Christ's example, said: 'Look at me! Learn from me! Copy me!' Looking to Jesus is also learning from the lives of his witnesses. Surround yourself with your own cloud of witnesses! If you battle addiction, don't hang around people with similar addictions unless they have conquered these areas. Visit places with zealous God-chasers who inspire hope. This good company will help you to get rid of the substitutes and instead be filled with the Spirit of Christ. Those who walk together with the wise become wise (see Prov. 13:20). If you want to excel and overcome, spend time in godly environments.

Church services, prayer meetings and small groups are all arenas where you can be discipled and trained for the work of the Kingdom. *"Come near to God and he will come near to you."* (James 4:8 NIV). Believing and belonging are different sides of the same coin. *"And these God-chosen lives all around—what splendid friends they make!"* (Psalm 16:3 MSG). It's a tragedy that myriads of Christians feel lonely and isolated. A church should be a place where we establish close relationships. The lame charade of impressing each other with our spirituality is farcical. Let us rather be as personable and genuine as possible. The mindless pretence game of being somebody we are not has to end. Connectivity is increased through vulnerability. If you are honest, you don't fancy a hip or funky church—you want friends! A living church is a self-evident place for socialising. In an appealing environment of faith and care, we develop a strong sense of community with meaningful and lasting friendships.

Communication ⟷ Vulnerability ⟷ **Connection**
Community ⟷ Sensitivity ⟷ **Closeness**

A church should be a place where we establish close relationships. Connectivity is increased through vulnerability.

The outcast of sinners and tax collectors flocked to Jesus, the Shepherd, whose life-giving atmosphere changed them. They sought proximity to the Son of God. When the Sun of Righteousness shone on them, these lonely stars defrosted and reignited in the close orbit of his kind warmness (see Mal. 4:2). Feeling lost, with nothing to lose, they went to King Jesus. They got lost in the ocean of his incessant love instead. In striking contrast, the religious elite shunned him because he exposed their hearts' hidden motives. They didn't fathom a God who loves us despite our wrongdoings, even if it's haughtiness. In closing the door on Jesus, they detached themselves from encountering the Father's deep love for them. Arrogance is a deceiving and divisive force: It disconnects us from other believers, whilst humility and openness pull us into the bosom of a loving community. As the Body of Christ, we are supposed to be preaching the good news. In fact, we are called to demonstrate the good news by developing wholesome habits of believing and belonging. We exemplify the gospel when we enter the mighty vortex of God's love. Isn't that what church is all about?

Keys to the Kingdom

Jesus told Peter he would give him the keys to the Kingdom (see Matt. 16:18-19). There has been a lot of speculation about what these keys are, and in verse 19, we read: *"I will give you the keys of the kingdom of heaven; whatever you bind on earth will be bound in heaven, and whatever you loose on earth will be loosed in heaven."* Keys traditionally represent access because being a keyholder embodies authority. If you present somebody with the keys to your house, you entrust responsibility to them. In the previous verse, Jesus declared to Peter that he would build his Church and the gates of Hades would not conquer it. The word church in Greek is *ekklesia*. The expression ἐκκλησία *ekklesia*—meaning assembly or community, is equal to the Hebrew קָהָל *kahal*. The kingdom of Heaven is accessible through the wonderful person of the Holy Spirit (see Rom. 14:17, Eph. 2:18). The keys represent authority to bind and to loose. To bind is to forbid, and to loose is to allow it. We invoke Jesus' name the same way, and it's fairly common among believers to take authority in the name of Jesus. Is it possible to unleash what is deposited in Heaven here on earth? We usually release Kingdom realities through prophetic declarations. In the process of spiritual activation, we attentively seek to be sensitive to the Holy Spirit and his methods in any given situation. Prophetic and powerful means to initiate change is speaking what he shows us through images or thoughts. The keys of the Kingdom are voice-activated keys—activated through prayer, praise and prophecy!

PRAYER   PRAISE   PROPHECY

While attending a gathering at church at the end of June 2019, the Holy Spirit gave me a vision of a huge white flag. I saw how the beautiful flag was waving in the wind, and it was dazzling white. I was immediately taken aback by its purity and power. It was like God himself was waving the flag. In my spirit, I felt it represented how the Lord will bring a renewed freshness and healing to the United Kingdom. It was an invitation for God's people to partner with him by yielding and surrendering to his priorities. It was like Heaven created an unspoiled moment by wiping the slate clean. When I declared it in my own words, I felt God's presence in a special way. This happened on the last day of Pride month. That's when the LGBTQ+ community celebrates their uniqueness. I observed how the Pride flag has only six of the rainbow colours, as the nuance of indigo is left out. I pondered that white light scientifically displays all the seven colours of the spectrum when dispersed through a glass prism. By spinning a colour wheel with a full scale of colours, they will appear white again, but making use of only six colours gives a blurred appearance. Because the rainbow is a covenant sign, it reminded me that we are all incomplete apart from Jesus. *"And God said, "This is the sign of the covenant I am making between me and you and every living creature with you, a covenant for all generations to come: I have set my rainbow in the clouds, and it will be the sign of the covenant between me and the earth."* (Gen. 9:12-13 NIV). If sin enslaves us, can living 'our truth' actually be a lie? To me, Jesus is the Truth. He is God's standard for humanity, and he sums up the objective reality of absolute truth. A disciple of Christ should refer to the Truth that sets us all free.

The *gospel* presents Jesus as our *identity*. God alone can heal our identity issues. On receiving it, we joined Christ through covenant, signing the contract of his radical love. His holy love is a love that saves, heals and delivers, nothing less. Rather than self-identifying, we freely access our actual identity in Jesus. That said, it's hypocrisy if we vilify fellow human beings with other sexual preferences while hiding behind pretentious and self-righteous façades. If we try to reach out in love, we cannot be appalled and judgemental in the process. We must get out of our Christian 'ghettos' and readily open our hearts and homes to people from all walks of life. Alternatively, we can meet at a café or at church, but we require *a conversation* where people can be heard and grow. Let us *relieve* pain instead of increasing it by creating safe spaces. We fail miserably if we cowardly abandon those who wrestle in these areas, whether they belong to a church or not. In this ongoing war about identity and dignity, our rival wants to stamp out God's sacred image in us. Shared human experience shows that it's very common to sexualise a lack of love or other basic needs for recognition because of emotional deficit or trauma.

Whatever the reason may be, I believe that Jesus, our Saviour, lovingly redeems our identity, but also our sexuality. More testimonies at: changedmovement.com.

When confronted with what we as Christians might perceive as sin or darkness, we should never publicly vent our frustration, fear or anger. Reacting superficially only distorts our God-given mission. As believers, we don't have the right to be disgusted or disown other people. We can boldly face our phobias through Christ's unfailing love (see Rom. 8:35-37, 2 Cor. 6:3-10). To respond with compassion, without any condemnation, is shining God's light on those in need. We should be trendsetters, through a loving demeanour, expressing the Father's affection towards everybody and showing the way back to him. *"As he is, so are we in this world."* (1 John 4:17). In Revelation, we discover that Jesus holds the keys to Death and Hades. Hades is the realm of the departed souls. The living and triumphant Lord declares that he is in total control of these keys (see Rev. 1:18). Did Jesus prophesy to Peter about this future reality? He may have referred to a hereafter where malevolent powers were defeated and deprived of their past authority, granted them through sin and death. It seems like Peter would receive keys similar to those Jesus got back from the devil. The gates of Hell will not prevail because the keys to overcome them were given to the Church, leading to conversions, healings, deliverances and resurrections from the dead. The Serpent fooled Adam in the Garden and snatched the keys, whereas Yeshua Ha Mashiach rightfully won them back. Hallelujah! We can boldly plunder Hell and populate Heaven by reclaiming what was stolen and lost. Through Jesus, we hold the keys to the Kingdom! These powerful keys of light dispel the darkness. When we use the keys strategically, they activate and release his glorious presence.

"Lift up your heads, O gates! And lift them up, O ancient doors, that the King of glory may come in. Who is this King of glory? The Lord of hosts, he is the King of glory! Selah." (Psalm 24:9-10 ESV).

Jesus also said he has *the key of David* (see Rev. 3:7). King David was a man after God's heart, as he constantly pursued his presence. David had a humble and contrite spirit. God delights in a sacrifice of praise, and David knew it (see Psalm 50:49, Heb. 13:15). God's *soft spot* is that he loves worship and inhabits the praises of his people (see Psalm 22:3). David unlocked the secret to the Lord's heart—transcending the sacrificial system—using the key of praise to access a grace that was yet to be revealed after Christ's death and resurrection. God may also give us keys in the shape of other ministry gifts. They won't necessarily suit our taste at first, but may be keys to our success! Let me mention a few examples. Paul's ministry got help from Titus, Silas, Timothy and Phoebe (see Rom.16:1, 1 Cor. 4:17, 2 Cor. 2:12-17). Revival history is full of preachers who effectively advanced God's kingdom through their good relationships, like the distinguished John Wesley and George Whitefield. These two brothers had a fallout but reconciled after some years. Others failed, as they refused help from their peers. Renowned healing evangelist John Alexander Dowie suffered from an envious and competitive mindset. When the Lord so graciously provided Maria Woodworth-Etter, a mother in the faith, to become a leaning pillar for him in the ministry, he declined her invitation. Regrettably, the much-touted Dowie later veered off course into strange beliefs. Without question, a healthy partnership with another seasoned servant of God could definitely have prevented his downfall. Alas, history repeats itself, as these are not isolated incidents. Humility comes with the fear of the Lord (Prov. 22:4). To welcome brothers and sisters in love and respect is to receive Christ because affability and accountability represent great blessings.

Keys to the Kingdom

Prayer Praise Prophecy   Authority & Access

Fellow ministry gifts   Affability & Accountability

Can keys to breakthrough be discovered by chance? The woman with an issue of blood touched the tassels of Jesus' tallit or tzitzit, his prayer shawl. Her brave act of faith led to her immediate healing. The fringed corners of the Jewish prayer shawl were called wings. Malachi envisioned how the Messiah, the sun of righteousness, would carry *"healing in his wings"* (see Mal. 3:2, Matt. 9:18-26). In the same way, Paul's handkerchiefs and aprons contained power. When applied to demonised and sick individuals, they were instantly delivered and healed. The unusual miracles and signs were atypical demonstrations of God's power (see Acts 19:11-12). In NLT, we read: *"God gave Paul the power to perform unusual miracles."* The surprising part of the story is that he didn't pray over or anoint these items in a deliberate or ceremonial way. He was going about his daily business as a craftsman of tents. Yet some scholars reckon that Paul manufactured [52]prayer shawls due to his rabbinical training. Producing shawls would require skilled craftsmanship and great attention to detail. These garments represented God's sacred Name and holy commandments. While he was working, the great anointing on Paul's life overflowed into his clothes and equipment—a remarkable sign! The Bible associates all labour with godly service. Work is more than an occupation to make a livelihood. This way, our workmanship can actually be our worship! Some years ago, I made a delicious apple cake. When my mother-in-law tasted it, she had an instant encounter with the Holy Spirit. She concluded that anointed revelation somehow resided within the yummy cake and curiously asked for the secret to this exceptional effect. I simply told her that I baked it without any prayer or agenda. God did the rest, as he can do whatever he desires whenever it pleases him (Psalm 84:11, Isa. 65:24).

The Bible associates all labour with godly service. Work is more than an occupation to make a livelihood.

We are entering a season of unparalleled signs, but so far, we have only scratched the surface. I am convinced that much greater things are yet to come in many areas and in unexpected ways. Do not easily discard proof of uncommon miracles. Of course, it's always wise to check the source and research whether the story is trustworthy or not. Some of the circulating stories are fabricated, but the others are the real deal. If something seems too good to be true, it's probably not true. Regardless, God is able to do above and beyond what you and I can reason or imagine (see John 21:25, Eph. 3:20). *"Jesus Christ is the same yesterday and today and forever."* (Heb. 13:8). Each new move of God was marked by forerunners and reformer revivalists—people he raised up in every generation. Many of these humble servants moved dynamically in

---

[52] **Prayer shawl**, called *tallit* with the four corners with fringes *tzitzit*. See the article "Tzitzit and the Mashiyach": bethmelekh.com/yaakovs-commentary/tzittzit-and-the-mashiyach

the miraculous, like Jesus, their beloved Master. Consumed by compassion for sick and hurting people, they stayed fully surrendered to God's will through intimate fellowship with the Lord. They knew him as both [53]the Covenant keeper and the miracle worker (see Deut. 7:9, Exod. 15:11, Neh. 9:32, Psalm 77:14. It's about time to join their ranks and continue their legacy!

```
      H
      E
P E A C E
      L
      I
      N
      G
```

"But He was pierced for our transgressions, He was crushed for our iniquities; the punishment that brought us peace was upon Him, and by His stripes we are healed."

(Berean Study Bible, Isaiah 53:5)

---

[53] **Covenant keeper:** In Hebrew, שֹׁמֵר הַבְּרִית וְהַחֶסֶד *Shomer Habrit v'hachesed* - it also means he who watches over his covenant of grace with his people (see Deut. 7:9).

CHAPTER 5 - PROPHETIC PRIVILEGES

A kingdom of priests

"Now if you will obey me and keep my covenant, you will be my own special treasure from among all the peoples on earth; for all the earth belongs to me. And you will be my kingdom of priests, my holy nation.' This is the message you must give to the people of Israel." (Exod. 19:5-6 NLT).

One of the most ground-breaking truths that were restored in the 20th century was *the priesthood of all believers*. It was recognised by the early Church and commonly applied across Christian communities. God's intent in the Old Covenant was to set up a kingdom of priests to represent him on earth. Initially, Yehovah, the Lord, sought to establish a new spiritual and social order for the People of the Promise. In fact, he intended his holiness and goodness to be displayed through Israel so all the surrounding nations could see his majestic power. The people resisted coming near to the Almighty, whose voice terrified them when he came down in glory on Mount Sinai (see Heb. 12:18-21). So, in their sinfulness and inadequacy, they asked Moses, Aron and the tribe of Levi to represent them before God. This elect group became mediators for the rest of the people when the sacrificial system was inaugurated.

After a series of failures committed by the tribe of Levi, God decided to pass on the priesthood to the tribe of Judah, king David's tribe. In fact, David had sons as priests - כֹּהֲנִים *kohanim*, something God approved of (1 Sam. 8:18). Priestly and prophetic patterns were fulfilled when Yeshua the Messiah arrived, a descendant of David. Christ's resurrection and ascension finalised the transfer of the priesthood from the priestly tribe of Levi to the kingly tribe of Judah. The office of the High Priest was changed from perishable men onto the immortal Son of God as well (see Hebrews chapter 7). Being a man of God's presence, King David facilitated a night and day worship service in the Tabernacle. He wanted to approach the living God, the One he loved, with undying devotion. When the priests worshipped, the Lord appeared in his glorious presence. King David fearlessly pushed the limits of the priestly office by accessing the New Covenant dimension by faith. He worshipped *"in Spirit and truth"* (see John 4:23-24). The Tabernacle he operated—or the tent of meeting, in

Hebrew מִשְׁכָּן *mishkan*—was the portable house of God. It translates as a dwelling or resting place. The tent became a prophetic prototype of how we, as individuals, would later carry his glory wherever we go, each one of us becoming a bodily temple of prayer and worship. In John 1:14, Jesus exemplified the very same principle when he came to *"tabernacle among us"*. Jesus *"went about doing good"* (see Acts 10:38). David's avant-garde and future-gazing ministry modelled, with prophetic precision, what to expect as Spirit-filled worshippers. How awesome is that?

THE MINISTRY OF THE BELIEVER

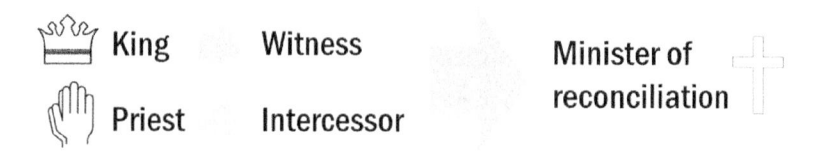

King Witness Minister of reconciliation
Priest Intercessor

Therefore, if anyone is in Christ, he is a new creation. The old has passed away; behold, the new has come. All this is from God, who through Christ reconciled us to himself and gave us the ministry of reconciliation; that is, in Christ God was reconciling the world to himself, not counting their trespasses against them, and entrusting to us the message of reconciliation. Therefore, we are ambassadors for Christ, God making his appeal through us. We implore you on behalf of Christ, be reconciled to God. (2 Cor. 5:17-20 NASB).

"... and from Jesus Christ, who is the faithful witness, the firstborn from the dead, and the ruler of the kings of the earth. To him who loves us and has freed us from our sins by his blood, and has made us to be a kingdom and priests to serve his God and Father—to him be glory and power for ever and ever! Amen." (Rev. 1:5-6 NIV).

In God's kingdom, we right now have the privilege to enter the Holy of Holies by the blood of Jesus (see Heb. 10:19). All believers can day and night come before the throne of grace and enjoy unbroken fellowship with the triune God. Being a royal priesthood, all born-again Christians are called to be ministers, enabled by Christ's sacrifice and the infilling of his Holy Spirit. We are a chosen generation, *ordained* by the blood of Christ and *activated* by the Spirit. When we speak, we choose to do so in harmony with God's Word and serve with his strength (see 1 Pet. 4:11). When looking at Eph. 4:11-15, we observe how God apportioned the gifts to his Body. It was for the equipping of all the saints, all who belong to him. Every child of God should become activated for ministry. Doing church with a bunch of demotivated, disillusioned and disempowered members filling the pews was never his intention! Having a church with paid clergy, where the so-called amateurs, on the whole, are reduced to passive listeners, volunteers, and financial contributors, is unbiblical. It's also boring and tiresome, a waste of potential and a loss for the people who depend on us. The surrounding community needs to see Christians rise up and move in the power of the Holy Spirit.

Being a royal priesthood, all born-again Christians are called to be ministers, enabled by Christ's sacrifice and the infilling of his Holy Spirit.

Do I discard the practice of employing full-time ministers to look after the local churches? No, but I do question the models of organisations and institutions where the 'professionals' are running God's house. My train of thought says that applying an Old Testament mindset to a New Testament reality doesn't pan out well. When a church is headed by apostolic leaders, who continually equip their members for service in God's Kingdom, it produces thriving believers. Soon, the ripple effect of an empowering and releasing church culture will translate into tidal waves of God's glory. Cities, regions and entire nations will feel the impact of it. No doubt, where fivefold leadership is commonly applied, churches follow an apostolic pattern.

In churches that have *the priesthood of all believers* as the benchmark, it may be hard to identify the leaders due to a professed *flat leadership* structure. Facilitating this kind of community requires dedicated leaders with a *long-term* commitment, with the intent to train and develop leaders of *a higher standard*. It demands discipleship that is challenging to achieve. Yet, having a community of mature believers properly schooled and released into ministry is a force to be reckoned with. It's the fivefold gold standard. Efficient models effortlessly yield the fruits of stability and increase. Organic growth takes place where smaller groups nurture tightly-knit relationships. Genuine oneness leads to transparency, care and recognition. Nine times out of ten, a high-functioning community will prevent people from slipping under the radar with their pain, sin or neglect.

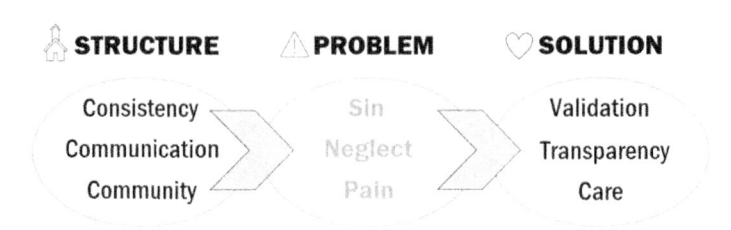

⌂ STRUCTURE	⚠ PROBLEM	♡ SOLUTION
Consistency	Sin	Validation
Communication	Neglect	Transparency
Community	Pain	Care

Now to another aspect of the priesthood of all believers. Nowhere in the Bible do we find the mention of a particular spiritual gift to intercede. Anyway, *intercession* is a part of our *priestly calling*. All believers are priests. Hence all are called to pray for others. But why are some renowned intercessors? One could also ask: Why are some athletes while the rest of the population isn't? It has to do with several factors like predisposition, specialisation and levels of exercise. God brings forth intercessors through extensive and focused prayer. I remember how I learned to pray in the Holy Spirit in my early teens. I used my prayer language because I was inwardly praying in tongues constantly. I wasn't always aware of this holy habit, but it was picked up on by prophetic people with *a spiritual radar*. In the late '80s, I attended a meeting arranged by all the evangelical churches in my hometown. The conference speaker, a Spirit-filled man, told me that he could discern how I, through prayer, lifted the atmosphere. He felt a strong support while he was preaching—making it effortless for him to share his message. The Holy Spirit used me in this persistent manner. For me, it was usual business, but it dawned on me that not all believers are familiar with [54]standing in the gap through intercession. While I attended Art College, a fellow Christian student registered a peaceful atmosphere among the students and teachers when I was present. On days when I was absent, she felt that the peace disappeared as conflicts emerged more frequently. I consistently took charge of the atmosphere of my school, through deliberate intercession, by claiming the territory for the Lord. In the morning hours, I undeniably felt the invisible resistance from evil spirits but

---

[54] **Intercession:** *Standing in the gap, or the breach,* is a phrase found in Ezek. 22:30. In times of upheaval, the prophets represented the people in prayer due to the general lack of righteousness. By taking responsibility before the Lord, they built a covering, or hedge, of spiritual protection around the nation to avert God's judgement. See also Psalm 106:23.

remained focused and persevering. Immediately after I had broken through, I could sense how a canopy of angelic presence and peace rested over the school.

Intercession is repeatedly referred to both in the Old and the New Testament: *"For the sake of his great name the LORD will not reject his people, because the LORD was pleased to make you his own. As for me, far be it from me that I should sin against the LORD by failing to pray for you. And I will teach you the way that is good and right."* (1 Sam. 12:22-23 NIV). *"Epaphras, who is one of you and a servant of Christ Jesus, sends greetings. He is always wrestling in prayer for you, that you may stand firm in all. I vouch for him that he is working hard for you and for those at Laodicea and Hierapolis."* (Col. 4:12-13 NIV). It appears like prophetic and apostolic ministries must take the strain of intercession and spiritual warfare. I base my conclusion on studies, testimonies and experiences. At times, I have interceded intensely, day and night, for weeks. I didn't volunteer for this kind of lifestyle. I knew it was a calling, as the Lord called me to do it and gave me the grace to cope. Many times over, I felt like opting out of it because of the insurmountable pressure on my soul. I sustained myself with God's Word and by claiming Jesus' blood for my protection. Whether we have light or intense spiritual warfare, it's our corporate calling. As a people of kings and priests, we contend in prayer to advance the Kingdom (see 1 Tim. 2:1-4). Since we are priests, we minister before God Almighty, at the Altar, on behalf of the people. When we steadfastly stand in his presence and earnestly seek him, our hearts become an altar. Our priestly ministry is twofold: 1) we offer sacrifices of praise and worship to the Lord, and 2) we intercede regularly for others by standing in the gap. (See Psalm 106:23, Ezek. 22:30, Col. 2:1, 1 Tim. 2:1-4, Heb. 13:10-16).

Is there a spiritual gift for being a witness, distinct from the office of an evangelist, specifically mentioned in the Bible? My answer is no, although being a witness is undisputedly a vocation and calling connected to our role as God's ambassadors and kings. The Lord has granted us full permission to influence our surroundings by spiritual diplomacy, and we succeed by following the etiquette of Heaven. If we rid ourselves of favouritism, quibbling and small-mindedness and instead focus on serving people, we gain their favour and trust. We serve the King of kings, as kings, by declaring his marvellous deeds, his glory and his majestic power. Kingly authority accompanies our royal assignment—a call to enforce his victory—reclaiming and repossessing what is his. That includes soul-winning, claiming God's lost property. We got the royal privilege to become witnesses after getting ransomed by Christ and reconciled with the Father. Encountering God and his goodness inevitably releases a generosity flowing out of his love for us. We *desire* to tell others about what he has done for us. As a matter of fact, it's a defined trait woven into our spiritual DNA and an integral part of the new creation (see 2 Cor. 5:17-18). Fused into our identity and our history with him is God's testimony about his Son (see also 1 John 5:5-12). Knowing our Lord, our Saviour, and our King comes from personal experiences. Having the testimony of Jesus, we also have the Spirit of prophecy. God gives us the urge to preach the good news—we want to get it out there for the world to see and hear! *"But you will receive power when the Holy Spirit comes on you; and you will be my witnesses in Jerusalem, and in all Judea and Samaria, and to the ends of the earth."* (Acts 1:8 NIV). The inclination to share the gospel builds up like an artesian well within us, a spring that surfaced the day we got born-again (see John 4:10-14). The moment we received the Spirit-baptism, the inner well burst into torrents of living waters (see John 7:37-38). It's an internal repository we can no longer contain because [55]a new desire erupts from our spirit to pray and worship constantly. We are brimming inside with a holy ambition to witness and evangelise. Suppressing it feels unnatural because of the living, dynamic and indwelling presence of the Spirit. *"But when the Helper comes, whom I will send to you from the Father, the Spirit of truth, who proceeds from the Father, he will bear witness about me. And you also will bear witness because you have been with me from the beginning."* (John 15:26-27 ESV).

Undeniably, the partnership with the Spirit makes us God's witnesses by definition. Actualising the priesthood of all believers is a natural outcome of applying fivefold ministry. These two concepts fundamentally incorporate the same idea. A church fronted by a few prominent leaders who are proponents of fivefold ministry, but fail to release its own congregants into ministry, is self-contradictory. That model is as insufficient as an established church with paid administrators and clergy. If people

---

[55] **My comment:** If the desire to pray or witness wanes, this should be a warning to us. *"Above all else, guard your heart, for everything you do flows from it."* (Prov. 4:23 NIV).

don't get to exercise their gifts and move freely in the Spirit, it creates felt 'ceilings' of spiritual oppression in a church's atmosphere. It stops expansion and holds back the release of other anointed fivefold ministers. Sadly, this is often the case even for churches claiming to espouse a fivefold vision. A competitive mindset, entrenched in ambition and entitlement, clashes with the selfless Kingdom attitudes. So also does favouritism. Setting the high-water mark for visionary leadership necessitates specific action. Good intentions aren't enough. The leaders in charge shouldn't feel threatened by other competent leaders in the same church but need discernment and humility. Close bonds, transparency and accountability foster mutual trust and dependability, and humility shows stalwartness. It effectively deals with jealousy. If we cultivate loving relationships, we override the fear of rejection, lack of attention and envy in our churches. We invalidate comparison and competition by zooming in on function and not on rank and position. The orphan spirit cannot survive, but we expunge it if we bond through vulnerability and unhesitating love. Compassion breeds community and togetherness. If we prioritise relationships over a paltry (!) pecking order, the emphasis changes from *me* to *we*. Insecure leaders typically build barriers, while mature leaders build bridges. Fear divides, but love unites.

Actualising the priesthood of all believers is a natural outcome of applying fivefold ministry.

Ability to understand the dynamics of family, community and corporate blessings should filter into how we approach the famous prayer 'Our Father'. We don't pray exclusively for ourselves and our own comfort. Our perspective is much wider as we think of the common well-being of our neighbours. We contend on behalf of the *soul* of our community. This eminent and priestly prayer beautifully sums up our unity with the Father and how we, as citizens of the Kingdom, are called to bless our surroundings. It contextualises the commandments by encapsulating our daily lives at a spiritual and societal level. The first part is pointed towards God and the latter towards each other. When I intercede and give praise to the Lord and treat his name respectfully, it is worship. Working, resting, nourishing myself and others, forgiving wrongdoings and living with integrity is also true worship. *"And whatever you do, whether in word or deed, do it all in the name of the Lord Jesus, giving thanks to God the Father through him."* (Col. 3:17 NIV). *"Finally, brothers and sisters, whatever is true, whatever is noble, whatever is right, whatever is pure, whatever is lovely, whatever is admirable—if anything is excellent or praiseworthy—think about such things."* (Phil. 4:8 NIV).

In common parlance, 'whatever' is a slang term meaning 'whatever you say', 'I don't care what you say' or 'what will be will be'. For a Christian, it's the total opposite. Whatever the Bible says, we want to follow, and whatever we do for God is an act of *worship*. We should refrain from actions that aren't aligned with Jesus' holy name. The Bible radically exclaims that what we don't do by faith is sin (see Rom. 14:23). We fail to worship if we avoid the nice things we could have done. *"If anyone, then, knows the good they ought to do and doesn't do it, it is sin for them."* (James 4:17 NIV). Don't be fooled. Our worship doesn't begin when the church service starts. Why is that so? It's our lifestyle twenty-four-seven. We worship from a house of flesh and blood, not one of brickwork. To show others what the Church really is about in our everyday life is a continual act of worship in God's eyes (see Rom. 12:1, Heb. 13:15).

True royalty and excellence
"But you are a chosen race, a royal priesthood, a holy nation, a people for his own possession, that you may proclaim the excellencies of him who called you out of darkness into his marvellous light." (1 Pet. 2:9 ESV).

"For if you remain silent at this time, relief and deliverance for the Jews will arise from another place, but you and your father's family will perish. And who knows but that you have come to your royal position for such a time as this?" (Esther 4:14 NIV). *"It is the glory of God to conceal a matter, But the glory of kings is to search out a matter."* (Prov. 25:2 NASB).

Let us look closer at *royal identity*, including our calling and privileges. Israel was the only nation on earth blessed with God's presence, as witnessed in the covenants with Abraham, Moses and David. A sacrificial system was the outcome, with priests as mediators between God and the people. The Lord chose Israel as a Kingdom of Priests, an example of his majesty and splendour. Through Israel, the surrounding Gentile nations would see a large-scale demonstration of God's redemptive power. It reached its highest point during king Solomon's impressive reign:

No citizen was destitute, violence was non-existent, and Israel enjoyed spectacular opulence within secure borders. With abundant blessings came prosperity in every area of social life since Israel's nationwide obedience prompted an unusual favour. Because Solomon revered the Lord's ordinances, the impact was felt throughout the land. Let us not forget that his father David's zeal for the Most High's presence laid the foundation for all of it. David prepared a place for the Ark of the Covenant by receiving the prophetic blueprint for the Temple, which Solomon later built.

We will not dwell on specific details but investigate the mindset behind exploits like these. To help us to further release God's glory, Holy Scripture gives us *patterns* to follow. Our best asset is a royal mindset. History shows that the Lord endowed his people with a priestly and kingly anointing to influence entire nations, like Moses, who, from boyhood, was brought up as royalty. In the land of Egypt, he was raised to be confident and brilliant in science, linguistics and political and military strategy. Did he suffer from low self-esteem? We don't know, but he seemed alarmed—afraid of being snubbed by his own people, despite being hand-picked by God (see Exod. 3:1-18, 4:1-17). The prophet Samuel likely mentored David, but his countless trials produced a character in him worthy of a monarch. Solomon was later groomed to be a skilful regent. The Book of Proverbs opens a window into Solomon's soul and his relentless quest for excellence. He was a child when David instilled in him a love for wisdom. Nehemiah, Mordecai and Esther all had a royal mindset, to name a few.

In developing a royal mindset, the Holy Spirit tutors us. He is our Helper, Advocate and Comforter who convicts us of righteousness. Scripture describes righteousness as the leading characteristic of a good king. He establishes his leadership on justice. To demonstrate his Kingdom in this world, God sets us apart to be his beloved sons and daughters, kings and priests, heirs and ambassadors. Are we, as a chosen people, distinctly marked by righteousness and preoccupied with the *majesty* of our King?

"But the LORD of hosts is exalted in justice, and the Holy God shows himself holy in righteousness." (Isa. 5:16 ESV).

"Righteousness and justice are the foundation of your throne; love and faithfulness go before you." (Psalm 89:14 NIV).

> [56] *"Majesty governs how we think about the Lord, our expectations of him, and our experience of his favour in our lives. When we develop a majestic understanding and experience of God's nature, we can know the absolute adoration of the Father, cultivate peace that surpasses understanding, and encounter a joy that becomes who we are."*

The Lord created us with royal dignity to represent him. The wrong response is to underrate ourselves (see Gen. 1:26-28). We were called to reign in life and to live in the overflowing grace of God (see Rom. 5:17). Does it suggest that we should pursue positions of power in politics or oversee influential organisations? Not necessarily. God can, and sometimes will, call us to occupy these positions, as he did with Daniel and Joseph. When we look at their examples, we clearly see their great integrity and unswerving commitment to serving the Lord and their community. Nevertheless, if Beelzebub can convince us to stay out of politics by considering it to be unpleasant and secular, he will be thrilled to dominate this battleground unchallenged. Neglect in the political arena has already caused many problems and explains in part why the Church, in many places, is losing the cultural war. That cannot be God's will. He wants us to serve and be close to the community and culture we hold so dear. Being Christians, we possess the power of our testimony regardless of our title, position or influence. If we understand the principles of God's kingdom, it will transform how we approach public leadership. Our high calling, as kingly ambassadors, is to release God's life and carry his light and presence in the territories he assigns to us.

Among many others, I dispute the so-called *dominion theology*. The thesis seems predicated on the assumption that we, as God's people, have an unlimited mandate to usurp all areas governing human life—often referred to as the seven mountains. Jesus commissioned us to go into all the world and make disciples of all nations (see Matt. 28:18-20, Mark 16:15-20). Naturally, believers should be represented within the ministry, the marketplace and the government. What I can't stomach is twisting the truth about sonship to hoard secular power and wealth. Isn't the purpose of fivefold ministry to build God's House? Using divine gifts to rule the kingdoms of this world corrupts our true mission. I think it is plain hubris to assume that our

---

[56] **Quote from Graham Cooke** - *Entering a Majesty Mindset* - www.brilliantperspectives.com

contributions to Christianise and reform society will somehow trigger Jesus' return. The Bible predicts a bright future where we will reign with Christ during a period of a thousand years on this earth (see Rev. 20:4-6). With resurrected bodies, we will govern the nations with his wisdom. As of now, the Kingdom is invisible. We access it through the cross in the blessed union we have with Christ (see Luke 17:20-21, John 18:36-37, Acts 1:3-7, Eph. 2:11-22).

Universally, the Church presently exercise a spiritual government based on Christ being the head. This reality provides the contextual backdrop for biblical dominion, with a consistent emphasis on *stewardship* and *servant leadership*. We violate these boundaries if we pursue worldly power and misinterpret the framework of God's Kingdom (see Matt. 20:25-28). At the outset of Christianity, it's noteworthy to find that regardless of the churches' size, they didn't operate under a unified structure. To tell the truth, the apostles explicitly maintained the house churches as self-governed units. They weren't organised networks under a strict oversight of some influential ministry gift, like Peter or Paul. Christian churches were relationally and organically connected in each city and region, neatly joined by love and the apostles' teaching. Since fivefold ministry teams looked after these fellowships with humility, they were respectfully received as Christ's messengers (see Acts 15:36-41, 1 Cor. 4:15-17).

We understand the royal aspect of our assignment as an apostolic and empowering concept. The devil doesn't want you to see yourself as a son and heir—the way God sees you (see Rom. 8:17). To him, the potential we represent is terrifying, as he, our foe, knows who we really are! To destroy us, he uses two tactics: The first is lying to us to keep us from knowing our God-given destiny. The second is to promote us too early or fool us to exercise our gifts outside our calling in order to abort our assignment. He tried to do that to Jesus: *When the people saw him do this miraculous sign, they exclaimed, "Surely, he is the Prophet we have been expecting!" When Jesus saw that they were ready to force him to be their king, he slipped away into the hills by himself.* (John 6:14-15 NLT). The Holy Spirit leads us all the way into maturity so that we, in due time, can bear the full weight of our calling and destiny. Strong gifts, but a lack of godly character, will put our assignment in jeopardy. The Father seeks the growth of the fruit of the Spirit in our lives and establishes in us a royal identity and mindset. He provides us with plenty of opportunities to further develop the skills and patience we need. Every time we go through trials, he is not playing a cruel joke on us but supplies us with real-life exercises to help us become his servants.

God's Spirit will lead us all the way into maturity, so we can bear the full weight of our calling and destiny.

Among the most important things in life is to understand our true identity as sons and daughters of the Most High. We move in our spiritual calling through ongoing worship, prayer and intercession. When we serve, our calling and gifts will surface. Are you prophetically inclined? Don't wait for others to recognise you as a prophet. Always focus on the *function* of your gift. Rest assured that the Father will use you regardless of your title. Stay faithful, and the Lord will affirm you at the right time. Serve in a fellowship where all the fivefold gifts are commonly accepted, and just be yourself. Your budding prophetic voice will soon blossom. Categorically refuse to get puffed up because of your gifts. Stay consistent and humble. Far too often, we overemphasise gifts but forget *how* to carry them and *whom* we represent. We are *vessels*. From God's perspective, you are *his* present to your surroundings. *You* are the gift! You are the blessing taking on flesh. A church's collective calling is to carry his heart in any given situation, being a tangible expression of the Father's love.

The Book of Esther is an illustrious tale of splendour—a testimony of great courage. Esther lost her parents early on and was raised by her uncle, Mordecai. Despite being her guardian and not her biological father, he became the dad she trusted. Mordecai was brilliant and supportive because he passed on a solid foundation in the faith and taught her how to live a life full of integrity. After becoming independent, she still heeded Mordecai's advice and observed his instructions to a tee. The girl Esther was well-behaved, incredibly beautiful and utterly glamorous. Without knowing it, she had been tutored for a place in life beyond imagination. When the monarch met with Esther, her vibes were better in comparison to the other ladies he courted. He was completely smitten by her. Was it because of the favour of the Lord that rested on her? Or was it more to it than that? Esther's eminent yet modest mindset created an environment where God was pleased to beautify her from the inside. *"For the LORD takes pleasure in His people; He will beautify the afflicted ones with salvation."* (Psalm 149:4 NASB). The king saw mutual traits in Esther. She had royal attributes of dignity and excellence that seemed spectacular and familiar at the same time. Esther's gentle demeanour reflected the values king Xerxes admired and respected. He was besotted—swept off his feet by Esther's bombshell beauty and sophisticated elegance. The name Esther is derived from the Hebrew root *hester*, from *satár*/ סָתַר, which means hidden one, secret, or star. It equals the Persian setâre/ستاره. In Greek, it resembled the word for star, which is *aster*. Esther's Jewish name was *Hadassah*, from *hadás*/ הֲדַס meaning [57]myrtle tree. It's also associated with peace, prosperity and love. The Almighty hid his star in obscurity until the appointed time came to reveal his tremendous compassion! Because of God's foreknowledge, he strategically positioned Esther. Luxurious gemstones are often stowed away deep underground for aeons. Under extreme pressure, carbon crystallizes as choice diamonds. If they are unearthed, these jewels get very pricy. Likewise, the Lord prepares and preserves his chosen ones for his glorious purposes until he suddenly proclaims: *"Arise, shine, for your light has come, and the glory of the Lord has risen upon you."* (Isa. 60:1 ESV).

The beautifying process Esther underwent before she was presented to the king is quite remarkable. She was treated with myrrh for six months. Due to its earth-like aroma, the scent of myrrh has been compared to black liquorice. The thorny myrrh tree's bark was slashed to provoke the tree to leak the precious resin; it would form into tears once it set. In antiquity, raw myrrh was processed for perfume, medicine or incense. The ointment had anti-ageing properties and anti-inflammatory effects, with the ability to heal scars. For believers, it represents the tears that came out of Jesus' earthly suffering, the agony of the cross and his royalty. Being the sacred Tree of Life, he was slashed, bruised, scourged and maimed for us. Abundant healing and vitality now flow from Jesus' wounds to all who receive his salvation. God wants to make sure that his bride is healed and whole. His anointing heals us like refining oil. We are presented before his glorious presence, without blemish and with great joy, as a chaste bride prepared for her husband (Jude 1:24, Rev 21:2).

---

[57] **My comment:** *The myrtle tree* represents the righteous and the prophets, with its beauty and pleasant smell (see Isa. 55:13 and Zech. 1:8). Hadas myrtle from Tzfat, Israel (see illustration).

Esther's SPA regimen lasted for another six months, with additional perfumes and cosmetics. The Bride of Christ is being purified by *"the washing of the Word"* to stand perfect and unblemished before the King of kings (see Eph. 5:26). Her walk in love releases an intense fragrance pleasing to the Lord, full of life, love and devotion. His bride wears the crown of beauty instead of ashes, the oil of joy instead of mourning and the garment of praise instead of discouragement (see Isa. 61:3). Queen Esther radiated beauty and mercy but was tested in the area of *courage*. Courage is to do the right thing in the face of danger. If confronted with perils, we have to overcome dread and anxiety. The situation soon developed into a suspenseful real-life thriller: A vile aggressor, Haman the Amalekite, maliciously plotted to annihilate the Jews in all of king Xerxes' 127 provinces. When Esther heard about the edict to kill the Jews, she could have cringed in fear. Instead, she rose up and took charge, putting her own head on the block for the sake of her community (see Esther 4). Most of us are well-acquainted with the frequently quoted scripture: *"God didn't give us a spirit of fear, but of power, and love and a sound mind"* (see 2 Tim. 1:7). Esther didn't have that verse to cling to. However, she knew the documented stories of how the Lord delivered his people in ages past. During a prayer meeting, I had a vision of the Bride. I couldn't see her countenance, but her beautiful dress was glistening white. At that moment, I picked up the boisterous conversation in the room: "Isn't she beautiful?" "Isn't she blameless?" Then the Father said: "I will make her fearless!"

Queen Esther possessed both beauty and mercy but was tested in the area of courage. Courage is the ability to do the right thing in the face of danger.

Esther went on a fast to get the much-needed composure for what was ahead of her. The sacrificial act of fasting is a credible and powerful tool because it *fast-forwards* God's answers to our prayers. Esther knew the dire risks of appearing before the king unannounced—she risked the death penalty. Her exquisite looks didn't guarantee that she would escape unscathed. I understand why Esther was aghast at the idea. She implored Mordecai to gather the local Jewish community to fast on her behalf and decided to pray and fast for three consecutive days without any food or drink. She then received divine boldness and wisdom, along with a game plan to proceed with her cause. Esther's courage made her successful, and the Lord spared the Jews from calamity. *Purim* is observed in memory of their deliverance. Today, the Bride is caught in a war, and her position is challenged by the forces of darkness. The Lord's Warrior Bride needs to emerge as a Body. Preparation for the battle happens in the bleak circumstances of turmoil and crisis. The God of Ages is shaking and sifting his people, as he also did with Israel, because he wants our full attention. Through acts of redemptive discipline, he is determined to awaken his Church: *"Awake, awake, Zion, clothe yourself with strength! Put on your garments of splendour ..."* (Isa. 52:1 NIV). God doesn't want uncommitted Christians or a lukewarm runaway bride.

The following quotation prophesies about the Bride's holy audacity: *"Strength and dignity are her clothing, and she laughs at the time to come. She opens her mouth with wisdom, and the teaching of kindness is on her tongue."* (Prov. 31:25-36 ESV). The Lord's bride is called to *interpret* major world events through *the lens of prophecy* and declare the gospel to the unsaved. In this decade, God will test our devotion and our obedience. Similar to Esther, he compels us to rise up at the appointed time, bent on rescuing as many as possible. Now is the time to get prepared and positioned in prayer and repentance, dressing in the divine apparel of strength to overcome and fulfil our mission! Esther dealt with her situation promptly and without hesitation, and the Lord gloriously came through. The Church's rediscovery of repentance is pivotal because it redefines her purpose and redirects her walk with the Father (see 2 Chron. 7:14, Mal. 4:5-6, Rev. 3:19). We fight with our eyes fixed on the price. God will reward those with contrite hearts who diligently seek him (see Heb. 11:6). One day, we will carry the eternal and heavenly garments from Jesus, snow-white robes of refined linen—symbolising the acts done in the Lord's name. These royal raiments will be interwoven with the gold-coloured fibres of our intercession, perseverance, toil and suffering. We will even wear our scars with honour. What a day it will be!

"The King's daughter is all glorious within; Her clothing is interwoven with gold. She will be led to the King in embroidered work; The virgins, her companions who follow her, Will be brought to You. They will be led forth with gladness and rejoicing; They will enter into the King's palace. In place of your fathers will be your sons; You shall make them princes in all the earth." (Psalm 45:13-16 NASB).

Tetelestai - it is finished!

There are some interesting correlations between the cross of Christ and the Bride. In John 19:30, Jesus cried out: *"It is finished!"* These famous words of our Lord will resound throughout eternity and were said right before the ninth hour, or 3 pm. The people in Jerusalem then heard a temple priest blow the [58]shofar since the Passover lamb had been slain. Three English words were used to translate the phrase. In Greek manuscripts, only one word was applied. Jesus spoke Aramaic, a sister language to Hebrew. Biblical Greek uses τετέλεσται - *tetelestai*. The Hebrew/Aramaic term for 'finished' was *kalah*. In Strong's concordance, *Kâlâh* #3617 כָּלָה reads: Completion, termination, full end, complete destruction, consumption, annihilation.

The word is similar to כַּלָּה *kallah* #3618, which means bride. The Hebrew letters Kuf-Lamed-Alef are alike but with a slightly different emphasis. Jesus completed eternal salvation for us by bearing the brunt of the Father's righteous indignation because of our many sins. He then declared destruction to the realm of darkness. In the same minute, he cried out for his bride, the redeemed community of the present, past and future saints. What a wonderful Saviour! Again, it corresponds with what Jesus said: *"I will build My church, and the gates of Hades will not prevail against it."* (Matt. 16:18 BSB – *the last part of the verse*). The term 'church' in this verse more correctly corresponds with congregation, community and family, as discussed in detail in chapter 4. The Bride is like the godly wife in Proverbs 31. She is adorned with courage and dignity, laughing without fear of the time to come because she has tasted the victory that defines her future! Let us see how "tetelestai" was applied:

1. Tetelestai was used by artists

When a painter or a sculptor had finalised his masterpiece, the creator would usually say "tetelestai", meaning: "This is my contribution—there is nothing more I can add to it. It's complete." (See Eph. 2:10, Heb. 10:14).

---

[58] **Source:** thattheworldmayknow.com/shofar

2. Tetelestai was used by builders
When a builder of a house followed the architectural drafting to its completion, he also used this word. (See Eph. 2:22, Heb. 9:24).

3. Tetelestai was used by creditors
If a debt was paid off, the creditor would take his pen and write "tetelestai" across the debt document, which meant that the owed money had been "paid in full". (See Matt. 20:28, 1 Tim. 2:5-6, Col. 2:14-15).

4. Tetelestai was used by jailers and judges
If a man was sentenced to serve time for a felony, the following would occur: When the allotted time was completed, the jailer would open the cell door and hang a sign over it with the one word "tetelestai", as the crime had been atoned for.

The Church's rediscovery of repentance is pivotal, as it redefines her purpose and redirects her walk with the Father.

The Bible tells us how the Father publicly revealed his righteousness through Christ on the wooden cross (see Rom. 3:25). During his lifetime, Jesus clearly revealed the Lord's nature and many times beforehand explained to his disciples that he would face death. The Passover drama positions Jesus, the Lamb of God, on the stage as the main actor, with the Father as the director. Although the canvas was grim, with our redemption violently painted across it with the broad strokes of our marred Saviour's blood, it portrayed the captivating glory of God. This poignant drama reached its culmination through the crucifixion when our High Priest victoriously proclaimed: *"It is finished!"* God's masterpiece was matchless that day. The Father's ultimate showpiece was put on display as the dark spiritual forces were thrown into instant disarray by God's magnificent act of love for us at Calvary (see 1 Cor. 2:7-8, Col. 2:14-15). God piled our sins on Jesus, and our indebtedness was permanently settled. He wrote "tetelestai" with his innocent blood and legally freed us from the dungeon of sin and death. As promised, Jesus went away and prepared a place for us. The great architect and builder opened the access to the throne room of Heaven. In him, we were placed in righteousness, holiness and glory! We got a royal seat in the Father's house, but also became *his House*. Through the Crucifixion, God, the

Father, showed his unfailing, unending and unwavering love for us. He boasted: "Here is my best work ever; there is nothing to add to it. My contribution is perfect and complete!"

The first prophetic glimpse of the Bride can be found in the Book of Genesis, where the Lord decided to fill the void in Adam's life. Adam recognised that he was missing an equal by his side, one who could match him in both dignity and brilliance (see Gen. 2:18-20). Most translations use the word עֵזֶר *ezer* - 'helper'. A more precise translation is [59]help, rescuer or protection. God gave Adam what he deeply longed for, someone to complete him: a woman. The Hebrew אִשָּׁה *isha* is derived from the word אִישׁ *ish*. *Ish* means 'man'; hence *isha* means 'of the man'. God performed history's first anaesthesia by surgically removing one of Adam's ribs, closing up the wound with flesh. An incredible miracle ensued: With the rib's DNA, he fashioned a woman. The mysterious relationship between man and woman is seen in Christ's relationship to the Church (see Gen. 2:20-23, Eph. 5:26-33). After his death, the last Adam was pierced between his ribs (see John 19:34). The blood and water leaving Jesus' side on the cross is viewed by some scholars as a sign of the Bride's birth. The correlations between Adam and Jesus are astonishing (see also 1 Cor. 15:45-48).

Let us look at the story in Gen. 24:1-27. Abraham, the patriarch, had to preserve his bloodline by securing a proper bride for his son. He wanted to find a lady from his native country. If Isaac chose to marry a Canaanite woman, it would have destroyed his legacy. Canaan hints at a worldly system. It means 'what humbles and subdues' or 'merchant'. So, Abraham sent his head servant Eliezer, a man he trusted, on an expedition to procure a suitable match. Eliezer means 'the Help of my God'. Eliezer reveals how the Spirit goes out from the Father and the Son to serve them both (see Gen. 15:2). When Eliezer arrived, he met young Rebekah, who was soon to become Isaac's bride. The symbolism is conspicuous. God longs for a bride who draws living water from his well, who seeks him and is sustained by the life he emits (see John 4:4; 7:37-38, 15:26, Rev. 22:17). The innocent Rebekah was unsullied, a virgin. The Church is also described in the same way in Scripture (see Gen. 24:16, 2 Cor. 11:2).

---

[59] **My comment:** *Helper* - See this brilliant article: theologyofwork.org > search for: **God Created Woman as an Ezer Kind of Helper (Genesis 2:18)** Article / Produced by TOW Project

The expedition Eliezer embarked on would take six whole weeks. During the seventh week, Rebecca met Isaac. The six weeks may prophetically foreshadow six thousand years, with the seventh week representing Christ's millennial reign on earth, together with his bride. Eliezer brought a caravan of camels. The English word 'camel' comes from the Hebrew word גמל *gamal*. The third Hebrew letter, *gimel*, is named after *gamal*. Gimel (ג) resembles a man in motion. In traditional Judaism, it's a symbol of an affluent man running after a poor man to give him charity. Christ humbled himself to lift us up—he endured the punishment in order to get his reward, the Bride. *Gamal*, from which we get our word camel, is close to the word גְּמוּל *gimul*. It either means 'reward and punishment' or 'justified repayment'—it all ties in with Christ. The camels came for Rebekah—whose name means 'fat, or blessing'—and carried her all the way home. God's promises have the same ability. They elevate us and take us home to the Father's house. Camels have excellent eyesight, capable of traversing various terrains. Covenant promises open up the horizons of our future; they help us in every possible situation. On the camel, the rider is situated between the humps and rests close to the supplies and the power source. The big humps store all the camel's nutrition and fat reserves. Lastly, the camel has one extra joint in the leg, which enables it to bow very low and sit down with ease. This ability points to humility and servanthood, with promises accessible to those who earnestly seek the Lord. To save us and to elevate us to a prominent place of hope and a future, Christ stooped down lower than anyone else before him (see 2 Sam. 2:8, Jer. 29:11).

Eliezer claimed Rebekah for Isaac by bestowing costly jewellery on her (see Gen. 24:54). In ancient times, dowry was customary, with gifts given to the bride and her family. It's a phenomenal picture of how Christ is purchasing the Bride for himself! He paid the price for our redemption, cancelled our debt, and richly blessed us with gifts. For some decades, signs and wonders have occurred and remind us of this fact. In the Eighties, gold dust started to materialise in meetings in the U.S., showering down on believers. The recently deceased Henry Gruver related this phenomenon to an Israeli rabbi. The man hollered out: "Gold is falling on the Gentiles!" Seemingly flummoxed, he loudly repeated his own words. To the rabbi, this was an irrefutable sign of the Messianic era being introduced. These signs suggest that God is claiming his Bride because he wants to take her home to Heaven. Eliezer charged Rebekah's father, Laban, not to delay him in returning her to Isaac, his master (see Gen. 24:56).

God doesn't want his bride to be held back by worldly cares but arranged for a swift and sweet departure in order to quickly unite us with our heavenly bridegroom. *"For the Lord will carry out his sentence on earth with speed and finality."* (Rom. 9:28 NIV, and also Matt. 24:23-27, Rev. 22:7).

God's promises open up the horizons of our future.

The Lord is preparing his overcoming and fearless bride. Jesus told his disciples: *"Let not your hearts be troubled. Believe in God; believe also in me. In my Father's house are many rooms. If it were not so, would I have told you that I go to prepare a place for you? And if I go and prepare a place for you, I will come again and will take you to myself, that where I am you may be also."* (John 14:1-3 ESV). Jesus, the Bridegroom, gently addressed his beloved Bride. In keeping with Jewish traditions, the groom had to return to his father's house and make ready the bridal chamber for his bride. He usually built an extension to his father's house, which would take approximately one to three years to complete. If the father consented to the marriage, the following would happen: The bridegroom first escorted his bride home to receive the blessing from his father. Later, the wedding guests would arrive at the house with the bride and groom, accompanied by pomp, shouts and music and join the celebration. The newlyweds consummated the marriage in the new extension. It's a brilliant picture of our blissful union with our Saviour and bridegroom, Jesus Christ! Through the cross and the resurrection, he prepared a place for us in the spirit realm, founded on covenant promises and privileges. We now sit with him in heavenly places (see Eph. 1:3, 2:6). Christ also returned to Heaven to furnish our eternal dwelling places.

The Bride is like Rebekah, ardently longing for her awaiting Isaac. She is like Ruth, emerging into her destiny at the appointed harvest time. She is like Esther, showing royal strength in a time of opposition and persecution. She is like Deborah, at the forefront of the battle—securing the victory in advance. The Bride must prepare for the harvest and the pushback that will follow the wake of the immense outpouring of the Spirit. We are in for a rough ride once persecution hits. In the days ahead, let us pray for a baptism of holy fire and unshaken confidence. Let his bride arise and be radiant!

The Bride is like Rebekah, ardently longing for her awaiting Isaac. She is like Ruth, emerging into her destiny at the appointed harvest time. She is like Esther, showing royal strength in a time of opposition and persecution. She is like Deborah, at the forefront of the battle—securing the victory in advance.

God parades his goodness through righteousness, truth, justice and mercy. Shrouded in the prophetic passage about Israel's and Jerusalem's future redemption, we detect a pattern of how the Bride is called to reflect Christ:

For Zion's sake I will not keep silent, And for Jerusalem's sake I will not keep quiet, Until her righteousness goes forth like brightness, And her salvation like a torch that is burning. The nations will see your righteousness, And all kings your glory; And you will be called by a new name Which the mouth of the LORD will designate. You will also be a crown of beauty in the hand of the LORD, And a royal diadem in the hand of your God. It will no longer be said to you, "Forsaken," [Azuvah] Nor to your land will it any longer be said, "Desolate"; [Shemameh] But you will be called, "My delight is in her," [Cheftzi-Vah]

And your land, "Married"; [Beulah] For the LORD delights in you, And to Him your land will be married. For as a young man marries a virgin, So your sons will marry you; And as the bridegroom rejoices over the bride [kallah], So your God will rejoice over you. On your walls, O Jerusalem, I have appointed watchmen; All day and all night they will never keep silent. You who remind the LORD, take no rest for yourselves; And give Him no rest until He establishes And makes Jerusalem a praise in the earth.

The LORD has sworn by His right hand and by His strong arm, "I will never again give your grain as food for your enemies; Nor will foreigners drink your new wine for which you have laboured." But those who garner it will eat it and praise the LORD; And those who gather it will drink it in the courts of My sanctuary. Go through, go through the gates, Clear the way for the people; Build up, build up the highway, Remove the stones, lift up a standard over the peoples. Behold, the LORD has proclaimed to the end of the earth, Say to the daughter of Zion, "Lo, your salvation comes; Behold His reward is with Him, and His recompense before Him." And they will call them, "The holy people, The redeemed of the LORD"; And you will be called, "Sought out [Derushah], a city not forsaken [Ir Lo Ne'ezavah]." (Isa. 62 NASB).

By comparing the text from Isaiah with the Book of Revelation, we discover some interesting similarities. *"You will be called by a new name"* (see Rev. 2:17 and 3:12). *"And to Him your land will be married. For as a young man marries a virgin, So your sons will marry you; And as the bridegroom rejoices over the bride, So your God will rejoice over you."* The Marriage Supper of the Lamb speaks of Christ and his chosen bride (see Rev. 19:6-9). The Church doesn't by any means replace Israel and the Jewish people, but we have been grafted in and partake in the same destiny and inheritance (see Rom. 11:17-18, Eph. 2:15). This spiritual union will soon become evident. Loving our Saviour is undeniably reflected in our love for Israel. The devil has sought to obliterate the wonderful connection between Gentiles and Jews, but God joins these two peoples of promise—completing a process of reconciliation and healing. In the coming harvest and outpouring, Messianic Jews will minister side by side with Gentile believers with one spirit. [60]Since 1948, Messianic congregations and synagogues in Israel have risen from 0 to approximately 300, a wonderful sign. These are truly times of great restoration! I believe we will see salvations, signs, and wonders break loose. Miraculous power will erupt as a result of a stronger corporate anointing. *"Behold, how good and pleasant it is when brothers dwell in unity! It is like the precious oil on the head, running down on the beard, on the beard of Aaron, down on the collar of his robe. It is like the dew of Hermon, which falls on the mountains of Zion! For there the LORD has commanded the blessing, life forevermore."* (Psalm 133:1-3 ESV). In the sermon on the mount, Jesus charged his disciples to be like an illuminated city: *"You are the light of the world. A city set on a hill cannot be hidden."* (Matt. 5:14 ESV). Isaiah chapters 60-62 connect redeemed saints with the heavenly Zion, the city of God, the new Jerusalem. When we compare them, they are identical to the depiction found in Revelation chapter 21. Somehow, it looks like the believers and the City have merged into one sphere. God's people are the Bride, and the Bride is the City, united as two indivisible entities. Words like righteousness shining forth, burning and radiating all describes the characteristics of Holy Spirit-filled believers.

God parades his goodness through righteousness, truth, justice and mercy.

---

[60] **Source**: The article "Findings of New Research on the Messianic Movement in Israel" Website: oneforisrael.org

The New Covenant reality culminates in God sending his only Son at the appointed time. Through the gospel, he reveals his righteousness (see Dan. 9:24-26, Rom. 1:16-17, Gal. 4:4). When we receive Christ, we become a part of the gospel message and a demonstration of its power. The gospel is highly infectious. Once you are smitten, it changes you! Christ's redemptive work gives us his spiritual DNA, and we become ministers of reconciliation. God moulds us into his likeness. By receiving the Light, we become light. *"The true Light who gives light to every man was coming into the world."* (John 1:9 BSB). God's light, through his Word, increases its brightness, all the while his Spirit sanctifies us. Christ, the hope of glory, lives inside and lights us up! Jesus described this inward change: *"No one after lighting a lamp puts it in a cellar or under a basket, but on a stand, so that those who enter may see the light. Your eye is the lamp of your body. When your eye is healthy, your whole body is full of light, but when it is bad, your body is full of darkness. Therefore be careful lest the light in you be darkness. If then your whole body is full of light, having no part dark, it will be wholly bright, as when a lamp with its rays gives you light."* (Luke 11:33-36 ESV).

The expression 'healthy' also means 'generous', as opposed to the [61]evil eye, which is covetous. When beholding God, who himself is light, we start to emit the essence of who he is. Eventually, we take after the One we gaze at with undying admiration. [62]Spouses unknowingly mirror each other's faces. How awesome to think the same is true about us and our Lord Jesus! We find this principle in the New Testament:

"Now when they saw the boldness of Peter and John, and perceived that they were uneducated, common men, they were astonished. And they recognized that they had been with Jesus." (Acts 4:13 ESV).

"And fixing their gaze on him, all who were sitting in the Council saw his face like the face of an angel." (Acts 6:15 NASB).

---

[61] **See also:** *"A person with an evil eye hurries after wealth and does not know that poverty will come upon him."* (Prov. 28:22 NASB).

[62] **My comment:** According to psychologist Robert Zajonc from the University of Michigan, the older a couple gets, the more similar they look because people in close contact with each other tend to mimic each other's facial expressions. When people stay together for a prolonged time, their actions, thoughts and appearance will align as the relationship progresses.

When beholding God, who himself is light, we start to emit the essence of who he is.

A close, loving relationship with Jesus leaves a distinct imprint of his glory in us that can be easily recognised and validated. Even the disciples' adversaries acknowledged this. With prophetic sternness, Stephen rebuked the Sanhedrin for rejecting Christ and his glory because they renounced the Chief Cornerstone, Jesus, the promised Messiah (see Acts 4:11). The Council looked intently at him and saw a face glowing like the face of a heavenly angel. Knowing he had their attention, Stephen fittingly addressed this phenomenon in the opening words of his speech, saying: *"The God of glory appeared to Abraham."* He referred to how Moses, as a prophet, received the Law via angels. Like Moses, Stephen moved in signs, wonders and miracles. His face radiated the genuine glory of the Lord. He was a marvel to them, yet they hated him. In the hour of testing, he fulfilled what our Master prophesied: *"But when they hand you over, do not worry about how or what you are to say; for it will be given you in that hour what you are to say. For it is not you who speak, but it is the Spirit of your Father who speaks in you."* (Matt. 10:19-20 NASB). Stephen ended his powerful testimony with unflinching courage, undismayed by the horrors of death. I recommend that you read his anointed speech in Acts chapter 7.

A close, loving relationship with Jesus leaves a distinct imprint of his glory in us that can be easily recognised and validated.

Earth is supposed to mirror Heaven through our attitude and way of life. Most believers think of Heaven as God's holy dwelling and our final destination when we die. It rightly is. That said, we partake in a heavenly reality at this very moment. The Bride of Christ should radiate his glory in righteousness, beauty and favour. The king delighted in Queen Esther, and King Jesus delights in us. Let us pursue the Bridegroom, our Lord, with intense longing and unceasing love! Expecting Christ's soon return is an attested sign of a healthy bride. We will get new bodies when Christ comes back, ready to enter the perfectly pure atmosphere of the highest Heaven. On a renewed earth, we will access the heavenly city forever (see Rev. 21). Through the centuries, people scorned and ridiculed believers for preaching the message: **'Jesus is coming back soon!'** Knowing how deep-seated scepticism would be one of the end time signs, Peter wrote: *"Most importantly, I want to remind you that in the last days scoffers will come, mocking the truth and following their own desires. They will say, "What happened to the promise that Jesus is coming again? From before the times of our ancestors, everything has remained the same."* (2 Pet. 3:3-4 NLT). Hesitant theologians scoff at the idea of Jesus coming back during our lifetime. I recall a story where a pastor tried to comfort his congregation. He concluded his speech by saying that Jesus would most likely *not* return very shortly. Many Bible-believing churches would have found this statement almost blasphemous two decades ago, but times have changed indeed. Some seeker-sensitive churches consider The Second Coming invasive because people could get upset and frightened. If the outcome of preaching the Lord's imminent return is repentance that leads to life, how can that be bad?

The scoffers Peter prophesied about claim everything remains the same, implying that no judgement is looming on the horizon. Their view of history is strictly linear, but the biblical pattern is both cyclical and linear. Many ancient cultures used the cyclical model, like the Mayans, with their famous calendar. Ecclesiastes underlines a similar paradigm: *"Whatever is has already been, and what will be has been before; and God will call the past to account."* (Ecc. 3:15 NIV). To brazenly assume that this evil age will continue undisrupted is not biblical. Cataclysmic events, like Noah's flood and the destruction of Sodom and Gomorrah, disprove such a simplistic view. Jesus linked ancient history to corresponding and future events: *"When the Son of Man returns, it will be like it was in Noah's day. In those days, the people enjoyed banquets and parties and weddings right up to the time Noah entered his boat and the flood came and destroyed them. And the world will be as it was in the days of Lot. People went about their daily business—eating and drinking, buying and selling, farming and building—until the morning Lot left Sodom. Then fire and burning sulphur rained down from heaven and destroyed them all."* (Luke 17:26-29 NLT).

Expecting Christ's soon return is one of the sure signs of a healthy bride.

The rise and fall of ancient civilizations demonstrate how the Lord resolutely dealt with unrighteousness. I oppose the argument of a world currently so depraved that Jesus has to snatch us out of it, where most people are headed for destruction. No doubt, the conditions are rapidly worsening, with increasing wickedness. Our Lord predicted dire times of apostasy and lawlessness. He is the King, who ultimately will bring judgement because of sin. Lawlessness leads to lovelessness because people have believed the deceiving prophets of the Post-Christian era. A cesspool of godless philosophies arrived with the Age of Enlightenment, and presently these pernicious ideologies haunt our society with their deadly cause-and-action effect. Jesus and his apostles prophesied about it (see Matt. 24:10-14, 2 Tim. 4:1-2, 2 Tim. 3:1-9). For some believers, it seems like the Rapture, or the catching away, is a suitable reason for evasion of duty. The late Leonard Ravenhill said: 'Today's church wants to be raptured from responsibility.' Do we barely tolerate sinners, or do we pursue them with the Father's love? The Lord is slow to anger because he wants to show mercy, not judgement. Indeed, judgement is coming, and the fear of God motivates us to show mercy, mixed with fear—to snatch people from the flames (see Jude 1:23). God wants us to rescue as many people as possible from eternal damnation. *"Since, then, we know what it is to fear the Lord, we try to persuade others. What we are is plain to God, and I hope it is also plain to your conscience."* (2 Cor. 5:11 NIV).

To my mind, Jesus will come back sooner than we expect. I will not waste time by speculating whether [63]the rapture will happen before, after, or in the middle of the Tribulation period. Is it worthwhile upsetting each other over a contested subject? However, we are told to be eagerly and patiently waiting for the Lord's return (Rom. 8:23, 1 Cor. 1:7, Phil. 3:20, James 5:7-11). God's people must be prepared, whatever the future holds. Our sails are already set for Heaven's shore. Jesus, in describing the end of this age, told us that we can expect a great harvest of souls—a major sign (see Matt. 13:29). Soul winning seems to be the ultimate end time sign. The Bride will not be speechless but declare the good news boldly! The gospel will be displayed in remarkable ways, leaving people without excuse: *"They perish because they refused to love the truth and so be saved"* (2 Thess. 2:10 ESV). Prophetic predictions reveal that multitudes of people will get the opportunity to repent because the earth will be flooded with the knowledge of the glory of the Lord (see Isa. 11:9, Hab. 2:14). Jesus said: *"And when I am lifted up from the earth, I will draw everyone to myself."* (John

---

[63] **My comment:** I belong to a Pentecostal tradition where we generally believe that Jesus will return before the Tribulation, based on 1 Thess. 4:13-18, 5:1-11. You may have a different background and opinion than me, whether you think the rapture will occur pre-trib, mid-trib or post-trib. In my walk with God, my response today is more pragmatic: In due time we will all know for sure!

12:32 NLT). When we finally decide to set our eyes on the crucified Nazarene alone, worshipping him with total abandon, one of the most glorious manifestations in the Church will be evangelism. *"Surely you will summon a nation you do not know, and nations who do not know you will run to you. For the LORD your God, the Holy One of Israel, has bestowed glory on you."* (Isa. 55:5 BSB). Everything shifts when the glory of the Lord shows up: *"It was in the year King Uzziah died that I saw the Lord. He was sitting on a lofty throne, and the train of his robe filled the Temple."* (Isa. 6:1 NLT). His weighty presence convicts on a scale traditional evangelism can't achieve.

The Bride won't be speechless but declare the good news boldly!

Jesus returns as Saviour for his chosen ones while appearing as King and Judge to the world. The Lord's millennial reign will disrupt the lifestyle of modern citizens, terminating this present evil age (Gal. 1:4). It will be an unexpected and perplexing event for some but a great relief for others. Jesus, the Messiah, will upend the system of macabre abortions, human trafficking and pointless wars. God's final judgement will prove his extraordinary love. God instituted physical death to curb evil when Adam and Eve fell. In his mercy, he closed off the portal to the Garden and the Tree of Life to prevent us from being sealed in our unredeemed condition indefinitely.

God will terminate wickedness out of love for his dear children. It's his response to the prayer *"Your kingdom come"*. The yearning for Jesus' second coming is, at the same time, a cry out of love and a clarion call for righteousness. The Bride can't help her deep longing for the Bridegroom—it's in her spiritual makeup! *The Spirit and the bride say, "Come!" And let the one who hears say, "Come!"* (Rev. 22:17). Our spirit testifies together with the Spirit of God, saying *"Abba, Father"*. In like manner, we all cry out, *"Come, Lord Jesus!"* (See Rom. 8:14-15, 1 Cor. 16:22). Jesus is looking forward to the eternal union with his redeemed and beloved ones. Our Saviour is the lovesick bridegroom! *He who testifies to these things says, "Yes, I am coming soon." Amen. Come, Lord Jesus.* (Rev. 22:20 NIV).

The yearning for Jesus' second coming is, at the same time, a cry out of love and a clarion call for righteousness.

Prophetic ministry and purpose

We all need to be loved, to belong and to feel significant. But, in regard to the visible ministry in God's Kingdom, we must be very conscientious about how we present ourselves. We are believers and first and foremost children of God, deeply loved by our heavenly Father. In the same way, the Father affirmed Jesus as his beloved son, he wants to affirm us as we daily feed on his love. Service springs from our fellowship with him. Prophecy was never meant to be an end in itself—it's a toolkit of grace to advance God's kingdom—flowing out of intimacy with him. It's incredibly vital to value the prophets and to honour those who carry prophetic gifts. Paul wrote, *"do not despise prophecies"* (1 Thess. 5:20), and Jesus said, *"Whoever welcomes a prophet as a prophet will receive a prophet's reward, and whoever welcomes a righteous person as a righteous person will receive a righteous person's reward."* (Matt. 10:41 NIV). In my case, I do have prophetic friends in the Lord, people I respect. I happily receive encouragement from them. They are dear, and their gifts are great blessings to me.

We all need to be loved, to belong and to feel significant.

I am wary when people in the prophetic community commend other ministers for being great prophets, which is every so often echoed from the pulpits. Paul advised us to *"test everything"* within the prophetic dimension (1 Thess. 5:20). Accepting the prophetic gifts is important, and in various churches, it's quite common to be called a prophet—out of respect for the office. The apostle Paul's desire was, in fact, that everyone would prophesy (1 Cor. 14:1-5). I, for one, think it's a danger in over-elevating the office by making prophetic ministry exclusive and not relatable to the common churchgoers. The flattering comments about other preachers' ministries are seemingly harmless. Wouldn't it be wiser to maintain a more low-key approach? Personally, I don't call out fellow preachers as prophets publicly, nor do I let them refer to me in that way. If we want to build an *honourable culture* within the Body of Christ, it's indispensable to love each other in healthy ways when we recognise and affirm *identity*. That certainly goes beyond verbalising gifts, callings and offices. Is it beneficial to depend on these things for validation of our identity? How do we view ministry today? Do we emphasise function over position? Do we have a career mentality or a servant mentality? Is ministry done selflessly or selfishly? We all know that Jesus rebuked the Pharisees for picking the best seats in the synagogues and at the banquets. Insisting on being praised as 'Rabbi', they believed they were more spiritual than the rest of Israel (see Matt. 23:5-8, Mark 12:38-39). These aristocrats patently ignored the well-being of society's underlings. Not unlike several of today's affluent Christian ministries, this entitled fraternity had become conceited and vain, preoccupied with status, visible positions and titles. Let us refuse this madness!

Today, there seem to be two main developments within charismatic Christianity: super-ministries and grassroots-ministries. Super-ministries, because of their size, have leaders that sometimes are seen as elevated above the organisations they head and unapproachable to normal churchgoers. Some have become wealthy from the merchandise they promote, which adds to this sense of grandeur. Needless to say, we expect to pay full-time ministers because it is fair and biblical. Is it a sin to prosper financially? Not at all. If a person becomes a brand or a widely acclaimed celebrity in the Church, it may be hard to stay humble and down-to-earth. Jesus very much disliked being famous. He chose to stay outside the cities by dint of his popularity and was determined to keep publicity to a minimum (see Mark 1:45). He wanted Israel's citizens to approach him with ease. Isaiah predicted this about the Messiah:

"He will not shout or cry out, or raise his voice in the streets. A bruised reed he will not break, and a smouldering wick he will not snuff out. In faithfulness he will bring forth justice." (Isa. 42:2-3 NIV).

It's indispensable to love each other in healthy ways when we recognise and affirm identity.

Paul also kept a low profile, trying to be as accessible to people as possible. Fivefold preachers, apostles, prophets and others frequently need to mingle and network in order to build good friendships, model Christlikeness, and nurture and mature believers (see Acts 20:28-31). To reproduce robust believers is a more urgent task than passing on information. In this season, God wants to release entire companies of fivefold ministers. We need the fathers and mothers of faith to reproduce their gifts as Paul did with Timothy. God wants prophetic revelation to be everywhere because without it, people will *cast off restraint*, and judgement will come (see Prov. 29:18). In preparation for revival and awakening, the Lord wants us to effectively prevent the agony of fatherlessness. If you are seasoned in the prophetic, your focus is on love and transparency. You understand how to equip the believers the Father teams you up with. But prophetic communities for the privileged few, engrossed in self-promotion and navel-gazing, are unfit to train the next generation of prophetic voices. Let us be relatable like Amos. He never sought recognition or fame but only prophesied when led by the Spirit, fully content to be just *"a herdsman and a tender of sycamore-fig trees"* (Amos 7:14-15). Yet Amos confidently knew his identity. If we demystify the prophetic realm, we actively empower those who desire the next move of God. The prophetic will erupt when we couple it with hunger and pure motives.

In this season, God wants to release entire companies of fivefold ministers.

Moses got a glimpse of what it is like to have a community filled with the prophetic Spirit: *But Moses replied, "Are you jealous for my sake? I wish that all the LORD's people were prophets and that the LORD would put his Spirit on them!"* (Num. 11:29 NIV). Moses understood the immense privilege of having the Spirit of God resting on his life. Besides, he wanted others to share in the blessing. Let us include people the same way Elijah did with Elisha. He didn't deny Elisha the double portion of the anointing he was chasing after. Elijah charged him to be extra vigilant, so he wouldn't let go of the blessing, but no rebuke was given (see 2 Kings 2:1-15). For that reason, Elisha ignored the flaming chariots while fixing his eyes on Elijah when he quickly departed into the churning whirlwind. He eagerly wanted to get hold of his precious mantle, whatever the cost. Today's younger generation is insatiably hungry for God, and their passionate pursuit of the Holy One will cause the prophetic revelation to dramatically increase and invade society in the years preceding Christ's return!

Kingdom radicals

Prophetic revelation always creates drastic shifts. Through the ages, God raised up awesome men and women. They changed atmospheres and shaped cultures. *"And what more shall I say? I do not have time to tell about Gideon, Barak, Samson and Jephthah, about David and Samuel and the prophets, who through faith conquered kingdoms, administered justice, and gained what was promised; who shut the mouths of lions, quenched the fury of the flames, and escaped the edge of the sword; whose weakness was turned to strength; and who became powerful in battle and route foreign armies. Women received back their dead, raised to life again. There were others who were tortured, refusing to be released so that they might gain an even better resurrection."* (Heb. 11:32-35 NIV).

Because it also is the Spirit of faith, the prophetic Spirit inevitably stirs us to do great exploits for God's kingdom (see 2 Cor. 4:13). Let us take a gander at Jonathan with his armour-bearer. You find this gripping story in 1 Sam. 14. The tantalising tale is literally a *cliffhanger!* Jonathan said: *"It may be that the Lord will work for us, for nothing can hinder the Lord from saving by many or by few."* (1 Sam. 14:6 NASB). Emboldened by faith, they scrambled up the steep hillside to pounce the Philistine outpost. Strategically speaking, their daring attempt was bonkers, but because God inspired their improvised action, they won a great victory. Faith is spelt *risk,* and its undertakings are always prophetic by nature. Faith comes by hearing or seeing God's voice (see Rom. 10:17, Rev. 1:12). Stepping out of our comfort zone can be scary but immensely rewarding if the Spirit leads us. The Israelites who earlier sided with the Philistines unexpectedly returned to the fold, heavily impacted because of this brave prophetic enterprise. And what about fellow Jews who hid in the hill country? They came out of the woodwork and joined the battle against their enemies!

Similarly, God empowers champions of our generation to cause the backslidden and lost to leave the enemy's camp and rejoin his people. Courageous individuals on fire for Jesus will awaken destiny and affirm God-given identity, thrusting them into the Kingdom of Light. Holy courage made the earth shake. It was an identical sign the Jerusalem church experienced when they petitioned the Lord for more boldness (see Acts 4:31). The praying assembly, without dithering, wanted more of the ingredient that initially triggered their persecution. If you know God, you only wish for the real deal! The congregation prayed like this: 'More, Lord! Give us more boldness to preach Christ crucified along with healings, signs and wonders!' You are a radical when you pray for something that brings you double trouble. These tough believers' mission was nowhere near a theoretical concept—they trusted a baptism of fire and love. These Kingdom fanatics didn't rely on their human ingenuity or meticulously prearranged campaigns. With a gospel message ignited by the mighty Holy Spirit, it was evangelism set on fire! With intense devotion, they sought the earth-shaking power of God, putting their lives and reputation at risk for it.

If you know God, you only wish for the real deal!
You are a radical when you pray for something that brings you double trouble.

Let us look at another character, Jehu. He was indeed a radical; fast, furious and ferocious! The anointing made him go berserk against idolatry. He was the hardliner who finally got rid of the evil queen Jezebel. The term *"driving like Jehu"* has absolute merit, as he drove his chariot like a complete madman (see 2 King 9:20). Jehu moved in the Spirit of power and might (see Isa. 11:2, 28:6). He eradicated idolatry in Israel with brusque but swift resolve. He did away with the corrupted royals and the pagan priesthood. Jehu's anointing turned him into a violent wrecking ball, as he acted quickly and without hesitation. Disruptors of this stature tend to ruffle a few feathers because they are mavericks and unconventional truth-tellers.

King Josiah heard the Book of the Law read and tore his clothes. He sobbed because the Word had been so grossly neglected. He celebrated Passover like no king before him and removed all the pagan shrines and the high places. Josiah rededicated Judah to the Lord. The kings of Judah utterly failed to demolish the high places because they wanted to appease their subjects. Sadly, some contemporary pastors refuse to take issue with believers they know to live in compromise. The high places are the things competing with devoted worship of God in our lives. Modern idols usually lack physical form but are somewhat vaguer: *"For everything in the world—the lust of the flesh, the lust of the eyes, and the pride of life—comes not from the Father but from the world."* (1 John 2:16 NIV). We dethrone our false gods by daily submission to the Lord and dying to selfish impulses. *"The weapons of our warfare are not the weapons of the world. Instead, they have divine power to demolish strongholds. We tear down arguments and every presumption set up against the knowledge of God; and we take captive every thought to make it obedient to Christ."* (2 Cor. 10:4-5 BSB). Josiah moved ahead with godly character, undeterred by the formidable challenges he faced. *"Never before had there been a king like Josiah, who turned to the Lord with all his heart and soul and strength, obeying all the laws of Moses. And there has never been a king like him since."* (2 Kings 23:25 NLT). Josiah was totally sold out for

God! To keep Israel faithful to Yehovah and not corrupted by foreign deities, David acted like a man after God's own heart. Being a great warrior, he protected both the nation's outer safety and inner integrity, yet he wasn't as extreme as Josiah in his day.

Let me add that God's Word repeatedly warns against idolatry: *Do not be yoked together with unbelievers. For what do righteousness and wickedness have in common? Or what fellowship can light have with darkness? What harmony is there between Christ and Belial? Or what does a believer have in common with an unbeliever? What agreement is there between the temple of God and idols? For we are the temple of the living God. As God has said: "I will live with them and walk among them, and I will be their God, and they will be my people."* (2 Cor. 6:14-16 NIV). *For freedom Christ has set us free; stand firm therefore, and do not submit again to a yoke of slavery.* (Gal. 5:1 ESV). Church leaders should warn their members to steer clear of all forms of idol worship and dabbling in the occult, which includes yoga, Eastern meditation, reiki, astrology, crystals, a wide range of alternative medicine, etc. These methods lead to spiritual bondage as they yoke their practitioners to demons. I also deem that Martial arts related to Zen Buddhism should be off-limits for Christians. Have you thought and prayed about these things?

Modern idols usually lack physical form but are somewhat vaguer.

Let us look at another heroine of faith, Jael, who was a calculating and shrewd woman. By defeating the high-ranking general Sisera, she was capable of toppling governments (see Judges 4:16-23). She had the courage and strength to act despite an agreement between her household and king Jabin, the Canaanite. It's ironic. Jael's neighbours probably shunned her. Distrusted because of her husband's treaty with the enemy, they probably treated her like a scandalous traitor. She moved in stealth mode and suddenly launched a deadly attack on Sisera with a tent peg: She was not afraid to carry sharp instruments *with intent!* Nobody questioned her loyalty after her gritty deed. She will go down in history as one of the most valiant women. To this very day, due to their epic legacies, typical Israeli girls' names are Jael, Deborah and Hadassah. They exemplify righteousness, virtue and valour. In Jewish culture, names prophetically define and capture essence.

Radicalism in the Kingdom isn't measured by the boldness of one's statements, even if it is tempting to suppose so. Words marked by bravado might not match the high standard the Bible sets for our lives. At times, we tend to compensate for the disparity between our internal convictions and our actual achievements. Of course, the devil will make every effort to agitate us to utter arrogant confessions—using pride to trip us up. He traps us by enticing us to say something we cannot master the capacity to sustain. Sometime later, he forcefully hits us when our guard is down. Satan wants us to become a laughingstock to the cynics and the sceptics and an embarrassment to those who look up to us. We need checks and balances: *our radical opinions* must be followed through by *an equally radical surrender* to the Lord. From time to time, we hear rallying cries from the pulpit, like: "We will take back what the devil has stolen!" I understand the noble intentions behind these slogans, although they seriously annoy me quite a bit because of their consequences. Some churches treat spiritual warfare very foolhardy because the corresponding actions to back their outspoken statements are in short supply.

The devil fears consistent commitment but not rash casual confessions. Just look at Job's consistency: He always sacrificed to the Lord on behalf of his close family by constantly interceding for his sons and daughters. Job's righteous deeds truly shook the kingdom of darkness, so much so that [64]Satan attempted to destroy him (see Job 1:4). Let us be cautious with our words. A *radical lifestyle* builds on being *radically loved* by God. What can be more radical than the Father's love, mirrored through Christ's sacrifice for us? His shedding of blood on the cross was history's turning point, the most radical act ever performed by anyone. Jesus disarmed the forces of darkness while he quietly hung on the cursed tree and wiped out our long record of sins (see Col. 2:14-15). Each time and moment we love radically, compelled by the Spirit of Christ, we enforce the victory won on the cross. Our spiritual enemies feel these actions as if we are violently wreaking havoc, causing them great harm. Jesus, our Lord, was revolutionary and radical to the core. He confronted corrupted attitudes and systems with undaunted resolve. Jesus didn't avoid fierce opposition but tackled it head-on. The rugged but competent carpenter from Nazareth bashed

---

[64] **My comment:** In the Bible, Satan is used as a title for an adversary, fallen angels or other entities. Our arch-enemy's name remains unknown. See: https://chasingalion.com/satan-is-a-title

injustice whenever he encountered it. God's House had been defiled as commerce had replaced true worship. With an outer temple court overcrowded with money changers and vendors, Jesus deliberately made a whip out of rope and evicted them from the premises (see John 2:15). Because he was a prophet, he showed righteous indignation. His actions and words were never untimely but aligned with Heaven.

Some theologians suggest that Jesus cleansed the temple not once but twice! Jesus emoted love and compassion in very dramatic ways and defended healing on every occasion—especially on the venerated Sabbath. He healed a man with a withered hand by asking him to stand up in front of the crowd in the synagogue and stretch it forth. Jesus made a public display of hypocritical religious leaders with hard and unbelieving hearts (see Mark 3:1-6). He often challenged the Jewish faith from within by addressing double standards, power abuse and frequent misapplications of the Mosaic Law. In stark contrast, his righteous revolt against these leaders was nothing compared to their wretched rebellion against the Father.

Jesus' unapologetic approach made him very popular with the people but equally despised by the religious and political hierarchies. Because Jesus gained clout, the ruling class instantly singled him out as the No. 1 Enemy of the State. *"And although they were seeking to arrest him, they feared the crowds, because they held him to be a prophet."* (Matt. 21:46 ESV). Jesus unmasked the sly tactics of the elite. He called it the *"leaven of Herod, the Pharisees and Sadducees"* (see Matt. 16:6, Mark 8:15). He strongly criticised their unethical mixture of politics and religion because their plotting unfavourably interfered with people's daily lives. In exposing them, Jesus stirred up a real hornet's nest. With today's depraved systems, history repeats itself. Society's upper echelons of power rapaciously protect their positions to ensure the status quo is unchallenged and to keep their big payouts. Influence peddling is their calling card. The high society brutes are bribing, bullying and lobbying to get what they want. Those who stand in their way are routinely steamrolled or silenced.

A radical lifestyle builds on being radically loved by God.

The New Testament, however, instructs us to respect authority and state officials (see Rom. 13:1-7, 1 Pet. 2:17). We should pray for them and influence them with godly wisdom (see 1 Tim. 2:1-4). Governmental decrees should only be disregarded if and when they oppose God's purposes. Christians worship the Lord and not the State! Let us boldly proclaim the gospel, regardless of censorship of ideas. Spiritual freedom is not to be conflated with civil rights, although these are vastly important. The irate members of the High Council tried to muzzle Peter for preaching in Jesus' name, but he said: *"We must obey God rather than men."* (Acts 5:29 ESV). Long gone was the fearful disciple, who disowned Christ in the High Priest's Courtyard (see Mark 14:53, 66-72). The transformed Peter was impervious to the Council's many threats: This brand, plucked from the fire, became a firebrand! (See Zech. 3:2). The new and revived Peter refused to be bullied or strong-armed. Forever changed, he emerged out of his crisis as a radical God-chaser. Apostles and prophets are fire-starters because they disrupt, innovate and pioneer. They are pushing the limits of what is possible; they inspire change—to take it to the next level. Led by a Kingdom vision, they can see which direction the church and society need to go to occupy the future according to God's eternal plans. These fivefold visionaries constantly birth new ideas, initiatives, movements and businesses.

Dr Mike Evans emphasises four main areas in which we demonstrate God's will for us: *radical obedience, radical forgiveness, radical humility and radical generosity.* In this way, Jesus reflected the Father, and when we follow in his footsteps, people will recognise Jesus *in* us by our example. Food for thought: Our modern term 'radical' is from the Latin word *radix*. The closest equivalent in biblical Greek is ῥίζα *rhiza*, interestingly connected to 'root'. The *'root'* supports us because we have a spiritual inheritance together with the people of Israel (see Rom. 11:18). Israel became God's radical conduit for transformation. Loving Jesus is reflected in our [65]love for Israel as salvation, Yeshua, came from the Jewish people (see John 4:22, Rom. 9:3-5). How

---

[65] **My comment:** Christians should stand with Jews and support their right to live in the area God promised Abraham. For further studies, see also: jewishvirtuallibrary.org/christian-zionism and factsaboutisrael.uk (this website has a lot of valuable information).

can we not care for those who gave us the Messiah and the Bible? We are immensely indebted to the Jewish nation. Jews and Gentiles have been reconciled and united in Christ as *"one new man"*. Radically rooted and grounded in love, being redeemed, both people look to Christ as the shared life-giving source (see Eph. 2:15, 3:17).

In reality, we are the radical ones, the new creation and the transformed humanity! [66]*Transhumanism* is the devil's counterfeit attempt to destroy mankind by using the hazardous scientific process of human germline engineering to indefinitely alter and [67]genetically 'enhance' the human species. This is extremely dangerous and goes explicitly against God's will. Some Bible scholars and researchers think this advanced and forbidden technology—tampering with the human genome—was God's main grounds for sending the Deluge. Beguiled by fallen angels, humans transgressed by defying the ethical and physical boundaries set by the Creator. These reprehensible activities gave rise to monstrosities and unequalled lawlessness. Ultimately, it led to utter destruction. Consistent with this view, God mercifully rescued Noah and his family to preserve the human race spiritually and genetically. Perhaps the term *"as in the days of Noah"* hints at a resurgence of the same kind of menacing technologies before Christ's return (see Matt. 24:37-41). If so, it proves that we haven't learnt from our past mistakes and are doomed to repeat them. Cutting-edge technologies, tainted by defiant ambition and a reckless quest for superhuman abilities, may cause the future demise of millions of people and conveniently coincide with a deranged elite's utopian goal to cull a so-called overpopulated planet (see Rev. 11:18).

---

[66] **Transhumanism:** Term coined by Julian Huxley. The global elite's '4th Industrial Revolution'. It began as the Eugenics Movement and is still thriving as the transhuman agenda. The plan is to force digital IDs and nanotechnology on us all. If our humanity is endangered as a result, those who interact with synthetic/alien DNA cannot be saved. Beware that persons who choose to receive the mark of the beast will most likely accept their humanity to be erased in the promise of perfect health and financial security. This final transaction will be anti-human, anti-God and guarantee immunity against salvation. Satan's end goal is clearly spelled out in God's Word (see Rev. 13:16-18, 14:9-11).
[67] **G.R.I.N.** is an acronym for Genetic, Robotic, Information, and Nanotechnologies. Cybernetics is another term for the same. See also the book by Thomas R. Horn: Forbidden Gates: How Genetics, Robotics, Artificial Intelligence, Synthetic Biology, Nanotechnology, & Human Enhancement Herald The Dawn Of Techno-Dimensional Spiritual Warfare.
My comment: AI (Artificial Intelligence) is a part of Information Technology. Another recommended article is: evolutionnews.org/2022/04/transhumanism-is-pure-eugenics/

In contrast, God's children believe in a supernatural transformation and a stunning enhancement by his Spirit alone! We only need the Lord; his anointing will suffice. If we seek to abide in the Father's love for us, our devotion to him will remain the same, regardless of promotion or persecution: *Then I heard a loud voice saying in heaven, "And I heard a loud voice in heaven, saying, "Now the salvation and the power and the kingdom of our God and the authority of his Christ have come, for the accuser of our brothers has been thrown down, who accuses them day and night before our God. And they have conquered him by the blood of the Lamb and by the word of their testimony, for they loved not their lives even unto death."* (Rev. 12:10-11 ESV). We were radically saved by Christ through the gospel. It makes us more than conquerors or super-winners, which is the literal translation of the Greek word ὑπερνικάω *hupernikao* (see Rom. 8:37). His radical love has overcome us, and as long as we keep overcoming evil with good, evil cannot overcome us (see Rom. 12:21). What can be a more radical lifestyle than that?

We are the radical ones, the new creation, the transformed humanity!

Loving Jesus is reflected in our love for Israel, as salvation, Yeshua, came from the Jewish people.

CHAPTER 6 - PROPHETIC PERSPECTIVE

Raising up an army

We discovered earlier that the people of God is like an army. The army concept isn't new. When the Lord delivered the people of Israel out of Egypt, he had to challenge their slave mindset. Instead, he wanted them to perceive themselves as sons and heirs and a people of priests. He successfully took them out of Egypt, but it was harder to take 'Egypt' out of them! The Exodus generation refused to part with their victim mentality—it became ingrained into their attitudes of the heart. Despite seeing all the signs of God, they didn't change their thinking. Relentlessly, he tried to school them into becoming his representatives, yet they provoked him ten times with their distrust, defiance and disobedience. Sermons commonly refer to the story. The Lord resolved to let them wander for forty years in the desert until the entire unbelieving generation had passed away. In their rioting, they accused the Lord, fully convinced that their children would waste away in this arid wasteland. Bizarre as it sounds, God mocked the mockers by literally proving them dead wrong. He decidedly swore he wouldn't let their children perish but safely bring them into the promised land. The real battleground wasn't the territory they physically traversed, but it was the mental landscape within their own minds. The next generation was raised in the desert and gained a different mindset: They learned to trust in the Lord and the strength of his might. They realised that spiritual focus was more crucial than battle techniques or wielding of weapons (Psalm 144:1, Eph. 6:10). They harnessed emotional resilience and honed practical skills to work as a family and a competent military unit due to gutsy Joshua's leadership. Taking on the task ahead was momentous: God's people had to seriously up their game because they would soon enough probe an eerie and uncharted terrain of giants, fortified cities and inhospitable tribes (see Jos. 3:1-4).

The next generation was raised in the desert and gained a different mindset: They learned to trust in the Lord and the strength of his might.

The battle is the Lord's—not acknowledging this is pure madness: *"The LORD is a warrior; the LORD is his name."* (Exod. 15:3 NIV). *When you go to war against your enemies and see horses and chariots and an army greater than yours, do not be afraid of them, because the LORD your God, who brought you up out of Egypt, will be with you. When you are about to go into battle, the priest shall come forward and address the army. He shall say: "Hear, Israel: Today you are going into battle against your enemies. Do not be fainthearted or afraid; do not panic or be terrified by them. For the LORD your God is the one who goes with you to fight for you against your enemies to give you victory."* (Deut. 20:1-4 NIV). *The LORD will march out like a champion, like a warrior he will stir up his zeal; with a shout he will raise the battle cry and will triumph over his enemies.* (Isa. 42:13 NIV). The Lord of Hosts, [68]Yehovah Tzevaot is the ultimate warrior, and teaming up with him by enrolling into his army is life-altering (see Jos. 5:13). The *war paradigm* is part of the Bible because we were called to be overcomers: *"Little children, you are from God and have overcome them, for he who is in you is greater than he who is in the world."* (1 John 4:4 ESV) *"Who is it that overcomes the world? Only the one who believes that Jesus is the Son of God."* (1 John 5:5 NIV). Through prayer, trust and obedience, we allow God to fight our battles.

Yehovah Tzevaot is the ultimate warrior, and teaming up with him by enrolling into his army is life-altering.

If we fail to act upon [69]a divine concept, the devil will strategically oppose us in that specific area. Through faithful obedience, we repel these attacks and hold our high ground. Once lost, it is much harder to regain old territory, albeit not impossible. If we don't listen to God, it will have dire consequences: King Saul refused to eliminate the Amalekites. Quite tellingly, it was an Amalekite who delivered him the sad and fatal blow on Mount Gilboa (see 1 Sam. 15:1-24, 2 Sam. 1:8-10). If we don't deal with sin, it will kill us! King David's neglect caused him to stay in his royal palace in a season when he was meant to conduct warfare against Israel's adversaries. David became susceptible to temptation because he was outside of God's perfect will and fell into sexual sin with the alluring Bathsheba. To make it worse, he arranged for her upright husband to be butchered in battle (see 2 Sam. 11:1-26). Much can be said about God's people's assignment as a spiritual army. Gideon was prophetically activated to be a warrior and a deliverer. His birth name means 'to cut down' and

---

[68] **Yehovah Tzevaot:** יְהוָה צְבָאוֹת The God of angel armies, the Lord of hosts (see 1 Sam. 17:45).

[69] **My comment:** We have spiritual laws, like the law of Seedtime and Harvest etc. When we stop to do the right things because they are inconvenient, we give up spiritual territory. The Bible is full of examples on how compromise is a temptation for God's people.

'to destroy'. First, he built God an altar and then destroyed idolatry by cutting down his father's Baal altar and the Asherah pole in his home village. Lastly, he cut down the enemy army. His calling and mission reflected his core identity (see Judges 6-7).

Once lost, it is much harder to regain old territory, albeit not impossible.

The Holy Spirit instructed Gideon to reduce a vast Hebrew army of 32,000 men to just 300. To conquer thousands, God intentionally chose to use a tiny unit to do the impossible. The Lord could get all the glory since Israel relied on God's power, not on manpower! 300 soldiers were hand-picked. It was personnel who passed the 'water test' (see Judg. 7:4-7). The weird but common denominator between the 300 soldiers was how they lapped water with their hands to their mouths. These troops' unorthodox drinking method was applied to keep their eyes open to spot the enemy from afar. The lapping men were vigilant and alert soldiers. 99% of the soldiers were oblivious and distracted, but not so with the unique remnant of 300! Gideon's army was remarkably focused, as each soldier had a watchful mindset. These selected few became elite warriors, men who could easily transition into battle mode at any given time, with undivided attention. God values the peculiar trait of single-mindedness. Paul advised Timothy to think like a soldier: *"You therefore, my son, be strong in the grace that is in Christ Jesus. The things which you have heard from me in the presence of many witnesses, entrust these to faithful men who will be able to teach others also. Suffer hardship with me, as a good soldier of Christ Jesus. No soldier in active service entangles himself in the affairs of everyday life, so that he may please the one who enlisted him as a soldier. Also if anyone competes as an athlete, he does not win the prize unless he competes according to the rules. The hard-working farmer ought to be the first to receive his share of the crops. Consider what I say, for the Lord will give you understanding in everything."* (2 Tim. 2:1-6 NASB).

Gideon's army was remarkably focused, as each soldier had a watchful mindset. These selected few became elite warriors, men who could easily transition into battle mode at any given time, with undivided attention.

An enlisted soldier has to be utterly devoted to his assignment. We need *alignment with the assignment*. We must also understand *the reason for the season*. Is it a time for war or a time for peace? (Eccles. 3:8). Well, it can be both. We have the authority to fulfil our mission in our capacity as Kingdom ambassadors, but cannot exercise our delegated authority fully unless we respond to God's voice, as *"faith comes by hearing"* the Word of God (Rom. 10:17). Do you want to hear what the Lord says? Then *listen* to him! (See John 10:27). Our goal is to please God because we are not people-pleasers. We know what our Commander-in-chief delights in, and submit to him (see 2 Tim. 2:4). Jesus aligned with the One who sent him, the Father: *"And you know that God anointed Jesus of Nazareth with the Holy Spirit and with power. Then Jesus went around doing good and healing all who were oppressed by the devil, for God was with him."* (Acts 10:38 NLT). Jesus led a lifestyle of love, fuelled by intercession and filled with miracles. It was his day-to-day battle mode. His many acts of mercy were felt as devastating blows to the kingdom of darkness (see also 1 John 3:8).

We need *alignment with the assignment*. We must also understand *the reason for the season.*

How do we expect to advance in Kingdom power and authority if we do not align with Christ by following his example? Our Saviour died, so we could release hope, love and grace to a hurting world. The template from the Sermon on the Mount is extremely powerful. This charter outlines our marching orders (see Matt. 5:1-15). We minister peace to others when we move with gentleness, mercy and excellence, but should never antagonise or criticise while sharing the gospel. That's a big no-no, a style we need to relinquish. Insulting remarks insulate people from encountering God's love and distort a hopeful message. Calling unbelievers to repentance tends to offend their minds and stir their hearts. Nevertheless, we must let the Holy Spirit convict people of sin; it's beyond our reach. The gospel itself represents actual and lasting change, which is challenging enough for many. We have to desist from inane remarks that lead to unwanted alienation. Through the ministry of reconciliation, our mission is faithfully proclaiming the gospel with love. God uses our testimonies for his Name's sake (see 2 Cor. 5:18-20). The gospel is [70]God's royal command *"to bring about the obedience of faith"* (see Rom. 16:26 ESV). As spiritual warriors, we

---

[70] **My comment:** The gospel announces God's government and is also called the gospel of the Kingdom (see Matt. 4:23 and 24:14). There is an emphasis on obedience because God is our King.

battle the forces of darkness and assert the highest form of dedication, fervour and submission to our Lord Jesus Christ. Beyond question, the finished work of Jesus guaranteed all future victories. As a part of our defined identity, we now restfully rule and reign together with King Jesus. What is Spiritual Warfare? It's certainly not heedless infighting under the guise of being spiritual. When we act as peacemakers, declaring the gospel of peace, the God of Peace will crush Satan under our feet (see Matt. 5:9, Rom. 14:17; 16:20, Eph. 6:15). We enforce the victory secured by Jesus when we use Kingdom authority. Peace is God's presence manifested: *"But if it is by the finger of God that I cast out demons, then the kingdom of God has come upon you."* (Luke 11:20 ESV). Like a soldier keeping watch from a high tower, the power of peace guards our mind and our spirit. If our peace vanishes, we should know why because God's Spirit usually alerts us through this internal function (see Phil. 4:7).

We should never antagonise or criticise while sharing the gospel.

Moving in spiritual authority starts with the baptism of the Holy Spirit. Every child of God is indwelt by his Spirit. However, being born of the Spirit isn't the same as the infilling of the Spirit. These are spiritual yet separate experiences.

> [71]*'Spirit-baptism marks the starting point of spiritual warfare. Once a believer has contacted the person of God via the baptism in the Holy Spirit, he then has his own spirit released. He now senses the reality of the things and beings in the spiritual domain. Only those who are spiritual perceive the reality of the spiritual foe and hence engage in battle (see Eph. 6:12). Such warfare is not fought with arms of the flesh (see also 2 Cor. 10:4). Because the conflict is spiritual, so must the weapons be. It's a struggle between the spirit of man and that of the enemy—an engagement of spirit [wrestling] with spirit.' 'Upon experiencing the baptism, his intuition becomes acutely sensitive, and he discovers in his spirit a spiritual world opening before him.'*

---

[71] **Watchman Nee 倪柝聲** *or Nee T'o-sheng*, was a Chinese church leader and Christian teacher who worked in China during the 20th century. Source: en.wikipedia.org Quote from The Spiritual Man, vol. 1.

Being victorious in God's holy war depends on invariable factors like sensitivity, obedience and perseverance. To accurately discern our actual position in the Lord requires spiritual insight. We dress for battle when we put on the full armour of God (see Eph. 6:10-18). The armour connects to our identity in Jesus Christ and how we exercise our God-given authority. Advancing the Kingdom of Heaven on earth is a serious affair. Jesus, the greatest warrior of all, came to terminate all the works of the devil (see 1 John 3:8). He preached in the synagogues and expelled evil spirits from many people. It's easy to skim through these passages, although the events of deliverances were revolutionary back in the day. I wonder if we would welcome Jesus' unconventional methods today. Truth be told, countless churches treat the deliverance ministry as highly controversial. Most denominations don't prefer any form of unsought commotion to interrupt their dignified and predictable services. Jesus frequently destroyed the domain of darkness everywhere he came with the help of aggressive spiritual warfare (see also Mark 1:39, 1 John 3:8, Acts 10:38). He spoke the truth, acted with mercy and healed whenever possible. We should move with the same power and compassion. In the Lord's eyes, his blood-bought Church is a living and impressive force, and the devil cannot stop its forceful advance!

The armour is connected to our identity in Jesus Christ and how we exercise our God-given authority.

In a well-organised army, soldiers know their designated place. Some individuals might be tasked with special missions when needed but otherwise act as one seamless unit. To further illustrate my point, Joel chapter 2 describes such a strapping army, intimidating and very efficient: *"Blow the [72]trumpet (shofar) in Zion; sound an alarm on my holy mountain! Let all the inhabitants of the land tremble, for the day of the LORD is coming; it is near, a day of darkness and gloom, a day of clouds and thick darkness! Like blackness there is spread upon the mountains a great and powerful people; their like has never been before, nor will be again after them through the years of all generations. Fire devours before them, and behind them a flame burns. The land is like the garden of Eden before them, but behind them a desolate wilderness, and nothing escapes them. Their appearance is like the appearance of horses, and like war*

---

[72] **My comment:** שׁוֹפָר *Shofar* – means *trumpet*. It's non-metallic and made from the Ram's horn.

horses they run. As with the rumbling of chariots, they leap on the tops of the mountains, like the crackling of a flame of fire devouring the stubble, like a powerful army drawn up for battle. Before them peoples are in anguish; all faces grow pale. Like warriors they charge; like soldiers they scale the wall. They march each on his way; they do not swerve from their paths. They do not jostle one another; each marches in his path; they burst through the weapons and are not halted. They leap upon the city, they run upon the walls, they climb up into the houses, they enter through the windows like a thief. The earthquakes before them; the heavens tremble. The sun and the moon are darkened, and the stars withdraw their shining. The LORD utters his voice before his army, for his camp is exceedingly great; he who executes his word is powerful. For the day of the LORD is great and very awesome; who can endure it?" (Joel 2:1-11 ESV).

Serving with your gifts is the best way of developing your ability in that area. What defines the range and influence of your skills is how you apply what God gave you. Above all else, we need to connect to the Father and his heart: *"God is faithful, who has called you into fellowship with his Son, Jesus Christ our Lord."* (1 Cor. 1:9 NIV). We must watchfully serve with our gifts in loyalty to our heavenly calling. Through focused prayer, we ask God to purify our motives and consecrate our talents. We are part of a family and an army and are on a journey with God and each other. Our place in the community will, bit by bit, become intelligible and evident. You will truly enjoy yourself in the Lord if you act on your God-given abilities. It gives joy and peace! A close community eliminates the fear of moving in our callings and gifts.

Highly evolved family ties replace a carnal culture, dominated by its comparison and competition, with a culture of love where we complete and complement each other. Building that kind of pure culture comes at a costly price, where we must choose to sacrifice our selfish agendas. The gospel becomes irresistible once we stop fighting each other for position and rather stay united as an authentic community. Preaching a gospel without disciples who demonstrate and validate the message risks the seeds we sow being pecked away or dying from lack of water. We should remember that the Lord saves us *from* sin, *onto* Christ and *into* his family on earth. Unless we build local churches that display the redemptive power of the gospel with tangible results, it will not bear fruit (see Col. 1:6).

The gospel becomes irresistible once we stop fighting each other for position and rather stay united as an authentic community.

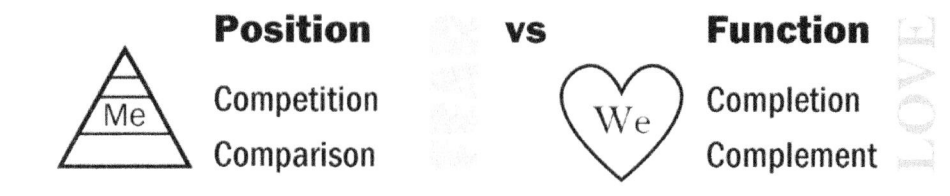

Position vs Function

- Me — Competition / Comparison
- We — Completion / Complement (LOVE)

Cultivating a culture where we all act together is like building an army. It's an army of God's love: *"A new command I give you: Love one another. As I have loved you, so you must love one another. By this everyone will know that you are my disciples, if you love one another."* (John 13:34-35 NIV). *"Greater love has no one than this: to lay down one's life for one's friends. You are my friends if you do what I command."* (John 15:13-14 NIV). These are the instructions from the great general, Jesus, the Lord of Hosts. The devil's absolute nightmare is an army of laid-down lovers! If we showcase unrelenting love, it causes lasting trauma to our enemy. The disciples of Jesus should be recognised by the world because of their great love and not for their giftedness. In 1 Corinthians, chapters 12-14, Paul explains how we effectively exercise our gifts through *agape* love. If and when we use our gifts for selfish gain, it will reflect very poorly on Christian ministry. If we humbly surrender these gifts, together with self-serving motives, God will let his anointing flow freely through us. That ability will advance the gospel and give us favour in our communities.

To tackle higher levels of warfare, Christians must learn to show both humility and accountability. To promote certain preachers or musicians as leaders too early is unwholesome for any leadership. These believers may be gifted but not mature and talented, yet lack integrity. If we expose immature believers to the limelight, they become easier targets for the enemy to take out, as they are unprepared for warfare. True anointing for service comes through crushing, by daily dying to self. Being set on a pedestal, celebrated or paraded without first undergoing the needed discipline will expose Christians as sitting ducks. If we treasure God's presence in our services, we must elevate character over talent and anointing over charisma. During praise and worship, some churches concentrate on creating emotional momentums rather than preparing hearts for genuine God encounters. Why this use of undue influence through mental distortion and emotional exploitation? Are they actually Christian business empires—entertainment industries disguised as churches? We don't need laser lights or smoke, only *"The anointing will break the yoke"* (see Isa. 10:27). That rhymes, yet the fact remains. The anointing breaks chains and transforms lives! *"The breaker goes up before them; They break out, pass through the gate and go out by it. So their king goes on before them, And the Lord at their head."* (Micah 2:13 NASB).

The Lord's anointing breaks chains and transforms lives!

Many of us long to see an army of Kingdom soldiers with power and authority. Are we ready to be tested? Are we able to serve with humility? Can we exercise authentic but invisible leadership? Can God entrust us with other people? All of us have been anointed and appointed, called and equipped. While we are moving forward in the holy fear of the Lord, we must allow the Lord to develop us. To kill off self-interest, he takes us into the darkroom—into dark seasons and tests—to make sure that the purified image of Christ is brought forth in us. Besides, shouldering responsibility takes time, and we have to start where we are. If we try to bypass the preparation process by taking some shortcuts, it will increase the potential risk of abject failure. Individuals without the proper discipline compromise the safety of the rest of the team. To serve a greater purpose, soldiers learn to lay aside inherent selfishness and self-preservation. *"Only let your manner of life be worthy of the gospel of Christ, so that whether I come and see you or am absent, I may hear of you that you are standing firm in one spirit, with one mind striving side by side for the faith of the gospel, and not frightened in anything by your opponents. This is a clear sign to them of their destruction, but of your salvation, and that from God."* (Phil. 1:27-28 ESV).

To kill off self-interest, he takes us into the darkroom—into dark seasons and tests—to make sure that the purified image of Christ is brought forth in us.

Top-tier armies prioritise taking urgent care of their injured soldiers. Lionhearted soldiers who put their lives on the line to rescue their wounded peers instil great courage into the rest of the battalion. Because they have learned the lessons of past mistakes, apt military leaders know that complacency quickly cripples battle morale.

These armies always deploy rapid response units with trained medics. Premeditated acts of instant mercy are as indispensable as any other strategy and exemplify a high-functioning community. We may steer clear of unsustainable losses by looking out for each other. Pushing reckless and radical agendas could endanger team members. Without decent care and protection, even experienced soldiers are in jeopardy. The sad death of hapless Uriah illustrates my point (see 2 Sam. 11:5-27). The Church has been brought into public disrepute by failing to care for those who faced adversity, illness or personal constraints. The harrowing ordeals some missionaries, evangelists and worship leaders suffered are heart-breaking. These precious people were forced out of the churches and the organisations they so loyally served. Facing inflexible board members and inhuman standards, they fell short. Some lost their faith, but many more lost their confidence in the church family. Such an outcome is against the culture we want to uphold in the Kingdom. Some of these wounded Christians now live a secluded life outside 'the camp', only left with a few trusted friends. They still love the Lord but have parted with church life at large—an agonising outcome.

Being inquisitive, some believers had the temerity to expect some accountability and transparency from their leaders. Instead, they got ridiculed, attacked and excluded from their local fellowships. These punitive leaders failed them. Seasoned spiritual leaders have integrity and humility and are not scared of scrutiny. Paul, the apostle, said: *"We have renounced secret and shameful ways; we do not use deception, nor do we distort the word of God. On the contrary, by setting forth the truth plainly we commend ourselves to every man's conscience in the sight of God."* (2 Cor. 4:2 NIV). Asking questions are frowned upon by many churches. Because they have a harsh culture, they view criticism as a betrayal. It's petty and controlling. It also makes one wonder why some congregants and entire churches and denominations accept this kind of senseless and cruel bullying. Sometimes leaders' arrogance will disguise itself as competence and charisma as anointing.

Leadership commands the natural attention of others, which explains why leaders should be evaluated and held accountable—and even more so in times of far-flung deception. To accuse church members of holding grudges or having a Jezebel spirit or a religious spirit, if they have the nerve to question leaders' conduct, is horrifying. It is gaslighting perpetrated by the ones who should have our backs. Yet fickle and domineering leaders see the same backs as easy targets, ready to throw the daggers bull's eye! In my opinion, we have inadvertently permitted a toxic environment. Instead of banishing it, we have often cradled and buttressed an abusive leadership culture—an avoidable predicament if we understood life and ministry better. What about preparing future leaders for realistic and warlike scenarios? I think most Bible schools aren't accustomed to training their students to become competent and resilient in taxing circumstances. The overall prioritised goal is to offer increased knowledge, their staple product. Although it seems quite admirable, this is the most undemanding part of an education. Building spiritual robustness to tackle life is not on their curriculums. It's high time we see an upsurge of another kind of leadership, focusing on creating a wholesome church culture able to withstand the test of time.

Toxic culture?

The full armour of God

Much has been discussed and written about the full armour of God (see Eph. 6:10-18). I will review each part of it by featuring some important aspects. The armour of God represents attributes of his own nature: *"He saw that there was no one, he was appalled that there was no one to intervene; so his own arm achieved salvation for him, and his own righteousness sustained him. He put on righteousness as his breastplate, and the helmet of salvation on his head; he put on the garments of vengeance and wrapped himself in zeal as in a cloak."* (Isa. 59:16-17 NIV).

Every believer partakes of God's divine nature (see 2 Pet. 1:4). We became one spirit with the Risen Lord (see 1 Cor. 6:17). *"And all who have been united with Christ in baptism have put on Christ, like putting on new clothes."* (Gal. 3:27 NLT). God wants us to live coherently, with our inner and outer worlds in balance. But this can only be achieved by putting off the old self and putting on the new self: *"But this is not the way you came to know Christ. Surely you heard of Him and were taught in Him, in keeping with the truth that is in Jesus, to put off your former way of life, your old self, which is being corrupted by its deceitful desires; to be renewed in the spirit of your minds; and to put on the new self, created to be like God in true righteousness and holiness."* (Eph. 4: 20-24 NIV). When it comes to putting on the full armour of God, the symbolism in the next passage conveys a similar message: *"The night is far gone; the day is at hand. So then let us cast off the works of darkness and put on the armour of light."* (Rom. 13:12 ESV). Our full armour consists of light, as we belong to the kingdom of light: *"and giving joyful thanks to the Father, who has qualified you to share in the inheritance of his holy people in the kingdom of light."* (Col. 1:12 NIV). Putting on the armour of light is indeed putting on Christ, with his righteousness, his holiness and his goodness. As long as we live yielded, we remain shielded. By surrendering to his Lordship daily in prayer and obedience to his Spirit, we choose to partner with his will and nature. Mechanical recitation of some Bible verses isn't enough. A result of being dressed in the armour of God would naturally be to expect more loving behaviour and less offence within our Christian communities. Sadly, where pride and hurt dominate, the armour is missing. Simply put: No *amour* means no armour. Walking in the Spirit is consistently walking in light and love.

As long as we live yielded, we remain shielded.

Let us keep our peace by not provoking each other, as we *"make every effort to live at peace with everyone"* (Eph. 4:3, Heb. 12:14). In a time of widespread social media use, we should be tactful and prayerfully consider what to post. Behind the screens are fellow human beings, but we sometimes forget basic facts like these. Deliberately choosing to move in the gentleness of the Prophetic Spirit helps us to disengage with the pervasive political spirit. We don't fight flesh and blood, but the dark spiritual forces of wickedness in the heavenlies. The enemy of our soul often uses the highway of unsanctified attitudes to get to us through the different people we socialise with. Responding in love and in the opposite spirit is critical. Christ inside us will not be offended, and constantly relying on him will help us to hold our tongue—and our ground. To better relate to his audience, Paul used the Roman armour as a helpful analogy. Careful study will reveal several truths regarding our identity and how we effectively activate God's protective presence in our lives. To know the written truth is not sufficient in itself. The Israelites focused on the oracles of God practically. The Greeks sought insight to discuss a topic. Governed by the latter mindset, we use theology as an excuse for our practical apathy, as we believe a theoretical analysis is satisfactory. Will the Lord ask us to do something only based on our understanding? No, he will ask us to do what he commanded us! Parents use the same approach with their children. Isn't this why we warn kids against playing on busy streets or going too close to waterways? The armour of God has to be rightly applied to work. Above all else, we should guard our heart as the issues of life flow from it (see Prov. 4:23). By examining the armour, we see that it focuses on the person of Jesus. Ultimately, it encourages having reputable attitudes of the heart. To put on the armour is to clothe ourselves with Christ's nature. *"But since we belong to the day, let us be sober, putting on faith and love as a breastplate, and the hope of salvation as a helmet."* (See 1 Thess. 5:4-9).

To know the written truth is not sufficient in itself.

THE ARMOUR OF GOD:

1. The breastplate of righteousness symbolises righteous living, being loving and considerate. Jesus is our Righteousness because righteousness is one of the primary principles of the Kingdom (see Matt. 6:33, Rom. 14:17, Gal. 5:22). Righteousness provides us with holy boldness, making us as intrepid as lions (see Prov. 28:1). We were made righteous by the blood of Jesus, and have the courage and confidence to enter into his presence by faith (see Heb. 10:19, Psalm 95:2).

2. The belt of truth represents speaking, thinking and living the truth. Jesus is the Way, the Truth and the Life. Truth, as a belt, manages to keep the rest of the outfit together. We develop humility when we willingly receive the truth with our hearts. Transparency and truth are closely linked to a Kingdom mindset, as those who walk in the truth come to the light (see John 3:21, 14:6).

3. The shoes of readiness represent a lifestyle of reconciliation, submission and peace. If we have an honest walk, the God of Peace will crush Satan under our feet (see Rom. 16:20). We should always be at God's disposal, ready to share the gospel and our testimony (see Rev. 12:11). In Eph. 2:13 we read that he, Christ, is our peace. Peace is not the absence of unrest; it is God's restful *presence*. God will come and establish peace where we receive him as *royalty*. One of his many names is Prince of Peace, in Hebrew שַׂר־שָׁלוֹם *Sar-Shalom* (see Isa. 9:6; 60:17).

4. The shield of faith represents our trust in God. Jesus is the Author and Finisher of our faith—the Spirit of faith lives in us (see 2 Cor. 4:13, Heb. 12:2). God told Abram, whom he later renamed Abraham: *"Fear not, I am your shield."* (Gen. 15:1). *"His faithfulness is a shield and buckler"* or our body armour (see Psalm 91:4). Faith stops the enemy's incendiary missiles; it overcomes the world (see Eph. 6:16, 1 John 5:5). Jesus is called *"Faithful and True"* (see Rev. 19:11 ESV). Faith, in Greek πίστις *pistis*, is equal to the Hebrew אמונה *emunah*. It means trust, committed faithfulness and steadfastness. Trust repels fear. We feel safe when God is close, much like a child suddenly realising the presence of mummy or daddy. Once we voluntarily connect our vulnerability to the Lord, it helps us deepen our relationship with the Father.

5. The helmet of salvation speaks of guarding our minds by never losing our hope. We firmly rely on God's intervention. We find comfort and rest in knowing that we have a loving Father who assists and rescues us (see Psalm 91:15). The helmet is the unassailable Hope of Salvation (see 1 Thess. 5:8). Jesus is our hope, the Hope of glory. The anchor of hope reaches within Heaven's veil, opened by Christ, the New and Living Way. Through this redemptive Hope, we now access God's presence and enjoy an intimate relationship with the Lord (see Heb. 6:19). Hope precedes faith because, without hope, people give up as they feel unloved. Faith, hope and love are a threefold divine formula, with love as the main component (see 1 Cor. 13:13).

6. The sword of the Spirit is the freshly spoken, energetic and Living Word. It's a mighty and versatile weapon used for defence and offence. Jesus is the personified Word of God. In Rom. 10:8, we read: *"The word is near you, in your mouth and in your heart," that is the message of faith that we preach.* Here it says that God's *rhema* is prophetic by nature, as we boldly declare the specific truths the Spirit reminds us of in different situations. Jesus overcame all the devil's temptations with prophetic precision. By quoting the Scripture, he effectively cut through the enemy's cunning lies (see Matt. 4:4).

7. **Praying in the Spirit** at all times is a hidden secret weapon which completes the armour. Jesus is the great Intercessor, praying at God's right hand on our behalf. We are instructed to pray constantly, the same way he does. Like a javelin, prophetic and anointed prayers pierce through the darkness—soaring into the heavens. Eph. 6:18 instructs us to pray at <u>all</u> times with <u>all</u> prayer, with <u>all</u> perseverance for <u>all</u> the saints. Please observe the word *all* in this passage. Four types of prayers are listed. Are these prayers somehow connected to the four levels of spiritual opposition Paul referred to in prior verses? Namely, principalities, powers, rulers and spiritual forces of wickedness. I don't believe that to be a coincidence. Paul describes Satan's highly organised chain of command as follows:

1) **Principalities** - in Greek ἀρχάς *archas*. These are the generals, the princes or chief rulers.
2) **Powers** - in Greek ἐξουσίας *exousias*. The commanders or governing rulers.
3) **Rulers** - in Greek κοσμοκράτορας *kosmokratoras*. These are world rulers, controlling specific areas of human life.
4) **Forces of spiritual wickedness** - in Greek τὰ πνευματικὰ τῆς πονηρίας *ta pneumatika tes ponerias*. Satan's hideous army covers the inhabited world of human life. We, the community of believers, exercise authority over all the hordes of the enemy! *"Behold, I have given you authority to tread on serpents and scorpions, and over all the power of the enemy, and nothing shall hurt you."* (See Luke 10:19 ESV).

We should intercede at all times in the Spirit—praying in tongues. We pray to release the right time for God to intervene (see Eph. 5:16). Why is that? Our opponent seeks to infiltrate God's plan and insert his agenda, as he persistently attempted with Jesus (see Luke 4:13). The devil is the 'sneaky snake' that schemes within carefully selected times and seasons. To prevent them from entering into temptation, Jesus asked his sluggish disciples to hold a vigil in the Garden of Gethsemane and diligently watch and pray. When they failed to keep watch with him for just one hour, he voiced real disappointment (see Matt. 26:41). Through prayer, we seize the time to sanctify the moments ahead. We prepare for battle by securing the outcome, and we stop the evil snake from harming us. Jesus prevailed, under extreme duress, in Gethsemane. In anguish, he interceded, seized his destiny and finally sealed the victory on the cross. All prayers mean all kinds of prayers or a full arsenal of weapons. When we move with the prophetic, led by the Holy Spirit, he teaches us how to pray in strategic ways. It may take a while to deflect the enemy's attacks, so we must pray with all perseverance. Quitting during spiritual warfare due to pressure and fatigue remains a distinct possibility. We should wear out the devil and not the other way around! Strip fear of its power. Desist from moping, worrying and bellyaching. Don't forget that you are much tougher and braver than you think! The Lord endowed you with the abilities to endure suffering, resist temptation and wage war.

Through prayer, we seize the time to sanctify the moments ahead. We prepare for battle by securing the outcome, and we stop the evil snake from harming us.

Through prayer, we clothe ourselves with the full armour of God—we remind our intellect of our true identity in Christ. We activate our spiritual force field through constant and prayerful dedication to the Lord! Lastly, we pray for *"all the saints"*. Paul urged his audience to pray for every disciple they knew. That naturally includes local believers as well as the global community of saints. We should pray for all in our sphere and not forget about the persecuted Christians (see Heb. 13:3).

Praying it forward

If you operate fivefold ministry gifts, prayer covering is essential. Having personal intercessors is a great asset. Have you heard the expression 'to pay it forward'? It is when a beneficiary of a good deed repays kindness to others instead of to the original benefactor. As beneficiaries of prayer, we pass on this gift by repeatedly 'praying it forward'. Intercession can be tiring at times, but for those at the front-line, in severe spiritual combat, it's a lifeline. The Everlasting God has chosen to cooperate with us through prayer for his will to be fulfilled on earth. Therefore, it's not optional. Jesus addressed his audience by saying: *"when you pray"*, *"when you fast,"* and *"when you give"*—not *"if you pray"* and so on (see Matt. 6). Jesus defined these occupations as effective worship. Our activities are all interwoven in the fabric of life. Christ's love spurs us, and we can choose his sacrificial approach as the template we follow. Have you ever heard about a 'prayer addict'? I doubt it! The Holy Spirit is compelling but never compulsive. Addictions are associated with a carnal and selfish lifestyle and other underlying causes, like trauma. We break addictions by fervently seeking God. In his presence, we partake of his holiness. If we let the Father love us, it changes us from within. In this way, we replace the ugliness of lies, fear and sin with purpose and the beauty of his holiness. Leonard Ravenhill nailed it when he said: 'A sinning man stops praying, a praying man stops sinning.'

We activate our spiritual force field through constant and prayerful dedication to the Lord!

Learning to put on the full armour of the Lord involves several key components: Awareness, identity and sanctification. The factual *shielding* is not so much about the *wielding* of authority or weapons as it is about the *yielding* of attitudes. Walking in the Holy Spirit is to demonstrate the ninefold fruit of the same Spirit. By clothing ourselves with Christ's nature, we become fully armed and dangerous, dressed in the full armour of God. The armour of light reflects Christ but deflects the accuser!

Some years ago, I had a powerful vision of a colossal sword being fashioned on an anvil, brightly glowing, heated by the fire. The blacksmith forged it into an elegant two-edged sword. It was superbly shaped, sharp and polished. The sword's flawless steel blade perfectly mirrored the clear blue sky when a hand skilfully turned it. The intense reflection instantly bathed the capital in brilliant sunlight. The incandescent city I saw was the world metropolis, London. To release his glory on earth, the Lord is forging the Body of Christ into this fabulous sword. God's grand vision is to wield us as his mighty weapon, as a united force. He is capable of punishing every act of disobedience through us if we rightly align with his Word. That is an awe-inspiring thought. We should clench the weapons of righteousness in the right hand and in the left (see Rom. 6:13, 2 Cor. 6:7; 10:6). Jesus, our Lord, is the ultimate weapon of righteousness. His judgement brings the final end to sin, death and Satan.

While he visited Athens, the apostle Paul got *"provoked in his spirit"* when he saw all the idols; this matches the Greek literal translation. Behind the foreign gods, he felt hostile and demonic oppression. But not for a second did Paul call a truce with the realm of darkness. In his spirit, he immediately started to push back these powers (see Acts 17:16). Kingdom soldiers are never passive. They display the raw spiritual aggression that is needed to possess their allotted inheritance: *"Every place that the sole of your foot will tread upon I have given to you, just as I promised to Moses."* (Jos. 1:3 ESV). *"From the days of John the Baptist until now the kingdom of heaven has suffered violence, and the violent take it by force."* (Luke 16:16, see also Matt. 11:12). The glorious Kingdom currency is faith that seizes the moment. It never rests on its laurel but goes forth and forcefully acts on God's promises. Did Jesus criticise people who pressed in on him for healing, deliverance or provision? Absolutely not, but he commended them for their unabashed faith! The Almighty delights in the spiritually bankrupt and radical zealots, the feisty individuals who freely sacrifice their comfort. Overcoming great adversity, they are storming God's Kingdom in prayer to advance his heavenly cause. Incentivised by the Father's steadfast love, the poor in spirit conquer opposition through their holy hunger (see Matt. 5:3).

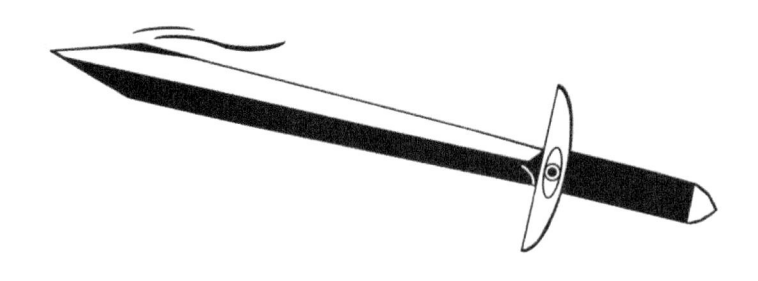

"For the word of God is living and active, sharper than any two-edged sword, piercing to the division of soul and of spirit, of joints and of marrow, and discerning the thoughts and intentions of the heart."

(English Standard Version, Hebrews 4:12).

CHAPTER 7 - PROPHETIC PRINCIPLES

The foundation of faith

God left his imprints and blessings in every culture, ethnic group and nation. He did so that we might seek his face and find him in each place we were born. To live a life fully blessed according to his Word, God arranged the times and locations for our arrival to make it possible one day to reach out to him: *From one man he made all the nations, that they should inhabit the whole earth; and he marked out their appointed times in history and the boundaries of their lands. God did this so that they would seek him and perhaps reach out for him and find him, though he is not far from any one of us. 'For in him we live and move and have our being.'* (Acts 17:26-28 NIV). To survey the surrounding culture to see if it aligns with the Kingdom is always wise. God wants us to cooperate with the cultural values and practises we can agree on. As ambassadors of Christ, you and I were supposed to influence and not succumb to ungodly standards set by a secular society. We settle for less if we merely view faith through a human lens, reduced to doctrines and traditions. God told Paul: *"I will rescue you from your own people and from the Gentiles. I am sending you to them to open their eyes and turn them from darkness to light, and from the power of Satan to God, so that they may receive forgiveness of sins and a place among those who are sanctified by faith in me."* (Acts 26:17-18 NIV).

The above passage relates to Paul's ministry. It also deals with a much deeper issue. The Lord prophesied that he would deliver him from his nation and the Gentiles. The profound deliverance he had to undergo was both spiritual and cultural. Christ could then use him as his apostolic vessel, or in Paul's own words: *"to reveal his Son in me"* (see Gal. 1:16). All dominant cultures have incorporated mechanisms and systems contrary to God's will and values. It implies that the seeds of a corrupted and wicked culture sometimes hold back believers from experiencing spiritual and emotional liberty. The Bible tells us not to *"be conformed to this world or age, but be transformed by the renewing of our minds."* (Rom. 12:2).

As ambassadors of Christ, you and I were supposed to influence and not succumb to ungodly standards set by a secular society.

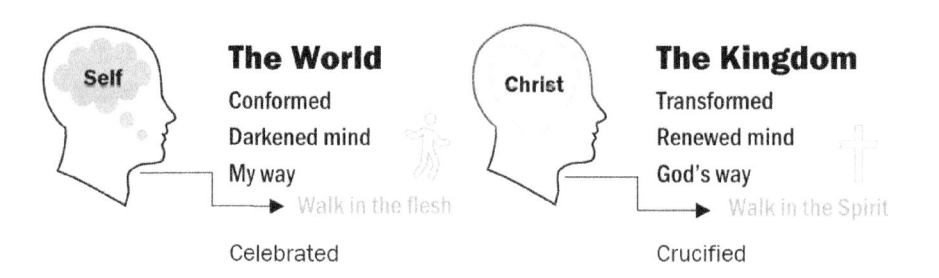

The World	The Kingdom
Self	Christ
Conformed	Transformed
Darkened mind	Renewed mind
My way	God's way
Walk in the flesh	Walk in the Spirit
Celebrated	Crucified

It should come as no surprise that Satan has infiltrated the nations' cultures with his oppressive apparatus. These devious and demonic systems conform individuals and people groups to trust in other entities than God. Although worldly and sinful, they are almost imperceptible as they blend with the existing culture. The most potent lies always have some truth to make them more deceptive and useful for evil puppet masters, but divine revelation enables us to identify and uproot these philosophies. *"See, I have appointed you today over nations and kingdoms to uproot and tear down, to destroy and overthrow, to build and plant."* (Jer. 1:10 BSB). Across-the-board, innumerable nations and people groups embrace mindsets and traditions in conflict with the gospel. Followers of Christ should be delivered from these immoral values and focus on the good things culturally (see Phil. 4:8 NLT). Christians profess Christ as their solid foundation. He is the Bedrock whom we trust (see 1 Cor. 3:11). Many of us still have blind spots, as some of the deceiving elements in the prevailing culture have become deeply entrenched in our personal lives.

The most potent lies always have some truth to make them more deceptive and useful for evil puppet masters.

The late apostle and teacher Derek Prince listed these specific issues in his original sermon, **Founded On The Rock** (4160), at derekprince.org. I have borrowed his brilliant outline as a launching pad for my own reflections:

1. Traditions
2. Prejudices: racial, denominational, social
3. Preconceptions
4. Unbelief
5. Rebellion

To establish Lord Jesus as our true foundation, Prince advised us to dig deep. We put God's Word into practice through repentance and surrender in every area of our soul. We get a heart of flesh from God when we allow him to remove a heart of stone (see Ezek. 36:26-27). Sanctification happens by intent and not by accident because we *"work out our salvation"*. It's wise to ask ourselves some difficult questions if we want to be transformed into the likeness of Christ (see Phil. 2:12-13). To change our attitudes, we must cooperate actively with the Holy Spirit.

1. Traditions

Historically, the Church often failed to correctly identify problematic and ungodly traditions and effectively deal with them. Several of today's traditions and customs arose from age-old Babylon and spread to the planet's existing cultures and empires. One example is the Roman empire. Its influence didn't crumble, but it adapted by slowly absorbing itself into the world systems, affecting theology, governmental structures, traditions and everyday life. We gather insight by studying the Bible and history to unravel and root up the disturbing influences derived from previous generations or the present-day contemporary culture. Worldwide celebrations of unholy traditions authorise demonic principalities access through agreement. One example is Halloween, or Samhain (Sah-ween), originally from Babylon. People in occult circles are fully aware of this synergy effect because of their evil participation, whereas many Christians wilfully ignore it. These mega rituals permit the devil and his fallen angels to establish strongholds over people's minds, even over cities and nations. Focused intercession into these issues is, therefore, of great importance.

Sanctification happens by intent and not by accident, as we *"work out our salvation"*.

Paul alerted believers about idolatrous traditions and their danger (see Col. 2:8-23). To be contingent on these in place of God's presence makes people vulnerable to deceptive spirits—more about this topic in chapter 8. Spirits of tradition, religion or the occult create a counterfeit atmosphere to true worship. They will attempt to oppose the Holy Spirit, to stop him from moving. To frequently encounter God on a deeply personal level and remain filled by his Spirit is very important. We should refrain from a superficial Christian life. When we draw near to God, he draws near to us. He protects us from ungodly traditions and empty rituals, leading to spiritual bondage (see James 4:8). As Christians, do we shrug our shoulders, pretending the issue is unimportant? If we pray for revival, we should take it seriously. Over time, traditional heathen influences seem partly weakened by Christianity. We better not underestimate the redemptive power of the gospel. The conventional [73]Christmas holiday, Yule, was a period when the sun god, Mithras, was worshipped, but now it is a season to remember and worship the one and true *Son of God*. At least some paganism has departed from our culture, although not entirely.

2. Prejudices: racial, denominational, social

As Western colonialism was forced on different groups and cultures, certain ethnic groups suffered generational wounds. On the one hand, the cause of civilising the 'heathens' was promulgated, an enterprise where rich nations sent missionaries and political emissaries to lands where they had vested interests. On the other hand, the wealthy establishment utilised governments as pawns in the ruthless pursuit of natural resources and cheap slave labour. Colonialism, if compared to the ancient Roman invasion of Britain, generated innovation and growth by bringing some improvement for the affected culture—this is how conquest works. Was it right? No! In hindsight, exploitative colonialism is a shameful piece of history. *Race* was twisted into an unscientific and crippling idea to justify the most recent slavery and later [74]eugenics. On a positive note, Britain later paid a high price in getting rid of the slave trade globally. In seeking to address deep-rooted racism and injustice, let us repent and let God reconcile, restore and bring healing. Any kind of prejudice and racism is incompatible with biblical faith. Some churches may lack ethnic variety due to attempts to evade the subject or the inability to confront their own biases.

The black Jesus idea probably emerged because of generational trauma imposed by colonialism. Undeniably, Jesus was not fair-skinned, but he was a Mediterranean

---

[73] **Paganism in the church:** Unfortunately, the Church of Rome 'Christianised' pagan holidays instead of observing and acknowledging the biblical feasts. Hence, they interfered with and changed the biblical calendar. We inherited these traditions, rooted in Babylonian sun god worship - an abomination to the Lord. The chosen Passover Lamb, Jesus, was not born on Christmas Day but in the spring, close to Ephrata, where the sacrificial lambs were raised by the Levites (see Micah 5:2).

[74] **Eugenics** is the practice or advocacy of improving the human species by selectively mating people with specific desirable hereditary traits. www.history.com > topics > germany > eugenics

and Jewish man, probably well-built from his carpentry, despite the anaemic, weedy imagery in Mediaeval paintings! Let us detect the deeper moral issues and get rid of ugly prejudice. Racism still negatively affects our world's cultures, but categorising entire Western societies as being systematically racist or downright oppressive is an unfounded and unhelpful claim. We shouldn't denigrate the historical records, with a dark past of segregation laws and countless atrocious deeds, nor the hurdles people of colour still face in society. It's the truth, but we can't deny that we live in a society where ideologically motivated groups stoke racism to sustain their self-serving goals. I think they were *founded* and *funded* to do so. Blinded by their own cognitive bias, two-faced and twisted activist factions widen the chasm between black, white, Asian and other ethnicities. Touting *diversity, inclusion and equality,* they hide behind the mirage of 'social justice' while inciting violence, mayhem and anarchy. Their reverse racism also disproportionally hurt Jews, Caucasian and Asian citizens. In the US, they harm marginalised black communities and misuse donations. Increased racial tensions come in handy as major talking points in glib politicians' intemperate quest for power and domination. Let us firmly expose and confront these diabolical and divisive efforts to confine citizens into hampering stereotypes of groups or ideas.

Let us repent and let God reconcile, restore and bring healing.

I regard critical race theory as dangerous because it fundamentally misappropriates the concept of [75]intersectionality. Trying to divide humanity into fixed groups of oppressors and oppressed by victimising black people and demonising white people is an ill-advised approach. Catering to group identity at the cost of individuals' rights by playing into the hands of political bigotry or activism is detrimental to churches and society. Socialist and fascist constructs pave the way for tyranny in how they devalue faith and human dignity. The civil rights movement is bound to implode if its aspirations aren't defined by an ethical sense of profound *personal* ownership. In a groupthink or conformist culture, independent thinking is considered a betrayal

---

[75] **My comment:** *True intersectionality* considers all contributing factors of discrimination to present a complete picture of the unjust treatment of individuals or groups. It also exposes oppressive systems and hidden power structures. It seeks to define and empower the disenfranchised to restore rights and opportunities and include them in society based on human rights, free from institutional, political, racial and economic biases.

of this community's cardinal goals or core values—a mentality unfit for targeting the underlying problems of discrimination, as these will largely remain unsolved. Naïve [76]Christians, who pander to ideological tribalism—left or right—are being fooled. They are blind to the establishment's sinister games. An antidote to flawed political concepts is to connect the Christian faith and its social thought tradition within the right historical and theological framework. Believers should stay vigilant and avoid reading political ideologies into their understanding of the Bible. We need true enlightenment. Awakened believers who earnestly seek God for sanctification and wise strategies are part of the solution. Cleaning up the dilemma of racism and injustice requires more than good intentions. The cross ends all discrimination. Full stop. A vertical reconciliation of sinners with God results in the horizontal effect of the gospel, which is loving our neighbours (see Eph. 2:14-16, Col. 1:19-23). Social programs, politics or money will never fill the God-shaped holes inside our hearts.

We should not despise each other's faith. We have established common values for fellowship when we believe in the divinity of Christ, the cross and his resurrection. Having the Spirit of God and genuine faith in the Bible create true oneness among believers. We will spend eternity together and will benefit from interaction with our lovely brothers and sisters during our earthly voyage. Pastors and preachers should more frequently come together to seek God and switch pulpits. There are plenty of possibilities to cross-pollinate with the good things from other churches. Embracing a plethora of cultural and ethnic diversity enables us to tear down fences and reduce dissent. God then meshes his people together as a beautiful mosaic of his love.

Social prejudice, or classism, is another challenge for the Body of Christ. Within the church, we often socialise with like-minded people. Leaders set a precedent and should avoid nepotism because of their preferences. We frequently assess and judge people based on social rank, background, education and income. Discrimination of this kind is pathetic, but it also grieves the Holy Spirit. Intolerance, prejudice and looking down on dissimilar people are things that God loathes (see James 2:2-4). We should cautiously review how we treat each other. Is it based on upbringing and

---

[76] **Politics:** Right-wing and left-wing identity politics harm people, particularly Millennials. Both bigoted views collide with the gospel by bringing division and disunity. To welcome healthy discussions without trying to silence dissenting voices reveals if you are a true libertarian or not.

social circumstances? Keen attention is also required when we address more delicate matters like sexuality and gender. Still, I don't think we should fear controversy and become submissive to whatever stance is the most politically promoted, but express our pastoral concern in love. Many individuals struggle in these areas, and Christian fellowships are not exempt. Because we are ministers of mercy, our mission is to stay connected to God's heart, praying for the Holy Spirit to intervene. Our eagerness to voice our biblically based [77]opinions might deter people from seeking counsel from the local church as they feel judged by us. It's damaging and counter-productive. May the Lord help us to remain unafraid and loving and not treat sexual sin more harshly than other sins. Let us counter judgemental thoughts and vow not to forsake fellow humans. Our sacred duty is to love everybody by allowing God to fix them.

The wonderful gospel transforms lives, but it only works if we speak truthfully and filled with love. Manifesting the Father's heart by having the mind of Christ is our single option if we want to support each other as a community. It's an oxymoron to antagonise and evangelise at the same time! If we fail to represent the Kingdom, we stop people from receiving healing from brokenness and identity issues rampant in our generation. Whenever we proclaim the gospel, our mission is to build bridges, not barricades. Hence we should always pray for words and actions rightly aligned with God our Father's redemptive plans and purposes.

3. Preconceptions

Is it possible to be misled by our assumptions because we think we have a good sense of judgement? Beyond question! Even Samuel, the great prophet, was fooled by his prejudice when he showed up to anoint as king one of the sons of Jesse. Israel's God rebuked his misjudgement and carnality: *But the Lord said to Samuel, "Do not look on his appearance or on the height of his stature, because I have rejected him. For the Lord sees not as man sees: man looks on the outward appearance, but the Lord looks on the heart."* (1 Sam. 16:7 ESV). By then, the Lord had rejected Saul as king, a man with all the traits Samuel admired concerning his external attributes. Predictably,

---

[77] **My comment:** The right to express one's private opinions has become idolatry for many people today, including some professing Christians. They feel compelled to share what they think, regardless of the outcome. Hence they lack insight and empathy. That's a result of the political spirit. We should bridle our tongue and speak in line with God's Word (see James 3:1-12).

we remember with fondness the last move of God and anticipate a repetition of the past. We are often experts in natural judgement but fail to discern a spiritual reality beyond the obvious. Being predisposed towards a fixed outcome, we seem inclined to trust our sensory abilities. It's imperative to train our spiritual senses. We should also remind ourselves that we gradually develop character and maturity (see Phil. 3:15, Heb. 6:1-3, James 1:4). Revelation and refined intuition increase when we seek the presence of the Lord (see Psalm 25:14). Time in prayer enhances our sensitivity towards a spiritual reality—it diverts attention away from the visible realm. People we don't like at first will usually improve on closer inspection. Shouldn't we ask God for his perspective? What a delightful surprise when we understand what precious individuals he created! Appearances can be deceiving.

Revelation and refined intuition increase when we seek the presence of the Lord. Time in prayer enhances our sensitivity towards a spiritual reality—it diverts attention away from the visible realm.

4. Unbelief

Unbelief is placing trust in things other than God. By faith, our hope is anchored in his unseen reality, and we cultivate trust through a relationship with him. The Father loves when we lean into him by faith, as humble trust is *his* love language (see Heb. 11:6). Let us discuss divine healing: We rely on the Word for healing and forgiveness because Jesus purchased both for us on the cross. We detect disease in the body by observation but discover healing by revelation. Through faith, we apply a higher law than peripheral laws, the same way as lift overcomes gravity. It allows for a 300-tonne aircraft to take off and fly. When we praise and magnify the infinite majesty of the Lord's name, he powerfully intervenes. Relying on our faculties more than his Word limits God in our lives. Constant complaining and worrying accompany unbelief. Unbelief originates from fear and self-righteousness and creates toxic thoughts and attitudes which shut down our ability to receive from God. Jesus had to stand up to unbelieving believers—our Lord *"marvelled because of their unbelief."* (Mark 6:4-6 ESV). What a tragedy this is! It's startling to observe a large number of unbelieving believers, yet there are many believing unbelievers! Joking apart, maybe ministering healing could prove easier outdoors than within a church building. Non-Christians are usually willing to give the Saviour a chance when they are loved on and prayed for because of their disillusionment. I have overheard banter where Christians lively discuss their infirmities right after receiving prayer for healing, seemingly indifferent to the sacred act they just partook in. It dawned on me that easy access to treatment and physicians may lead to complacency, albeit unintentionally.

There are two ditches to fall into, 1) To make hasty conclusions based on personal let-downs. If we don't get healed at once, this is tempting. We could instead choose to press into God's promises by giving him *time* to build hope and faith in us.

2) Some churches elude responsibility by creating guilt in the person they prayed for. They allege the healing was lost due to a lack of faith when it failed to manifest physically. These churches are playing the blame game. That said, God responds to spiritually hungry people. Such hunger should arguably transition into perseverance while we patiently wait for our breakthroughs. I love to encounter God's presence in church gatherings, seeing people ablaze for him, with the atmosphere pulsating with holy anticipation. Our responsibility is to keep that fire burning!

By faith, our hope is anchored in his unseen reality, and we cultivate trust through a relationship with him.

5. Rebellion

Rebellion is closely related to disobedience. It's a stubborn attitude, causing us to distrust God and oppose authority. We counteract this by practising submission to the leaders of our church. Of course, not blind submission because God wants us to retain our discernment and critical thinking. If we struggle in this area, we learn by serving with a loving attitude. The sin of rebellion is also related to witchcraft and idolatry (see 1 Sam 15:23). On that note, we need to contemplate all involvement our family line has had with the occult or pagan worship. Being born again doesn't automatically remove the access the devil has to your family's bloodline. That might come as a surprise to some believers. How we address these matters is critical if we want to experience personal freedom and spiritual growth. Do prayerfully consider if you have any ungodly activity in your family line. If that is so, please renounce any involvement as thoroughly as possible, especially freemasonry. Also, confess which types of sins your family members or ancestors were involved in, then disavow them in Jesus' name. Start to repent on behalf of your lineage, then ask for the blood of Jesus to cleanse your family (see also Acts 19:18-20). If you feel uneasy and restless on the inside when doing so, you may need further help to get delivered from these bondages. Deliverance is a normal process to experience because the enemy usually fights back to keep his strongholds. Seek mature or trained ministers for help. When deliverance has happened, firmly resist the adversary in the area he once controlled. After being evicted, the foe usually returns to try to retake his former territory. Act calmly, without fear. Keywords are: *Repent, renounce, refuse* and *resist.* You can rest assured that the devil no longer has any rights over you because of the redeeming blood of Jesus. We exercise our God-given authority, in Jesus' name, by deliberately resisting the devil and claiming back our bloodline.

To confess Christ as our foundation is easy. Living a life where we demonstrate his nature is more challenging. The Greek word for truth is ἀλήθεια *aletheia*—the same as *reality*. It means unconcealedness, the state of not being hidden. In God, we are hidden with Christ but not hidden from his truth. One description of the Church is *"the pillar and foundation of the truth"* (see 1 Tim. 3:15 NIV). Our calling is to display the truth. When we feel loved, we have no need to hide from God because Jesus is the personification of truth (see John 14:6). Once we set out to dig, to hit the bedrock, we first penetrate the turf and soil and then unearth more. By his grace, we uncover a fair amount of dirt. That can be a horrid business. It takes some elbow grease to remove it as we search for truth and the face of the Holy One. When delving into the darkness of our hearts, we may be tempted to quit. However, the Holy Spirit is the *Spirit of Truth.* He leads us into *all truth* because he provides us with his light and revelation—he also brings out the gold in us! (See Psalm 43:3, John 16:13).

To confess Christ as our foundation is easy. Living a life where we demonstrate his nature is more challenging.

If the governing culture of our hearts hasn't been properly revised in the first place, it's impossible to change nations' cultures. We shut out the revelation required for a victorious lifestyle if we dodge the truth about ourselves (see Psalm 139:23-24). By honestly embarking on the pilgrimage of truth, we will soon enough bump into the Father's beautiful heart. *"My son, if you accept my words and store up my commands within you, turning your ear to wisdom and applying your heart to understanding—indeed, if you call out for insight and cry aloud for understanding, and if you look for it as for silver and search for it as for hidden treasure, then you will understand the fear of the LORD and find the knowledge of God."* (Prov. 2:1-5 NIV).

The Spirit of Truth

Jesus said what would happen after his departure. He promised to send his Advisor, the Advocate, the Helper—to live within his children. The Spirit glorifies Jesus, his death, resurrection and his ascension. He leads us into all truth, and we saw earlier how the word for truth equals our word for *reality*. In regard to a thoroughgoing reality check, the Holy Spirit is unrivalled! He searches our inner motives and knows all things. Nothing is hidden from him (see also Rom. 8:27, 1 Cor. 2:10). And, the kindness of God leads us to repentance, as *"the fruit of the light"* consists in all goodness, righteousness and truth (see Rom. 2:4, Eph. 5:9). God, in his goodness, reveals the secret things of our hearts. To make us Christlike, he facilitates the much-needed transition. The Father knows and loves us at the same time. A friend of mine once said: 'To be known and still be loved is to be truly loved.' By plumbing the depths of who God is, he shows us who we really are. The more we get to know him, the more we will understand ourselves—in whose image we were created.

When it comes to a thorough reality check, the Holy Spirit is unrivalled!

The Holy Spirit generally focuses on two realities: **1) Our new identity in Christ and 2) The state of our hearts.** On the one hand, we have the revealed truth, our position in Christ—seated with him in heavenly places. On the other hand, we have our experienced truth—our walk with Christ. When the Holy Spirit shows us our identity, he focuses on justification by faith. He then transfers our *positional* reality into *practical* realisation. Through intimate relation with him, he convicts us of his holy righteousness, built on unwavering covenant promises. Absolute righteousness is a manifestation of God's Spirit. In his presence, he exposes sin as a consequence of his perfect righteousness. A strong conviction of sin may unexpectedly open the abyss of eternal despair beneath us, and our only hope lies in holding fast to God's matchless grace provided in Jesus. Persistently pointing us to his cleansing blood is the remedy for our afflicted hearts. As his children, God is determined to show us our new and wonderful identity in Christ. He wants us to share in the abundant life he has granted us. Focusing on our human shortcomings and sin could cause the opposite of what we want, thus reinforcing failure. Food for thought: Adam and Eve showed no sign of sin-consciousness in the Garden of Eden. They were totally preoccupied with God's presence and provision and weren't self-absorbed in any way. They were unaware of their nakedness—comfortably cocooned in his glory. The situation drastically changed after the fall. Their spiritual eyes shut the moment their 'eyes were opened'. Their innocence vanished, as sudden self-awareness caused them to feel guilt and shame, and they hid from the Lord (see Gen. 3:6-12). God's Spirit seeks to move our focus from shame and guilt attached to our fallen state and redirect it to our new standing in Christ, where we are clothed in his righteousness. A believer is a *receiver*. God convicts sinners of sin to demonstrate their urgent need for a Saviour. With Christ as our Lord, the emphasis slightly shifts with a more direct focus on *righteousness* (see John 16:8, 2 Cor. 15:34). How awesome the Holy Spirit is! By faith, he gives us a new outlook as he reveals our new identity. By learning to see from Heaven's perspective, a believer is also a *perceiver*. The Helper is relentlessly wooing us to fall in love with Christ, our blessed Lord and Bridegroom.

Absolute righteousness is a manifestation of God's Spirit.

God knows that his grace can only flow from a place where we experience his love. We recognise that we love him because he first loved us (see 1 John 4:19). His love takes away our fear and the desire to try to live independently. *"And he died for all, that those who live should no longer live for themselves but for him who died for them and was raised again."* (2 Cor. 5:15 NIV). Living by faith is trusting God's enabling grace instead of our natural strength. It's something we have to practise again and again. No one possesses a moral inclination to live a strong Christian life. Faith only works when we connect with the right power source. Vehicles require fuel, and most gadgets and appliances run on electricity. Christians are *powered by grace* because we don't live for ourselves. It would be a grave mistake to disconnect from the harness in mid-air if you go on a tandem skydive with an experienced instructor! Your whole survival depends on clinging trustfully to your coach. In Tit. 2:11-14, *grace* appears as our private tutor, an instrumental tool in God's rescue mission. The Spirit of

Grace trains us for a righteous lifestyle. He helps us to live synchronised with God's plan for us. Life in the Spirit is a state of the heart where we depend on his grace and wisdom. Striving to live as Christians in our carnal strength wasn't the life our Lord intended (see 2 Cor. 5:15, Gal. 2:21; 3:1-3). We seek God and aim to help each other.

It doesn't require great faith to adhere to religious traditions and practices. Neither to acknowledge inadequacy, weaknesses, nor misbehaviour. It's common to admit one's shortcomings. But does it prove an understanding of biblical spirituality? Not in the slightest! Being downcast and self-deprecating is hardly built on esteemed Christian virtues. We are helpless apart from God's saving grace and can still admit our mistakes while recognising sonship. Repentance may bring us temporary grief because of our fallen state, but it produces lasting and genuine joy. Heaven's hosts celebrate when one sinner repents—the angels are rooting for us! (See Luke 15:7, 10). The Scandinavian countries left the Old Norse religion when they converted to Catholicism and rapidly embraced the novel faith. The underlying cause is no secret. The more lenient Vatican refused to interfere with the places of worship, and they built new sanctuaries exactly where the pagan temples once stood. The Holy See has operated along these lines through the centuries to achieve a smooth transition and fend off resistance from the population. Over an eighth of the Norwegian churches were initially erected at locations dedicated to the ancient Norse gods. The Vikings turned to Catholicism during their travels and shared their newfound religion when they returned. They also brought Christian slaves from the British Isles, particularly from Ireland. These Irish believers carried the genuine gospel because of their active, intimate faith in God. German missionaries later ushered in Protestant Christianity. [78]Catholicism and Protestantism were religious and well-structured efforts. On the surface, one attempted to supplant the pagan religions in Europe, like the renowned mystery cults of sun worship. It was really about centralisation of power. As a result, we got the state-controlled churches—institutions endorsed by the kings and the clergy. These churches held sway over the populace for centuries, with doctrines like christening, confirmation and the sinfulness of man. It also explains the historical context as to why beliefs like justification by faith and the baptism of the Holy Spirit

---

[78] **My comment:** The Vatican introduced the Babylonian/Chaldean pagan religion under the thin veneer of the Christian faith. To this day, we find Catholicism riddled with sun motifs and other occult symbols visible on the attire of the priest and cardinals and the objects used in worship.

don't get much attention within these church systems. The core beliefs held by these rigid institutions don't always represent what we find in the New Testament. Some doctrines, such as christening, seem to lull people into a false sense of security regarding salvation. These churches confuse their [79]sacrament with biblical baptism by sprinkling a little liquid on a child's head. The word *baptism* suggests otherwise, as it means 'to immerse' or 'to lower down into a body of water'. Baptism is for those who—aware of their sinfulness—desire to receive the power of new life through Christ. There are low church movements that encourage the need to be born-again, yet they insist on high church creeds. The Norwegian Lutheran State Church has this prayer in their worship ritual: *"Look upon me with grace, I, a poor sinful human, who has displeased you in thoughts, words and deeds and is aware of the evil desire in my heart! For the sake of Jesus Christ, have long-suffering with me, and forgive all my sins, and help me to fear and love you alone. Amen."*

The liturgical confession of sin the typical churchgoers publicly partake in has now become more than a creed. It's a well-rehearsed state of mind.

Without realising it, an inward gaze gets us stuck at the foot of the cross instead of embracing the feet of the Resurrected One—like lovely Mary Magdalene attempted (see John 20:17). It may result in a deficient and one-sided version of the gospel, that quickly becomes another gospel. In Gal. 2:20, Paul exclaims boldly: *"It is no longer I who live, but Christ who lives in me."* The result of believing in the cross is a changed perspective where we actively receive the empowering grace of God. Paul said: *"I do not set aside the grace of God ..."* (see Gal. 2:21 NIV). Not to make use of the grace made available through the cross is to disregard Jesus' sacrificial work and, in the end, neglect what the Father so lovingly provided for us. The liberal theologians' multiple efforts to reduce and redact the Bible have deprived crowds of the life-transforming force the gospel represents. If the gospel we proclaim doesn't bring a lasting change, *our version* must be fraudulent. God's will for us supersedes man-made respectable religion: He calls us to radical wholeness and holiness. It's a life where we follow the

---

[79] **A sacrament** is a Christian rite recognised as of particular importance and significance. There are various views on the existence and meaning of such rites. Many Christians consider the sacraments to be a visible symbol of the reality of God, as well as a channel for God's grace. Source: en.wikipedia.org

standards of the Word and not those of the world. Holiness is not the same as being subdued or void of joy and passion. Believers aren't duty-bound to push the 'mute button', keep up appearances or quell all emotions. Austere religiosity says we can't joke around anymore—especially not with God. But the gospel won't necessarily cramp your style or suppress your enthusiasm. If you were a notorious party animal, perhaps there is a wildness in you that the good Lord wants to redeem rather than sucking the life out of you. He purifies your passionate personality and then gently saturates your soul with his goodness. Experience indicates that the more untamed and outgoing converts simmer down a bit, whilst composed and timid individuals become more direct and social. God heals and restores us; it's a gradual change. He frees us from continuous cycles of rejection and shame. With that in mind, we want churches with raw authenticity, vibrant audacity and unashamed love. Owing to his exuberant energy, Jesus endorsed all these qualities—without hesitation. The snobs and moralising hypocrites hated it, but the crowd loved his zest for life.

We desire fellowships with raw authenticity, vibrant audacity and unashamed love.

There are two ways to receive the gospel: We can receive it with or without power. If we receive it without power, true repentance is absent. Some want to cherry-pick forgiveness of sins but fail to embrace the entire gospel. Unfortunately, they become Christians in name only and not radical followers of Jesus. They live in a critical state of deception—not realising they are spiritually dead—as a lasting change of heart never took place. During altar calls, I have heard preachers ask unbelievers present if they want 'to receive Jesus into their hearts'. They weren't taught how to surrender to the Lord, nor did they feel a conviction of sin by the Holy Spirit. Neither were they read the terms and conditions but were offered salvation for free. Who of us doesn't want to get free stuff in a consumerist society? This careless pursuit of new converts while betraying the foundation of the gospel has proven to be a disaster. Some of these individuals may later pose a risk to the churches they join and become like leaven. Why is this? Because they are professing Christians but haven't been regenerated or born-again by God's Spirit (see Rev. 3:4). The other breed is the real deal. By receiving the gospel openly, they set the standard for the rest of Christianity: *"For we know, brothers and sisters loved by God, that he has chosen you, because our gospel came to you not simply with words but also with power, with the Holy Spirit and deep conviction. You know how we lived among you for your sake. You became imitators of us and of the Lord, for you welcomed the message in the midst of severe suffering with the joy given by the Holy Spirit. And so you became a model to all the believers in Macedonia and Achaia. The Lord's message rang out from you not only in Macedonia and Achaia—your faith in God has become known everywhere."* (1 Thess. 1:4-8 NIV).

In the end, God sees our hearts. One of the thieves, crucified next to Jesus, asked for *a thought* but got *a Paradise* in exchange! The regretful robber didn't pray a sinner's prayer but entered the Kingdom with his plea for mercy (see Luke 23:42-43).

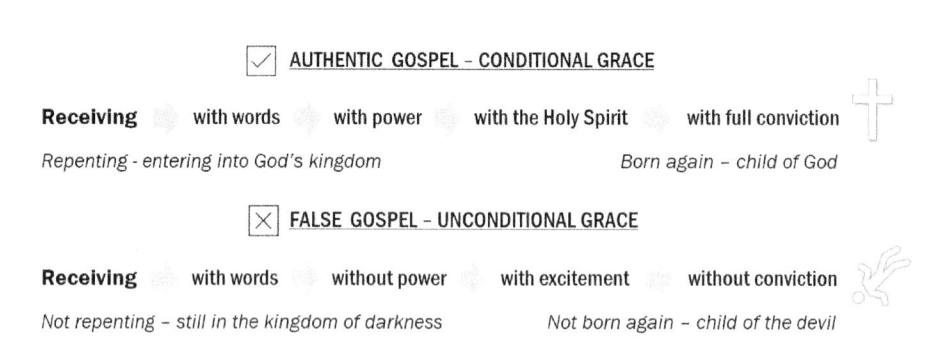

✓ **AUTHENTIC GOSPEL – CONDITIONAL GRACE**

Receiving   with words   with power   with the Holy Spirit   with full conviction

Repenting - entering into God's kingdom   *Born again – child of God*

✗ **FALSE GOSPEL – UNCONDITIONAL GRACE**

Receiving   with words   without power   with excitement   without conviction

Not repenting – still in the kingdom of darkness   *Not born again – child of the devil*

Anyway, repentance leads to fellowship with the living God, and his love starts to govern us through our walk in obedience. When Paul shared the gospel, he always purposed to bring people into the Kingdom and under the Lordship of Jesus Christ. *"Now to him who is able to establish you in accordance with my gospel, the message I proclaim about Jesus Christ, in keeping with the revelation of the mystery hidden for long ages past, but now revealed and made known through the prophetic writings by the command of the eternal God, so that all the Gentiles might come to the obedience that comes from faith— to the only wise God be glory forever through Jesus Christ! Amen."* (Rom. 16:24-27 NIV).

Here is another thing to ponder: It's ironic. Some Christian circles consider unbelief a sign of spirituality, making it virtuous to experience doubt on a regular basis. Some believers doubt their faith, but others have faith in their doubts! Of course, you don't lose your salvation if you occasionally waver. We all face personal ordeals and pitch-black seasons—some of the disciples had doubts after Jesus' resurrection (see Matt. 28:17). Our faith builds on a relationship of trust. Unbelief will naturally not be encouraged if we cultivate a culture of faith (see also Matt. 14:31, John 20:27, James 1:6). The following in-joke is a good picture: Three Christians without any forewarning found themselves in a predicament. They ended up in Hell. These churchgoers were a Lutheran, a YWAMer and a Word of Faith believer. Woefully overcome by grief, the Lutheran blurted out: "I knew it! I knew this would happen!" The YWAMer responded prayerfully: "Lord, what do you want me to learn from this?" Last but not least, the Word of Faith believer shouted: "I'm not here! I'm not here! I am standing on the Word—I'm not here!" Within these extremes, we will hopefully find a relevant representation of biblical faith.

Some believers doubt their faith and have faith in their doubts!

Undoubtedly, pun not intended, the person of the Holy Spirit is the leading key to growing churches around the globe. *"In the same way, the gospel is bearing fruit and growing throughout the whole world—just as it has been doing among you since the day you heard it and truly understood God's grace."* (Col. 1:6 NIV). Up-close encounters with the risen and living Christ, as well as dreams and visions, transform locations where missionaries are denied access—especially in Muslim countries. Salvations are frequently accompanied by signs and wonders, miracles and healings, which is the norm around the world. More often than not, spreading the Word of God spurs persecution. Preaching the gospel is not for the faint-hearted. However, most of these new believers are unfamiliar with a stale, passionless and uninspiring presentation of the good news. The Western concept of respectable religion is both passé and irrelevant and totally incongruous with reverence and awe. Traditional denominations could benefit from a closer look at the transformative moves of God with an unbiased and sympathetic mind. Many of these take place in the Southern Hemisphere. Today, Europe's empty churches show irrefutable evidence of spiritual decline. Europe was uncontested for hundreds of years as a pronounced Christian continent. Its elevated position was extravagantly expressed in fine art, architecture, science and education. Christian faith has been replaced in many places due to the arrival of Islam, atheism, Marxism and the New Age. Still, there is hope for a change. The new generation of teenagers and young adults are relational, open-minded and curious about the truth. They are searching and willing to hear our views on the end times but are also receptive to prayer for healing. The fires of revival will soon hit kids and teenagers in the millions across the world's many nations. The coming move of the Spirit will be transformative and virtually unstoppable. Positioning ourselves by getting up-to-date knowledge, with the ability to minister through spiritual gifts, is key when trying to reach our audience. It's a plus if you are well-informed but, more importantly, competent in pointing people to Jesus. Overall, be literally well-versed, especially in the books of the New Testament—TNT for short because it contains explosive power! That said, a little Internet sleuthing could also prove useful.

THE NEW TESTAMENT

When Paul testified to a heathen Roman official, he also included themes like end-time prophecy and judgement. But the Roman dignitary, Felix, was scared out of his wits on hearing this rather tough part of the gospel message (see Acts 24:24-25). Paul, the apostle, wasn't perceived as appeasing or seeker-friendly compared to some contemporary ministers. He preached the uncompromising message of the cross. As a rule, Christians are being scolded and told not to frighten people into Heaven. Is it really that bad to scare them out of an eternal Hell? It's a courtesy to caution our neighbours about impending dangers, like housefires. We should show care because God's kindness leads sinners to repentance, regardless of demographics. Heaven is delightful beyond description. Conversely, Hell is absolutely horrific. Shouldn't we, as followers of Jesus, do whatever it takes to keep people out of it?

"Death and Destruction lie open before the LORD—how much more do human hearts!" (Prov. 15:11 NIV). *"Rescue those who are being taken away to death; hold back those who are stumbling to the slaughter. If you say, "Behold, we did not know*

this," does not he who weighs the heart perceive it? Does not he who keeps watch over your soul know it, and will he not repay man after his work? (Prov. 24:11-12 ESV).

I know of individuals the Lord saved after conversations about all sorts of topics, like aliens and [80]conspiracies. Providing a biblical narrative for them brought them to faith in Christ. God often works in mysterious and even hilarious ways (see Num. 22:21-34, Jonah 4:5-10, Rom. 11:33). At any rate, we need the Holy Spirit to guide us in our research because several of these topics are infested and used by Satan to derail believers. They represent harmful demonic strongholds not to be trifled with. As for occultism, there are serious pitfalls one could stumble across. Despite their obvious danger, aberrant doctrines might exude some type of magnetic attraction: *"But I also have a message for the rest of you in Thyatira who have not followed this false teaching ('deeper truths,' as they call them—depths of Satan, actually). I will ask nothing more of you except that you hold tightly to what you have until I come."* (Rev. 2:24-25 NLT). Be careful, stay on track and avoid speculations. Love for Jesus and the Scripture must always have the pre-eminence of our lives (see 2 Tim 2:23). Don't consume all kinds of books or videos. Be selective and prayerful, and get advice from experienced Christians. My conviction is that all born-again believers should be able to share the gospel and their own testimony in a clear and simplified way.

Don't slide farther down the rabbit hole if you discuss a controversial topic instead of reverting to the gospel message. Many preachers began evangelising but ended up obsessing over politics or some fringe topics. Their attention got hijacked, and they stopped sharing God's Word with their audience. Some even fell prey to strange and deceptive doctrines and left the Lord. We have an overarching assignment to point people to Jesus, earnestly praying that they will experience his saving grace. Don't pull back, but stay focused, unwavering in your devotion to Jesus and representing him well. Soul winning is the sole purpose. We are on mission 3:16, and it's a rescue

---

[80] **Conspiracy theory** is commonly used as a weaponized term to either silence or counter any individual or group that challenges the establishment's increased implementation of clandestine programs and activities. It was first the Central Intelligence Agency (CIA), in the U.S., which invented the term and applied it through the many media outlets they owned or controlled.
In popular culture, it's often an umbrella term for allegedly unsubstantiated claims regarding politics, history and science, etc. I prefer to use the word conspiracy as a more valid term. There are some real *conspiracy facts* that can be confirmed by following the money, or via existing paper or data trails.

mission. Omission of the gospel means 0 mission. Got it? Satan has launched a string of vicious attacks against the Body of Christ as we approach the finale. He feverishly attempts to sideline the evangelists because he doesn't want them to gather the great harvest of souls. We should diligently devote ourselves to prayer and be ready in season and out of season, and at all times be prepared to share God's goodness and the unambiguous message of the cross (see 2 Tim. 4:2). To drift away from our given assignment is a price too high to pay.

We are on mission 3:16, and it's a rescue mission. Omission of the gospel means 0 mission. Got it?

Paul's sound and wise words to Timothy, his son in the faith, contain good advice: *"But you, man of God, flee from all this, and pursue righteousness, godliness, faith, love, endurance and gentleness. Fight the good fight of the faith. Take hold of the eternal life to which you were called when you made your good confession in the presence of many. In the sight of God, who gives life to everything, and of Christ Jesus, who while testifying before Pontius Pilate made the good confession, I charge you to keep this command without spot or blame until the appearing of our Lord Jesus Christ, which God will bring about in his own time—God, the blessed and only Ruler, the King of kings and Lord of lords, who alone is immortal and who lives in unapproachable light, whom no one has seen or can see. To him be honour and might forever. Amen."* (1 Tim. 6:11-16 NIV).

How we respond to the prayer Jesus asked his disciples to pray is crucial: *"Ask the Lord of the harvest, therefore, to send out workers into his harvest field."* (Matt. 9:38 NLT). To send, in Greek ἐκβάλλω *ekballo,* is to thrust forth or violently throw out. Matthew used precise gospel terminology about Jesus casting out demons. Neither harvest workers nor demons will leave their comfortable position unless they feel firmly compelled to do so! God gave me a prophetic picture: I noticed a tidal wave of evangelists hitting the earth. In another vision, I saw a large cathedral on fire. Horses and chariots shot out from it, carrying the evangelists. Moving with great speed, they extracted flames from the building—being on fire for the gospel! The Lord has orchestrated a full-scale victory ahead of time, and the fiery evangelists play a vital part in it. Besides, God tasked evangelists to train other believers as witnesses by releasing the anointing to win souls into the churches they belong to. Building personal ministry opportunities can't be relevant compared to an activation of the evangelistic anointing in the Body of Christ. Jesus won't build without the servants he commissioned to build his House, who carry fivefold offices (see Psalm 127:1). I don't think criticising churches for their lack of evangelism—in a black-or-white fashion—is part of an evangelist's ministry. Without a doubt, an evangelistic church culture is mission-critical. The world's growing churches should encourage and inspire us. I am a strong proponent of leading by example. Is it somehow possible to adapt our know-how into show-how? Various organisations and ministries provide churches with evangelistic programmes, but if we don't love and live like Jesus, these efforts will yield meagre results. Leaders and pastors must pray for the Holy Spirit to guide them with the right approach for their unique fellowship.

Without a doubt, an evangelistic church culture is mission-critical.

Evangelism is about building relationships and bringing others into God's family. Sadly, some Christians have a sense of superiority. Being 'churched', they think they are morally better than those who don't know Christ. It's an attitude that hurts our mission—people are put off by it. My point is this: Let us refocus our attention on *community* by resisting the temptation to schedule evangelism as an activity where we volunteer some hours and then conveniently ease our conscience. Seeing fellow humans as mere 'projects' or 'souls' is wrong. Although hectic, daily life is bustling with moments to build lasting and loving relations with family, friends, neighbours and work colleagues. God will make sure that our testimony doesn't fall on deaf ears but is eventually received by those who trust and respect us. Christ will gently pull them into his glorious kingdom if we allow his light to shine through us. As the old adage goes: *"Preach the gospel as often as you can, and if necessary, with words."* Some churches successfully reach younger generations. Appealing music and meaningful messages keep them in step with contemporary culture. These churches master to attract all kinds of people because of their effective evangelistic approach. They also have a biblical stance on lifestyle, including marriage and sexuality. One of the main arguments these churches underscore is this: Church is the place to promote what we are *for* and not against. I totally agree because Christianity is too often defined by what not to do instead of modelling a righteous lifestyle. This argument instantly draws fire from both legalistic conservatives and progressive liberals. The castigators conclude that holding a view of being conservative and inclusive is unworkable. To me, these concerned responses explain the tension we presently face: 1) to accept individuals without promoting godless lifestyles or 2) mixing our teaching with political slogans—which then turns into a false and futile gospel. It's impossible to side with all the social agendas of our day and still insist on being biblical. If we get accused of being intolerant, it's inescapably the price we must pay for standing our ground as believers. When we reverently bow to the Lord, the gospel draws the same demarcation line as we draw. He offers real opportunities for profound change and discipleship to truth-seeking pilgrims (see Matt. 4:17, Rom. 12:1-2, Gal. 1:6-9, Jude 1:3-4). We need to contend for the faith because a diluted gospel will hinder people's salvation and cause us to misrepresent Jesus. The true gospel is holistic in the best sense of the term: God makes us whole by his Spirit to bring wholeness to others!

In our churches at large, ambitious agendas abound. Our selfish agendas must go if we want to be a part of the new wineskin God is creating. There is, in fact, no other way forward. Some people leave churches because they can't play first fiddle. Have these Christians become a bit pampered—wanting to be served instead of learning to serve? Community requires service and sacrifice. Commitment to God and each other is the backbone of any fellowship, conducive to friendship, trust and care. When people feel genuinely welcomed and valued, it's easier for them to participate and invest their time and resources. The church leaders set the temperature for the community through their warm and inclusive behaviour. The outcome is treasured members who are faithful and contribute to the fellowship massively. They have the potential to become future leaders. Local churches are indispensable: Stay plugged into a local church. Don't leave unless pastoral care is absent or biblical teachings are abandoned. Walk out in cases of misconduct and unbalanced preaching, and flee churches where leaders cover up or promote abuse. Manipulators expect a free pass to excuse their double standards by trying to absolve themselves of responsibility. Leaders lacking accountability and transparency confirms volatile environments. It's heart-rendering to hear all the stories of victims who had to pull out of churches due to spiritual, emotional or sexual abuse. Churches with predatory leadership will pursue your time and resources and ruthlessly demand your compliance. Tyrant leaders will set forth hilarious statutes, often disguised as conservative and biblical teachings, to hinder you from staying self-governed and emancipated. They will not hesitate for a second to limit your freedom. It's cultish and evil—you better run!

We read in Acts that the early believers followed the Way. They also *"belonged to the Way"*, another name for Jesus and his entourage (see John 14:6, Acts 9:2, 22:4 etc.). Isaiah prophesied: *"a highway will be there; it will be called the Way of Holiness"*; *"the redeemed will walk upon it"* (see Isa. 35:8-9). What does the Way of Holiness symbolise? This highway is spoken for since the remnant of God will wander upon it. Holy people walk the walk and talk the talk. No unrepentant or sinful person will ever enter the sacred Way of ransomed and redeemed saints. Sadly, there are wicked people who ridicule God's Word and trample on it. Sharing the gospel with scoffers is like casting pearls before swine (see Matt 7:6). Let us not waste time and effort on Christophobic individuals who wilfully reject the holy Way God entrusted to us. Biblical salvation arguably culminates in sanctification. Far too often, the world sees division among us because we fail to manifest a highway where others can encounter Christ's love for them. In the process of becoming a highway for the Lord, we learn to be laid down, yielded and humble to serve a greater purpose. An integral part of keeping the faith untarnished is refuting spurious teachers and their false doctrines. We do so to preserve a pure gospel in brotherly love. In Jerusalem, the church made the highway of holiness visible to such an extent that we read:

"Now they were steadfastly continuing in the teaching of the apostles, and in the fellowship, in the breaking of the bread, and in the prayer." (Acts 2:42 BSB).

"No one else dared join them, even though they were highly regarded by the people. Nevertheless, more and more men and women believed in the Lord and were added to their number." (Acts 5:13-14 NIV).

Jerusalem's High Council treated the first Christians as defectors of the Jewish faith because these truth-loving Jews embraced Yeshua as their Messiah by perceiving him as the awaited Hope of Israel (see Jer. 17:13, Acts 26:6-8, 28:20). Their impeached leader, the Nazarene, wasn't a ringleader for a weird and dangerous sect, but the Son of God. Rabbis frequently and falsely claim that Yeshua attempted to bring another religion than the Jewish faith, but their timeworn rhetoric is a part of their ongoing cover-up and denial. The real truth? Yeshua fulfilled the many ancient prophecies and revived Judaism by introducing the New Covenant - בְּרִית חֲדָשָׁה *B'rit Chadasha* - as predicted by God through the prophet Jeremiah (see Jer. 31:31-34).

The High Council's strong antagonism couldn't disband the devout believers of the Jerusalem church. Oddly enough, Jesus previously instructed them to go and spread the gospel to areas that matched the cities and regions where they ended up because of persecution. The disciples were scattered geographically—reluctantly dispersed as salt and light, but not shattered spiritually (see Acts 1:5-8, 8:1-4). Because God's majesty powerfully manifested through a community unified by a risen and living Saviour, the revival spread like an unstoppable wildfire. Jesus' disciples intimately knew the Way. Therefore, their movement was called the Way. Thus, the resurrected Lord confirmed his Word wherever his witnesses came (see Mark 16:19-20).

[81] Ancient Messianic Seal, found on Mount Zion, in Jerusalem.

---

[81] **Source:** olimpublications.com/MessianicSeal.htm

CHAPTER 8 - PROPHETIC PRESENCE

Understanding the anointing

Understanding the anointing and how it operates is central to Kingdom ministry. Every born-again believer has the Holy Spirit indwelling in their spirit man (see John 3:3-5, Rom. 8:9, Eph. 1:13). The Father's equipping presence, the anointing—in Greek *chrisma*, meaning 'smearing'—is resting upon all God's true children. *"But you have an anointing from the Holy One, and all of you know the truth." "As for you, the anointing you received from him remains in you, and you do not need anyone to teach you. But as his anointing teaches you about all things and as that anointing is real, not counterfeit; just as it has taught you, remain in him."* (1 John 2:24, 27 NIV). In the Old Covenant, only a few individuals were anointed with oil to ordain them for office: priests, kings and prophets. Anointment with olive oil was associated with godly service—being equipped by the Spirit—for their individual assignment. After the anointing took place, God's Spirit would usually fall upon that individual with power and wisdom (see Num. 11:16-17, 26-29, Judg. 14:5-6). In the same way, the Spirit of God rested on the waters when God spoke Creation into being: *"the Spirit of God moved upon the face of the waters"* (see Gen. 1:2). God's Holy Spirit entered into, rested upon, and filled certain individuals during the period of the Law and the Prophets. We cannot know for sure whether the Spirit permanently resided in the spirits of these anointed kings, priests and prophets. Somehow, that elevated state seems to be a privilege reserved exclusively for the born-again believers of the New Covenant. John the Baptist seems to be an exception that proves the rule. While he was still a foetus, he leapt in the womb—moved by God's Spirit: *"For he will be great in the sight of the Lord, and he will drink no wine or liquor; and he will be filled with the Holy Spirit, while yet in his mother's womb."* (Luke 1:15 NASB 1995). *"When Elizabeth heard Mary's greeting, the baby leaped in her womb, and Elizabeth was filled with the Holy Spirit."* (Luke 1:41 NASB).

Right at the outset of the Old Covenant, the Lord filled the craftsman Bezalel with his Spirit: *"See, I have chosen Bezalel son of Uri, the son of Hur, of the tribe of Judah, and I have filled him with the Spirit of God, with wisdom, with understanding, with knowledge and with all kinds of skills—to make artistic designs."* (Exod. 31:2-3 NIV). Uri means 'my enlightenment', and Bezalel translates 'in the shadow or the protection of God.' This is the first instance in Scripture where a person was filled with God's Spirit. It's striking because Bezalel was not anointed to preach. He was an artisan of items for the holy Tabernacle, using his artistic prowess to furnish and decorate God's abode. Man was created *"in the image and likeness of God"* (see Gen. 1:26). As humans, we tap into divine creativity. We reflect God's attributes because we are his co-labourers. In our spirit exists a vast capability to visualise and create, an inherent desire inspired by the Holy Spirit. The Lord defines us in stunning ways: Through his brilliant design of our nature, through the cross, through his Word and also through our talents and gifts. Following the Spirit baptism, God sets about to activate the potential within—inspiring and empowering us to flow creatively. And if the flow stops, we should repent and revive the gifts again with the help of the same Spirit (see 2 Tim. 1:6-7). New Testament ministry is based on a supernatural lifestyle and cannot be separated from the outpouring of his Spirit. It's also evident that the revolutionising Pentecostal experience remains the principal catalyst for salvations and miracles and growing churches around the world.

Healing ⇔ Power ⇒ Creativity
Peace ⇔ Gift ⇒ Inspiration

Following the Spirit baptism, God sets about to activate the potential within—inspiring and empowering us to flow creatively.

When Jesus presented his powerful ministry, he did so with an announcement by quoting the prophet Isaiah's words: *"The Spirit of the LORD God is upon me, because the LORD has anointed me to bring good news to the poor; he has sent me to bind up the broken-hearted, to proclaim liberty to the captives, and the opening of the prison to those who are bound; to proclaim the year of the LORD's favour, and the day of vengeance of our God; to comfort all who mourn; to grant to those who mourn in Zion—to give them a beautiful headdress instead of ashes, the oil of gladness instead of mourning, the garment of praise instead of a faint spirit; that they may be called oaks of righteousness, the planting of the LORD, that he may be glorified. They shall build up the ancient ruins; they shall raise up the former devastations; they shall repair the ruined cities, the devastations of many."* (Isa. 61:1-4 ESV). An excerpt from Isaiah's scroll was read by Jesus in his hometown's synagogue, in Nazareth (see Luke 4:18-19). He finished reading, but ended with the words *"the Lord's favour"*. Jesus' emphasis was done with deliberate intent: He came to proclaim the Lord's favour! As predicted by Isaiah, a new era and reality were ushered in by the Messiah's arrival. Messiah means 'the Anointed One', and Jesus showed us how God's Spirit operates when he fully rests upon a human being. Jesus carried the anointing without limits because he was pure and without sin (see John 3:34). He performed God's work and taught God's words (see Acts 1:1). Because of his sacrifice, the same Spirit that raised Christ from the dead now dwells within us: *"The Spirit of God, who raised Jesus from the dead, lives in you. And just as God raised Christ Jesus from the dead, he will give life to your mortal bodies by this same Spirit living within you."* (Rom. 8:11 NLT).

Understandably, the anointing is not for personal gain but for godly service. What luxury compares to the mighty infilling by the Holy Spirit? When his majestic Spirit moves in and through us—overtaking our conditions with God's blessings—it's joy unspeakable. Our walk in grace is far from a mediocre, monotonous or conventional lifestyle, although our expressions of faith are vague, stale and mundane at times. That is never the case with the remarkable, larger-than-life and riveting Holy Spirit! There is constant energy, flow, light and creativity in him. Abiding in his glorious presence is sacred and indescribable. The Lord's anointing permeates atmospheres and attitudes. The three branches of government are also mirrored in the Godhead: the Legislative, the Judicial and the Executive. God's Spirit represents the executive branch of the Holy Trinity. He is the provider of forgiveness, healing, deliverance and peace and directly completes all God's actions and transactions. That is why the Bible urges us to revere him and be careful not to insult his royal dignity (see Matt. 12:31, Eph. 4:30, Heb. 10:26-29). It is comparable to mocking someone's mother, the ultimate disrespect in most cultures. God also carries a motherly side, revealed by his Spirit. Being born by the Spirit, we are definitely God's children. Does it imply that he is feminine? No, but the Spirit brings to the table a wide array of God's caring attributes, like a mother's bottomless compassion and empathy. Strikingly, the word compassion in Hebrew is רַחַם *racham*. The womb, or uterus, is רֶחֶם *rechem*. These are almost identical expressions. It cannot be accidental, as God very intentionally demonstrates his affection towards us. Driven by the Spirit, Paul told the Galatians that he suffered on behalf of them all, not unlike a mother in childbirth: *"Oh, my dear children! I feel as if I'm going through labour pains for you again, and they will continue until Christ is fully developed in your lives."* (Gal. 4:19 NLT). He prayed and interceded deeply for them, with signs of spiritual and emotional distress.

Isaiah chapter 61 describes at least three areas where the Lord intervenes through the anointing: 1) redemptive power 2) restorative power 3) reformative power. The redemptive power brings freedom through the gospel. It ends suffering, brokenness and oppression. Forgiveness, healing and deliverance from addictions flow from his redemptive power. It implies that the gospel does not become good news for people until its effects are noticeable—for spirit, soul and body. Its true power shows itself through reconciliation, with families reconciled and people beginning to lead lives full of integrity! Regrettably, some churches focus their core message on a health and wealth gospel—a distorted version of the authentic gospel. It's theologically fallible and closer to New Age doctrines. Most believers are God-fearing, loving and hardworking—not opportunistic, rich and entitled evangelicals.

I don't think our mission as Christians is to pursue every sphere of government and power. Neither do I claim that we should refrain from the decision-making arenas. There has to be a balance in our approach. The call to disciple nations isn't the same as dictating a country's national policies. Historically, the Judeo-Christian mindset brought great blessings to the world based on its biblical values. And, despite all our efforts, it's not the Church that will end the present evil age, but eventually Christ himself. He will establish his thousand-year reign of peace, as mentioned in chapter 5. I believe in revival and awakening, but I don't expect the Church to conquer the supposed seven mountains before Christ's return. Nonetheless, I trust the Lord to raise up righteous people within these important spheres of influence.

Our call to disciple nations is not the same as dictating all policies.

God's restorative power brings relief. It removes the scars of sin and despair from our lives. Where the Lord restores hope, he gives beauty for ashes and healing. In the Presence, we get the oil of gladness instead of mourning because loss and grief fade away. Holy laughter often manifests when God pours out his love on us. As former seasons of darkness peter out, he infuses us with new strength for the seasons ahead. Garments of praise mark our thankfulness and confidence in God's promises. The reformative power takes up residence in redeemed, restored and equipped saints who extend blessings to families, communities and cities. God gloriously transforms misery into ministry, testing into testimony and breakdown into breakthrough. He wants us to represent him in recognisable ways in this world and therefore shapes us into mighty oaks of righteousness for the sheer display of his glory. Christianity is more often described as 'seeing the light' rather than being the light, which is sad. Our assignment is to be the illuminated city on the hill, a shining lighthouse full of life (see Matt. 5:14). What we pursue is more than individual salvation. The Father wants transformation on a grand scale! A war consists of multiple battles, and we win souls one by one. God won't be satisfied until we, as an undivided community, corporately carry his light to the nations (see Isa. 42:6). Consequently, we should never count on Christian nations but on Christians being a holy nation *within* every nation! Together, we will explore the corporate anointing later in this chapter.

Pentecost caused a dramatic shift when the first believers of the New Covenant were baptised with the Holy Spirit (see Acts 2). Tongues of fire manifested and rested upon the heads of the disciples gathered in an upper room, those who waited for the fulfilment of the Father's promise (see Luke 24:49, Acts 1:4). After they had been clothed with power from the presence of the Lord, they left their prayer meeting and flooded the streets, declaring the good news in [82]different languages under the Spirit's inspiration. The supernatural event of Pentecost sparked a confidence to evangelise the Jews gathered in Jerusalem during Shavuot, or the Feast of Weeks. It marked a reversal of God's judgement at the tower of Babel, where he confused the languages of the peoples that rebelled against his lordship (see Gen. 11:1-9). People

---

[82] **Tongues:** Two different words are used for tongues: We find the first in Acts 2:6 - *dialekto*, meaning known language - (dialect comes from this word). The second, *glossolalia* appears in the New Testament, a combination of the noun γλῶσσα *glōssa* and verb λαλέω *laleo* (Mark 16:17, Acts 10:44-46, 19:6, 1 Cor. 14). Tongues ascribe to the operation of the Holy Spirit - a capability to articulate earthly and heavenly languages unbeknownst to the speaker (see 1 Cor. 13:1).

from these nationalities were now assembled in Jerusalem, and they heard the gospel preached in their own native languages. For obvious reasons, they marvelled. Most of Jesus' followers were manual and unschooled workers, although a few were wealthy, well-educated and synagogue-trained. They couldn't possibly understand foreign languages, let alone master them. Until this watershed moment in history, such a supernatural event was unheard-of. It was a dramatic sign to the crowd. The overwhelming result was three thousand people turning to the Messiah in one day, receiving new life in the Crucified One. That was the second reversal of events from the Old Covenant: When God appeared in glory at Sinai, during the first Pentecost, three thousand people perished at the time the Law was given (see Exod. 32:28).

Seeing the Light

Being the Light

Christianity is most often described as 'seeing the light' rather than being the light, which is sad.

The anointing rested upon the Spirit-filled believers when they assembled, albeit not as an impersonal force. Be sure to associate the anointing with him, the precious person of the Holy Spirit. The unrestricted anointing rested upon the Son of Man. It was the driving force behind all the healings, miracles and deliverances we read about in the four gospels. Totally depending on the person of the Spirit, Jesus Christ modelled for us how to do life and ministry. Our point of reference is: *"Jesus of Nazareth, how God anointed Him with the Holy Spirit and with power, and how He went about doing good and healing all who were oppressed by the devil, for God was with Him."* (Acts 10:38 NASB). Some charismatic camps interpret the practical bit quite one-sidedly because they presume that doing good is indistinguishable from healings and miracles. The answer can be both yes and no. Anointing is much more, it relates to serving with kindness—doing considerate, compassionate and unselfish deeds. The world longs to see credible Christians who aren't dodgy or two-faced! Of course, the unchecked narcissistic quest for miracle power has to stop. Like our Lord, you have power if you remain truthful and kind, despite persecution. For unbelievers, *that* is a miracle in itself. *"The Spirit of the LORD shall rest upon him, the Spirit of wisdom and understanding, the Spirit of counsel and might, the Spirit of knowledge and of the fear of the LORD, and He will delight in the fear of the Lord."* (Isa. 11:2–3 NASB).

Depending on the person of the Spirit, Jesus modelled for us how to do life and ministry.

The Spirit of the Lord rested on Jesus in a sevenfold way. We see this in the Book of Revelation: *"And out of the throne proceed lightnings and voices and thunders. And there were seven lamps of fire burning before the throne, which are the seven Spirits of God ..."* (Rev. 4:5 ASV).

These are the seven spirits of God:
1) **The Spirit of the Lord** - giving authority; 2) **The Spirit of wisdom** - giving discernment and skill; 3) **The Spirit of understanding** - giving perception and revelation; 4) **The Spirit of counsel** - giving guidance and instruction; 5) **The Spirit of might** - giving power and strength; 6) **The Spirit of knowledge** - giving facts and insight; 7) **The Spirit of the fear of the Lord** - giving holy integrity and self-control.

The anointing carries with it the absolute lordship of the Holy Spirit. We experience freedom where his lordship is welcomed. *"Now the Lord is the Spirit, and where the Spirit of the Lord is, there is freedom."* (2 Cor. 3:17 ESV). We can interpret this verse as follows: The remaining six functions of the sevenfold Spirit will be visible if we yield to the authority of the Lord. The result is liberty. Spiritual liberty manifests as peace, wisdom, understanding, counsel, might, knowledge and godly fear. Jesus said this: *"By the Spirit of God ... the kingdom of God has come upon you."* (Matt. 12:28). If his lordship is received—through the Spirit—the anointing will come on people and dispel dependency, demons and disease. Once more, we read: *"For God has not given us a spirit of timidity, but of power, love, and self-control."* (2 Tim. 1:7 BSB). Spiritual freedom will manifest as power, love and self-control, which proves authentic faith. In the epistle of James, we come across another description of the anointing: *"But the wisdom from above is first pure, then peaceable, gentle, open to reason, full of mercy and good fruits, impartial and sincere."* (James 3:17 ESV). The quoted passages perfectly explain the many important purposes and functions of the anointing. What does the anointing cause? The letter to the Galatians sums up the fruit of the Spirit: The first aspect is love (Gal. 5:22-23, Rom. 14:17). Agape love is the ultimate expression of God's nature and explains why Jesus ministered out of compassion. Jesus demonstrated the Father's love as he went about doing good. One of the early disciples, Barnabas, followed in the same steps as his beloved Master: *"He was a good man, full of the Holy Spirit and of faith. And a great many people were added to the Lord."* (Acts 11:24 ESV). Whereas the petrified company of disciples questioned Paul's conversion, the discerning and tender-hearted Barnabas vouched for him and safely introduced him to the church in Jerusalem (see Acts 9:26-28).

Much to my chagrin and disappointment, Christians regularly fail to show common courtesy in simple day-to-day settings, us preachers included. These clear disparities between our words and actions are disgraceful and damage our reputation. If we treat restaurant staff rudely or are unreasonable in business dealings, the apple has fallen far from the tree. Daily life provides plenty of opportunities to represent the gospel through selflessness and generosity (see Acts 10:38). Do we seize and sanctify those precious moments by the grace of God? *"You are the epistle of Christ ... "* (see 2 Cor. 3:3). Living with integrity, privately and publicly, is essential. Let us learn from our mistakes and instead try to *fail forward*. Compartmentalisation is dangerous and thrives when we justify and practise incongruent values and ethics. Our public persona and image may look immaculate, while we, at the same time, indulge in deviant behaviour in private. We feed a dominant dark side of our lives if we secretly entertain sinful habits. Jesus warned about this great danger: *"Woe to you, teachers of the law and Pharisees, you hypocrites! You are like whitewashed tombs, which look beautiful on the outside, but on the inside are full of dead men's bones and everything unclean."* (Matt. 23:27 NIV). The nature of hypocrisy is pretence—self-righteous attitudes are contrary to the gospel message. It's also a theological problem because by allowing unredeemed flaws in our character, we profane the Lord's holy name.

People should praise God because of us and not curse us. We were supposed to be Christ's love letters to our neighbours. (See Matt. 5:16, 1 Pet. 4:16). If we want our community to receive our testimony, sanctification is all-important. We should be wholesome and trustworthy ministers, whether we stand behind a pulpit or not (see 1 Tim. 3:1-12, 2 Tim. 2:22-26). However, it's possible to use gifts and anointings to build Christian ministries in order to gain both riches and popularity. Still, gauging a ministry's success based on favour or achievements isn't rock-solid proof of our obedience as ministers. God doesn't assess us purely on that basis but looks deeper. He adds more variables, like godly character and honesty. Can people see Christ in you? Are you wholehearted and reliable? Do you have an eternal perspective? God values this more than prosperity, the size of your ministry or your public image.

Compartmentalisation is dangerous.

We should exercise every God-given gift with a clean conscience before the Father. It's possible to operate the spiritual gifts despite our sinfulness because God's gifts are irrevocable (see Rom. 11:29). Some churchgoers are shocked on hearing this, but it's a sad fact supported by human experience. Because they engage in lawlessness, Jesus announced that many who call him Lord—and even work miracles in his name—will later be rejected by him (see Matt. 7:21-23). Jesus highlights two specific points: 1) 'I never *knew* you', or 'We didn't have an intimate friendship'. 2) 'You practised *lawlessness*', which means that [83]they practised iniquity or were living in habitual sins they refused to give up. Sins like lust, [84]avarice and unforgiveness have likely caused countless professing Christians to capsize on their spiritual journey and sink due to a lost faith. Such a grisly fate is unsettling, to say the least. Superficial, half-hearted confessions are never pleasing to the Father, who wants us to undergo a profound change of heart. Living in daily repentance is vital, as it keeps our lives unblemished. It helps us safely abide in the holy fear of the Lord. But what is daily repentance? It's constantly resting in the Lord's unceasing love for us by not hiding our shortcomings or sins. It's turning to God again and again, as he is our victory.

---

[83] **My comment:** The phrase *"I never knew you"* doesn't speak about false Christians but refers to a backslidden condition. For further study, read about it in Ezek. 3:17-21; 33:7-9, 12-20.

[84] **Avarice:** an extremely strong wish to get or keep money or possessions. Source: dictionary.cambridge.org/dictionary/english/avarice

Ask brothers and sisters to stand with you in prayer. Never give up! Let us focus on Jesus alone because he is the perfecter of our faith. He helps us to trust him more unreservedly day by day. Faith and holiness are about developing refined attitudes of the heart while receiving the Father's overflowing love for us. Jesus said this: *"Be perfect, therefore, as your heavenly Father is perfect."* (Matt. 5:48 NIV). Another passage reads: *"Be merciful, just as your Father is merciful."* (Luke 6:36 NIV). When combining these two passages, we see how loving with God's heart is *perfection* after Heaven's standards. Abba sculpts us into the image of his love-filled Son: Through the phenomenal work of the Holy Spirit, he forms Christ's nature within us. If we let him change us through repentance, he can even redeem our flaws and imperfections for his perfect purposes (see Rom. 8:28-29, Gal. 4:19).

James wrote about the wisdom from above. He depicted it as an anointing—which is first of all pure. Our motives are being purified by the Holy Spirit until our only desire is to please God. The early Methodists actively sought the power of the Spirit. They didn't pursue it for personal kicks or goosebumps but for sanctification! God's wisdom is always peace-loving, seeking harmony and reconciliation. It's gentle and attentive and helps us to behave politely—showing dignity and respect. Faith works through love, and the anointing flows through love the same way: *"Love is patient, love is kind. It does not envy, it does not boast, it is not proud. It is not rude, it is not self-seeking, it is not easily angered, it keeps no record of wrongs. Love does not delight in evil but rejoices with the truth. It always protects, always trusts, always hopes, always perseveres."* (1 Cor. 13:4-7 NIV). This quote characterises the anointing. God's love respects authority without hesitation (see Rom. 13:1-8, 1 Pet. 2:13-21). His love is full of mercy and good fruits—it makes hearts compassionate and generous. It never shows partiality. It's not judgemental or biased. God's love isn't hypocritical because it dismisses double standards through self-restraint and consistency. Through his mighty Spirit, God's love and wisdom transform us to become more like Jesus!

The purpose of the baptism of the Holy Spirit is to *empower us as witnesses* and to *host his presence*. God anoints our attitudes and character when we remain in a close relationship with him. Can Christians become a 'landing field' for the Holy Spirit, a habitation prepared for him? That mystery is unravelled by true worshippers, but yes! My attitude towards him should always be: 'I am seeking your face, not only your hands.' We should desire God *himself*, not merely his gifts or provision. Do we seek his blessings or the face of the Blessed One? Let us not use God as an excuse to achieve selfish dreams, but rather pray for *his* dreams to be fulfilled through us! (See Psalm 139:16-18, Jer. 29:11 and 1 Cor. 2:9).

Let us take a look at this statement: *"But you have been anointed by the Holy One, and you all have knowledge."* (See 1 John 2:20 ESV). Because the Holy Spirit lives in our hearts, we now access revelation through the anointing. This is how we know all things. *All things* refer to discernment to unmask deceptive beliefs and the devil's schemes. The baptism of the Holy Spirit helps us to develop a hunger for *the things of God*. In our longing for the authentic presence of Jesus, we learn to recognise his voice: *"My sheep listen to my voice; I know them, and they follow me."* (John 10:27 NLT). All believers should know the mind of Christ (see 1 Cor. 2:16, 1 John 4:13-16). God's pure love is shed abroad in our hearts by the Holy Spirit (see Rom. 5:5). The anointing is constantly operational when we discover how to bask in his love, abide in his words and seek his counsel. As Christians, should we fret about what is fake, false or phoney? Not at all! We learn to discern counterfeits, often in an instant, through the anointing, by seeking God's face. And, if a lie isn't detected instantly, the Holy Spirit will expose it gradually while we pray over it and study the Word.

Are you called to be a spiritual watchman, moving in the prophetic seer realm? Find out if what you see is something you can share with others or if God shows it to you strictly as a matter of prayer. When you pray, ask God to show you more and what to do with it. Revelations can be very powerful and impart huge blessings to others. The discerning of spirits is vital because this gift has been given to the Church both to warn and to safeguard us. At times, demonic spirits and people's bad intentions get exposed when we use it. That can be quite scary. Through this ability, I have also sensed the presence of angels or discovered other believers' gifts or callings (see Luke 2:25-35; 6:12-16, John 1:45-50, Acts 8:18-23; 13:6-12; 16:16-19 etc.).

The anointing is constantly operational as we discover how to bask in his love, abide in his words and seek his counsel.

We chase after Jesus because we love him! The romantic lover in Song of Songs sought her lover's face and her lover's voice (see Song of Songs 2:14). When we enjoy an intimate relationship with somebody, we recognise their face and their voice. We even sense their thoughts. So it also is with the holy interaction between us and our Lord Jesus: Our closeness with him grows daily, and we know that *"perfect love casts out fear"* (see 1 John 4:18). We are wowed and wooed by the inconceivable love of God! Our humanity plays out amid a breathtaking divine love story. Have you seen how a courting couple suddenly reacts if an intruder attempts to break up their close relationship or plots to divert their affection? Lovers only have eyes for each other. In our love for our supreme King and Bridegroom, we dispel the clamouring voices and mindsets that don't agree with our sanctified unity with him. We gaze at his face to receive grace for the race (see Heb. 12:1-2). King David wrote so beautifully: *"I have set Jehovah always before me: Because he is at my right hand, I shall not be moved."* (Psalm 16:8 ASV). Let nothing or nobody steal your gaze!

We experience oneness in the Holy Spirit when we gather in the Lord's name. While praying, worshipping, sharing the Word and using the spiritual gifts, the following dynamic unfolds: When we, as a Body, partner with his presence, we manifest and partake in a corporate anointing. In Paul's prayer in Eph. 3:14-21, he primarily prays about two things: 1) For all believers to encounter Christ's love on a *deeply personal level*. 2) For all believers to receive the revelation of God's love and be filled with the fullness of him on *a corporate level*. In the congregation, we appreciate the anointing released through individuals who use spiritual gifts and ministry gifts. It seems like Paul's desire was to contend for a greater corporate anointing within the whole Body of Christ. The Lord Jesus is present whenever we gather for his purposes—a reality that goes far beyond personal anointing. Jesus said: *"For where two or three gather in my name, there am I with them."* (Matt. 18:20 NIV). The union of two or three people is the smallest operational unit in God's kingdom. We can always expect the manifest presence of Jesus when a Christian couple comes together in the Name. What could be more formidable than that? A corporate anointing brings a covering. That *covering* is the person of *Christ*, who protects us and breaks through for us. Jesus regularly sent teams ahead of him, two by two, to every village and town he intended to visit. Jesus was resourceful and inventive—a strategist (see Luke 10:1).

It's like spiritual guerrilla warfare when he sends us on prophetic missions for his Name's sake, where small teams work as highly effective special operations units!

When we, as a Body, partner with his presence, we manifest and partake in a corporate anointing.

The apostle Paul knew very well that he carried a weighty apostolic anointing for breakthrough—indispensable when he ventured into unknown territories—yet he routinely worked within compact teams. What could be Paul's motivation? Well, he obviously understood spiritual relationships and their powerful dynamics in moving as one body through the corporate anointing. It's astonishing what we read:

"Now when I went to Troas to preach the gospel of Christ and found that the Lord had opened a door for me, I still had no peace of mind, because I did not find my brother Titus there. So I said goodbye to them and went on to Macedonia. But thanks be to God, who always leads us as captives in Christ's triumphal procession and uses us to spread the aroma of the knowledge of him. For we are to God the pleasing aroma of Christ among those who are being saved and those who are perishing. To the one we are an aroma that brings death; to the other, an aroma that brings life. And who is equal to such a task? Unlike so many, we do not peddle the word of God for profit. On the contrary, in Christ we speak before God with sincerity, as those sent from God." (2 Cor. 2:12-17 NIV).

Paul had a huge opportunity to preach openly in Troas, a Roman colony in Asia Minor. He distinctly discerned a climate welcoming to the gospel. Still, he moved on to Macedonia! At first glance, his tactic seemed somewhat irrational, but Paul was extremely strategic and wise. He had no peace of mind or *"peace in his spirit"* as his brother Titus was nowhere to be found. Like Paul, Titus was also an apostle. It was the selfsame Titus whom Paul tasked to complete his mission work in Crete by appointing elders in every town (see Tit. 1:5). In his letter to dear Titus, he greets him with these opening words: *"To Titus, the apostle"*. However, most translations lack the opening phrase. I believe this manuscript, used in my study Bible, to be authentic. Apropos of that, the ministry gift of the apostle is the most mentioned office in the New Testament. If you doubt me, check for yourself. Paul found it necessary to cooperate with the apostolic anointing Titus carried because something powerful happened when these brothers ministered together. Being inseparable, they became invincible! These brilliant men of God, like peas in a pod, *"spread the aroma of the knowledge of him"*, and were *"to God the pleasing aroma of Christ"*, as well as *"an aroma that brings life."* (2 Cor. 2:14-17).

To be a loner or a recluse is unscriptural. No man or woman is an island. For the sake of prayer, we only seek seclusion for some time. Apostles and prophets need to establish positive and steady friendships. The same relates to all ministry gifts. The Lord dislikes attitudes of independence and ambition. Revival history shows that pride and envy separated influential preachers. They pulled back when they should have sought closer relationships with peers. In unprecedented ways, God pours out his many blessings on us when we learn to be close-knit and choose *interdependence* through love. Growing in our gifts is imperative. Still, there is more land to conquer. God starts to release a mighty flow of the corporate anointing when we nurture and develop loving relationships. All our endeavours to excel in love will advance the Kingdom and bring corporate blessings upon churches, communities, regions and even nations. If we look at the Great Commission, we see how Jesus instructed his apostles to disciple nations (see Matt. 28:19). This great mission to evangelise had its beginning in Jerusalem and extended *"to the ends of the earth."* (Acts 1:8). God wants to revive that calling by raising up *apostolic teams* within cities and nations.

In unprecedented ways, God pours out his many blessings on us when we learn to be close-knit and choose interdependence through love.

Another glimpse of how the corporate anointing works in a church is found in the following passage: *"But if an unbeliever or an inquirer comes in while everyone is prophesying, they are convicted of sin and are brought under judgement by all, as the secrets of their hearts are laid bare. So they will fall down and worship God, exclaiming, "God is really among you!"* (1 Cor. 14:24-25 NIV). When Paul taught about the proper use of spiritual gifts, he stressed the distinctions between the gifts of tongues and prophecy. A situation where the limbs of the local church body flow together in prayer or the gift of prophecy can release the manifest presence of God. A dense cloud of anointing causes sinners to repent in an atmosphere effectively supercharged by prayer and prophecy. A distinguished Nordic preacher—at that time a glowing Marxist—attended a protest against the Vietnam War. It was freezing outside. A voice told her to go inside a church nearby to get warm. She was reluctant at first, but an irresistible pull brought her to a prayer meeting. These believers spoke with her and invited her to a gathering, where she later gave her life to the Lord. The Holy Spirit masterfully captivated a hungry heart. After this experience, she realised that her salvation was orchestrated by divine appointment and not by chance.

Under the Old Covenant, individuals got incapacitated by God's glory on several occasions. In one instance, the backslidden and demonised regent Saul was in hot pursuit of David because of his personal vendetta against him. Coming to Nevaioth, near Ramah, the king fell to the ground and began to prophesy (see 1 Sam. 19:19-24). Unknowingly, he went straight into a cloud of thick prophetic anointing. Saul, with his escort of soldiers, was disarmed by the prayerful environment Samuel had generated through immense intercession and prophecy. It created a place where the anointing rested, a hotspot where the Lord could move without restrictions. Before this, the young and anointed David brought Saul relief by skilfully worshipping on his lyre. When he shortly after had to duck the envious king's unforgiving spears, he hurriedly fled the court (see 1 Sam. 16:14-23, 19:9).

During a spiritual outpouring in my Norwegian hometown, Larvik, incredible reports came in: Christians visiting from other places got baptised with the Spirit the very moment they crossed the city limits! Apostles and prophets carry open heavens to impact locations the Lord sends them to. This enables angelic hosts to be dispatched and breakthroughs to manifest more frequently. God typically assigns specific geographical areas to certain ministries, as he did with the prophet Samuel.

Amid the well-known Azusa Street Outpouring (1906–1909), it was very common to find people struck down by God's Spirit quite some distance from the sanctuary. People fell to the ground because they were undone by the mighty presence of the Lord. Unknowingly and unexpectedly, they had entered the 'Kingdom zone'!

A dense cloud of anointing causes sinners to repent in an atmosphere effectively supercharged by prayer and prophecy.

During the years of outpouring, many of the members in a small Pentecostal church on [85]Azusa Street moved in signs, wonders and healings. They saw instant miracles, like limbs and teeth growing out, etc. With their praying pastor and apostle, the black holiness preacher William J. Seymour, this flock carried a corporate anointing that brought glorious salvation to many, touching thousands of lives. Seymour, who was a dedicated servant of the Lord, prayed for 5–7 hours a day for years until he finally became a mighty vessel in his Master's hands. Influenced by divine encounters, godly wisdom began to govern the lives of countless individuals, breaking the moulds of human limitations. We might wish for people to be 'zapped' or enwrapped by God's Spirit, but maybe we should adopt a long-term perspective. Revival history shows that manifestations like being slain in the Spirit, having open visions, visitations, and other unexpected encounters don't have to end there. It's impressive to see how God changed ordinary people into conduits of transformative power. Their testimonies impacted the society around them for decades and sometimes centuries.

When God's Spirit is heavily resting on specific, territorial areas, the Bible refers to it as [86]*kratos* power (see Acts 19:20). In Ephesus, this category of power manifested through the preaching and miracles of Paul and his team. *Kratos* relates to the ruling and manifest presence of the Almighty. During the Welsh revival (1904–1905), God's holy presence moved from village to village, causing sinners to repent. Strong conviction, brought by the Spirit, hit people at home and on the streets. Repenting villagers sent for the priests to get right with the Lord. We should ask ourselves this question: Are we hungry for revival? Are we willing to contend in prayer and fasting

---

[85] **See also:** decadeofpentecost.org/ebooks/Azusa-English.pdf
[86] **My comment:** κράτος *kratos*. Other Greek words in the New Testament about power are δύναμις *dunamis*, ἐξουσία *exousia*, ἐνέργεια *energeia* and ἰσχύς *ischyos*.

for similar outpourings? God wants his incredible love, power and presence to be unrestrained. The knowledge of his glory should fill the earth (see Hab. 2:14). Day and night, his resurrection life in us is supposed to flow out from us: Jesus said this: *"Whoever believes in me, as the Scripture has said, 'Out of his heart will flow rivers of living water.'"* (John 7:38 ESV). God wants rivers, not stagnant and putrid ponds: The life that flows into you from him is most potent when it is *released*, not held onto like a lake such as the Dead Sea. Jesus said: *"Heal the sick, raise the dead, cleanse those who have leprosy, drive out demons. Freely you have received; freely give."* (Matt. 10:8 NIV). He also said, *"Whoever has will be given more; whoever does not have, even what they have will be taken from them."* (Mark 4:25 NLT). What you receive and release will increase. This is a rudimentary biblical principle. We initiate a release of God's saving power by saturating the atmosphere with testimonies and persistent prayer. When we build in the Spirit, it creates a climate full of hope and faith! If we rightly steward our personal encounters with God today, it will determine our level of breakthrough for tomorrow. Salvations and wonders will erupt in our midst!

According to research, Christians in the West rarely share their faith in Christ. These statistics are alarming! Cults, like the Mormons and Jehovah's Witnesses, are doing more to spread their twisted message. If we privatise our faith by only saying we are Christians when asked directly about it, do we have the actual right to complain when secular humanism or Islam flood our countries? To daily discuss politics or the latest sporting events doesn't seem to bother us in the least. But could we, by choice, commit ourselves to proactively sharing the eternal gospel? Telling the good news about Jesus should be a matter of love because his Holy Spirit compels us to do it. Let me illustrate with a personal testimony: An episode at a former workplace a few years ago comes to mind. I went on break, scanned my employee card and noticed the time. It was 10:35 am, to be exact. A verse from Hebrews 10:35 came to mind. It encourages us not to throw away our confidence as believers. I knew that God's Spirit prodded me to testify to my co-workers. Unsurprisingly, some well-timed minutes into the break, I got a golden moment to speak freely about my faith.

What you receive and release will increase.

The Lord wants rivers, not confined ponds. If rivers of living water constantly flow from us, people will associate us with the very thing we release: *"But let justice roll on like a river, righteousness like a never-failing stream!"* (Amos 5:24 NIV). The river symbolises God's holy presence and rich blessings. It also illustrates God-given opportunities. Our mission is to release overflowing life and hope to a dying world. We are called to move with God in order to become *the move* of God! We are all called, as a corporate Body, to demonstrate the River. I remember a dream: High up in the mountains, a handful of preachers convened in an office in a building. I saw the clear blue sky through a window nearby, and the sun shone brightly. From this elevated vantage point, we overlooked a big valley with lush and verdant forest. The room belonged to a famous preacher, whose name I will not disclose. It was what he signified that seemed pertinent in the dream. Although he is contested, he believes in nurturing an environment for miracles through testimonies, as it generates faith for stronger breakthroughs. By the way, most of our churches have inconsistencies and faults, but does it rule out the fact that our God encounters and uses individuals and groups who are chasing after him? In reality, the Lord uses fragile and flawed people all the time. This bothersome truth seriously messes with our beliefs because God is not as unbending as you and me. We often gloss over inconvenient parts of treasured Bible stories without realising that we would likely dismiss these fallible heroes of faith under similar circumstances today. I wonder if we would cordially welcome the racy Rahab, who lied about the spies, or the temptress Tamar, who seduced Judah and tricked him into getting her pregnant. (See Gen. 38 and Jos. 2). The point is, in my dream, the pastor addressed a young man and prophesied over him. He called him by a new name and boldly stated: "You are River!" The man shook violently and fell under God's power. To me, this dream confirmed that the Lord wants to raise up a generation of hungry believers possessed by his love. These believers are determined to *"follow the Lamb wherever he goes"* (see Rev. 14:4). Sold-out, courageous worshippers will carry the supernatural realm of the Holy Spirit in ways the world has yet to see and become a visible manifestation of his move.

Some time ago, the headline in a local newspaper spoke strongly to my heart. It was 'Roads turn into rivers'. A YouTube video about the same incident had the title 'Roads turn into rivers after biblical rain'. Roads represent God's Word, and rivers God's power. The Word and the Spirit will soon merge into one mighty stream. The picture is unmistakably clear: We live in a time and age where the Lord wants to manifest his glorious truth through signs and wonders in incredible ways. But signs and wonders were supposed to follow us, not us following them. As followers of Christ, we have to resist sensationalism. However, we should fully receive Jesus as our Saviour, Healer and Deliverer. The Holy Spirit works non-stop to convince and convict people powerfully through the gospel. The notion that a church becomes unwholesome once supernatural signs begin to occur is fear-driven. Of course, neither emotional outbursts nor miracles can by themselves generate a dynamic faith, but preaching the gospel should lead to repentance for sinners and recovery for sufferers. Many churches are afraid to lose their reputation as they want to pick and choose. A few churches are willing to take risks in pursuing a fuller expression of the gospel while enduring slanderous and untrue accusations in the process.

Resisting controlling spirits
The greatest threat against any move of God seems to be religious spirits. They want to put an end to all fivefold ministry. These menacing spirits are trying to side-track and seduce unaware believers. Religious spirits are identified as anti-Christ or anti-anointing spirits since they hate God's Word. Satan furiously seeks to assault what is devastating to him: The anointing. He understands that attack is the best form of defence. With his long-established and well-proven strategy, he secretly hides within the unsuspicious ranks of believers. Detecting controlling spirits and their trickery can sometimes be challenging. Let us describe their plan of action in three parts:

1. **Manipulation** - operating through guilt, seduction and self-pity.
2. **Intimidation** - operating through slander, threats and terror.
3. **Domination** - operating through force of personality, politics or other means.

Religious spirits prey on our human nature's inherent weakness and target victims struggling with fear, insecurity and pride. We all have a propensity towards self-righteousness, but a tender and loving heart is the best antidote to an arrogant mentality. Humility is the ability to acknowledge our errors, as it prevents us from developing a cold and unfeeling heart. Daily repentance helps us to abide in our first love with Christ and makes us responsive to his Holy Spirit. Our brains physically rewire in healthy ways during a spiritual renewal process, which also benefits our emotions. Repentance keeps the evil one at bay, but legalistic religiosity feeds on our instinctive selfish and judgemental proclivities. A fault-finding, hypocritical spirit gains access when you and I don't act on what God told us to do. A religious spirit also keeps believers in the *soulish realm* and *hinders discipleship*. I have battled this evil influence in churches I have been a member of for more than three decades, ever since I became a believer. Shortly after I received the baptism of the Holy Spirit, God trained me in the discerning of spirits. One of the reasons he equipped me with that ability was to prepare me for ministry as an elder, overseer, watchman and pastor (Acts 20:17-28). These functions and responsibilities are all connected to fivefold ministry in God's Kingdom, and they are actually working titles for serving leaders within the Body of Christ rather than being pretentious achievements on a CV. Our walk with the Lord is the basis for understanding and discernment (see Dan. 2:21). We grow in revelation and wisdom by nurturing a deeper relationship with the Lord through Spirit-led intersession and research. Encountering God's beauty and glory marinates us in the Spirit of Revelation. Seeking the King in his righteousness helps us recognise the patterns of Heaven. We gradually learn how to resist all the devil's schemes, usually expressed through conflicting spirits. These religious spirits fool us into building God around our lives instead of building our lives around God and the truth of his Word. Although unintended, our inner reflexes of self-preservation tend to push our blessed Redeemer out on the fringes of our lives. The fear of the Lord effectively enables us to deal with these reflexes by letting him take centre stage as our only source and safety (see Psalm 16:1-2, 11 and Psalm 139:1-12, Prov. 18:10).

Encountering God's beauty and glory continually marinates us in the Spirit of Truth and Revelation.

True Christianity is daily walking in the Spirit and not in the flesh. If we do ministry in our human capacity, apart from God's presence, we no longer live by faith. Those led by the Holy Spirit focus on his will and loving others, but controlling individuals within our churches focus on themselves and often lack empathy. I have assembled a list that shows the clear distinction between selfish works and the fruit produced by the Holy Spirit, with some main characteristics:

AUTHENTIC:	**COUNTERFEIT:**
1. Living relationship	Dead regulations
2. Divine revelation	Carnal reasoning
3. Supernatural anointing	Natural charisma
4. Self-reflective (perception)	Self-centred (projection)
5. Repentance	Rebellion
6. Ministry gifts	Merit list
7. Wisdom	Head knowledge
8. Spiritual gifts	Natural talents
9. Brotherhood	Allegiance
10. Obedience	Compromise
11. Encouragement	Flattery
12. Humility	Conceit
13. Holy hunger (power)	Carnal complacency (no power)
14. Sense of awe	Irreverent familiarity
15. Christlikeness	Narcissism
16. Compassion	Contempt
17. Transformed mind (godly)	Conformed mind (worldly)
18. Love-identity (spirit)	Performance-identity (flesh)
19. Spiritual function (authority)	Social position (status)
20. Fear of God	Fear of man
21. Affirmation from God	Attention from man

Please study the above list carefully, and pay close attention because it will help you to determine and differentiate between God's work and 'good' works. Religiosity may appear as godliness at the surface: Ponder on it and pray: You will notice that it clashes with biblical faith. Man-made religion is self-centred and sustained by self-righteousness. Myriads of believers live under the dark clouds of guilt, shame and condemnation. Perhaps they think they fail to pray or read the Bible enough. They also struggle with personal issues and lack confidence. This kind of introspection creates insecurity by focusing on sins or shortcomings. It prevents us from accessing the abundant grace and resurrection life in Christ. Then again, we have Christians who smugly salute themselves for being impeccable churchgoers. These believers arrogantly think they are contributing to the local church in countless ways. Yet they slight those they consider as less accomplished. Whether you identify with the first or the last category, they both end up in the ditches of condemnation or conceit. What is their error? They are performance-driven and legalistic. Legalism is defined as 'a strict conformity to the letter of the law rather than its spirit.' Paul reprimanded the Galatians because they left the gospel of grace. Living after principles rather than seeking the Lord is to replace the spiritual with the superficial. God's kingdom is about connectivity and identity, whilst human religion centres around activity.

We affirm identity by lending an ear to God's message about who he created us to be. When we figure out who we are in Christ, it helps us to reinforce his image in us. Looking at your face in the mirror of grace is a constant and positive reminder of your true identity. Look, and look again by intently gazing at your new self. Don't forget the person God designed you to be. Become what you are! Discover your _identity_—learn to walk in your full _destiny_. Acting on the will of the Lord will set you free! *"For if you listen to the word and don't obey, it is like glancing at your face in a mirror. You see yourself, walk away, and forget what you look like. But if you look carefully into the perfect law that sets you free, and if you do what it says and don't forget what you heard, then God will bless you for doing it."* (James 1:23-25 NLT).

To practise God's Word is fundamental, and our Lord Jesus also pointed out this fact: *"Therefore everyone who hears these words of mine and puts them into practice is like a wise man who built his house."* (Matt. 7:24 NIV). The NIV has the expression *"to put into practice"*. Our compliance requires mental focus and hands-on effort! Jesus told us to abide in him and his words (see John 15:7). Obedience and intimacy work hand in glove. We learn to recognise God's gentle voice and follow his will through intimacy. Intimacy, with the nifty wordplay 'into-me-see', describes how we are known by God and connected with him on a deep heart-to-heart level. By gaining information *about* God, most of us find it uncomplicated to comprehend faith on a theoretical level. At times, our theology conjures up a 'god' from thoughts about him. This rarely leads to genuine encounters with the living God. To espouse strong convictions about his Word is not the same as having solid faith. Because God is personal, he wants to connect with us individually. Do we humbly *allow* him to teach us? Are we heeding his voice? *"All your children will be taught by the LORD, and great will be their peace."* Peace is *shalom* - it means completeness, success, peace and safety. (Isa. 54:13 NIV). If we elevate feeble human reasoning over revelation, we will fail to grasp God's plans and purposes: *"My thoughts are nothing like your thoughts," says the LORD. "And my ways are far beyond anything you could imagine. For just as the heavens are higher than the earth, so my ways are higher than your ways and my thoughts higher than your thoughts."* (Isa. 55:8-9 NLT).

Keep in mind that a religious spirit is competitive, fuelled by self-interest and envy. *"For where you have envy and selfish ambition, there you find disorder and every evil practice."* (James 3:16 NIV). Selfishness easily leads to a [87]narcissistic attitude. When confronted, people heavily influenced by controlling spirits refuse to submit to the truth. Their hard attitude shows no sign of remorse or humility. Oftentimes there will be resentment and offence in tow, although God's Word instructs us to resolve issues between believers. This mentality has a warped perception, a distorted reality and a hypocritical desire for justice over mercy, ending in rows over petty things. Its fruits are destructive and hurtful. Jesus told us to go to the person who offended us (see Matt. 18:15-17, Luke 17:1-4). By walking in wisdom, we daily learn to overlook offences (see Prov. 19:11). We should focus on mercy and strive for reconciliation. *"He who covers an offence promotes love; but he who repeats a matter separates best friends."* (Prov. 17:9 WEB). Self-righteousness fixates on position and performance, as it shuts out others. It's contrary to discernment because it's driven by unhidden prejudice and accusation. Feeling peeved, controlling people elicit unreasonable and disingenuous behaviour and accuse you of having a religious spirit—the very thing they often manifest themselves.

Self-righteousness fixates on position and performance, as it shuts out others.

Religious spirits remain unexposed in most churches, as many members and leaders are frequently tethered to them. Disguised under the clever cloak of spirituality, they go unnoticed. Within Christianity, we suffer because of our ignorance. Believers

---

[87] **Narcissistic personality disorder (NPD)**— one of several types of personality disorders — is a mental condition in which people have an inflated sense of their own importance, a deep need for excessive attention and admiration, troubled relationships, and a lack of empathy for others. *18 Nov 2017* Source: www.mayoclinic.org › symptoms-causes › syc-20366662

have inherited these as generational religious spirits, or spirits of witchcraft, without even realising it. Satanic powers hide within respectable and charismatic individuals as a fifth column, detrimentally affecting many churches from the inside. They are widely tolerated because many Christians have experienced God's glory on a limited scale. Pertaining to what faith should look like, a great many of denominations have lowered their standards. Lifeless and predictable meetings are commonly accepted. These churches rarely encounter God's presence and the freedom of his Spirit.

If you install a dimmer switch in a room, it will help you to adjust the light source. At times, we gradually dull light to an extent where it is barely visible, and things get blurred. Quite a few appreciate a faint gleam of light with its cosy ambience. Due to fear or spiritual blindness, the light of God's Word has been routinely suppressed in church settings. A legalistic religiosity routinely replaces real faith once regulations relegate revelation to a repudiated status. In letting doctrine substitute relationships, believers will treasure theological principles over Presence—often without giving it a second thought. What a field day the enemy is having with congregants like these! It's baffling to me that many believers have never undergone *deliverance* from evil spirits during or after their conversion, and this explains the darkness in their souls. Seasoned ministers know the enemy's tactics and have convincing testimonies about Christians who got gloriously delivered. Countless churches erroneously conclude that accepting Christ as Saviour is sufficient, with an emphasis on forgiveness and eternal life. Salvation encompasses more than forgiveness because the gospel also includes deliverance, healing and walking in daily repentance. Every time we receive spiritual liberty, our love for God and each other increases exponentially. Another obstacle is theology: Some churches refuse to think that Christians can be bound by the demonic, although their own biblical framework is incomplete and inconsistent. Even worse, most fellowships neatly sidestep the question to fend off controversy. Sadly, it allows the enemy to keep the matter in the dark, which then leaves us with intense and unresolved issues. As a result, these suffering and unhappy Christians backslide or learn to slowly adapt to inner oppression. If individuals with spiritual yokes get promoted as leaders based on merit, gifting or popularity, it badly affects others. These newly appointed leaders tend to re-enact a cycle of control. Its effect is disastrous when this phenomenon hits churches from within because the Holy

Spirit cannot flow as freely as earlier. God's presence will subside if we don't use the gifts of the Spirit as frequently as we once did, and the decline soon become evident.

Those who sympathise with a religious spirit often join forces together, being duped and dominated by a rigid sectarian mentality. Ghastly cliques like this give the pastor a harrowing experience. *"The accuser of the brethren"* controls these believers (see Rev. 12:10). Because we humans are easily led astray, we desperately require the prophetic watchman function among us (see Acts 20:28). It's especially troubling if spiritual leaders come under identical spiritual oppression. God called us *"to keep the unity of the Spirit through the bond of peace"* (see Eph. 4:3 NIV). The glory of the Lord prevents division and brings unity. We forge an indestructible bond of love by seeking each other's well-being (John 17:22-24). The Lord commanded his blessing to dwell where brothers live together in melodious harmony (see Psalm 133:1-3). Christian fellowships suffer greatly if another influence than the Holy Spirit gains access. Some leaders and their allies create a feigned unity—much like the one we find in secular political parties, by yielding to another spirit. Any thought, idea or proposition this group fails to square with will be actively opposed or discarded.

Spiritual Warfare, lesson No. 1:
We don't wrestle against flesh and blood. There is nothing biblical in battling each other! Division and disunity strike where witchcraft or control materialise because the invisible war manifests in the visible and physical world. If we deal with serious issues, it would be unfruitful and unwise to discuss it with other members of the local church instead of the person it directly concerns. Before a conversation takes place, we must make it a matter of earnest prayer and spiritual warfare. We can leave our prayer closet, but only after being armed with God's love and truth to confront issues constructively, without accusation. How do we tackle the intolerable Jezebel spirit or other despicable and controlling spirits? If you have been held liable for manifesting this spirit due to evident control issues, own up to it. Make sure that you repent of it, renounce it and disentangle from its damaging influence. Break the chains! Afterwards, contact those hurt by your actions and ask for their forgiveness. Be totally honest on your journey and consciously surround yourself with apostolic leaders who love you and hold you accountable. Seek deliverance and healing in areas of insecurity, fear or rejection. Get it over and done with (see Rev. 2:20-23).

Spiritual warfare, lesson No. 1: We do not wrestle against flesh and blood. To battle each other is never biblical!

Faith works through love. Almost all issues can be dealt with if we are willing to roll up our sleeves and not shy away from healthy confrontations (see Gal. 5:6; 6:1-2). Please humour me: In the over-polite British culture, we face this odd phenomenon when dealing with a problem. At first, people discuss whether there actually is 'an elephant in the room'. During the deliberation process, those directly involved may ignore obvious facts confirmed by eyewitnesses. Reactions then follow:

1. Silence 2. Denial. 3. Blame. 4. Leaving the room (!)
Of course, there are always exceptions because some people take ownership and start a constructive conversation in order to come to grips with the unpleasant situation.

When we watch fellow believers trying to live out God's calling, some disagreement is healthy without necessarily considering it to be divisive. Churches should strive for unity, not drab uniformity. Beware that a 'Jezebel-spirit' may also cause conflicts through Christians who brashly insist on being more spiritual than the pastor or the entire leadership. Some title themselves intercessors—or prophets—while spreading poisonous slander within their social sphere. Members who do contest the pastor's authority will sometimes, and without forewarning, establish belligerent resistance squads. Individuals deceived by this spirit bring great harm to the flock. Break every spoken curse and sever ties of demonic assignments, in Jesus' name. Then plead the blood of Jesus over yourself and your church. Intercede for those who are involved and pray that they will repent. Besides, if an occult group targets a church, we should realise that these individuals are deluded in their search for power because they seek it in the wrong camp. The Father wants to save the lost, including those who spew out curses. Act in the opposite spirit, and thwart these attacks too. Quash all gossip, criticism and accusations. Inept and careless behaviour is toxic. It opens a gateway for the devil to harass the fellowship from within. Have you ever badmouthed other Christians without even considering praying for them? Most believers are probably guilty as charged. It's horrible, and we should all repent of this blatant sin by simply refusing the accuser in his attempts to divide God's beloved sons and daughters.

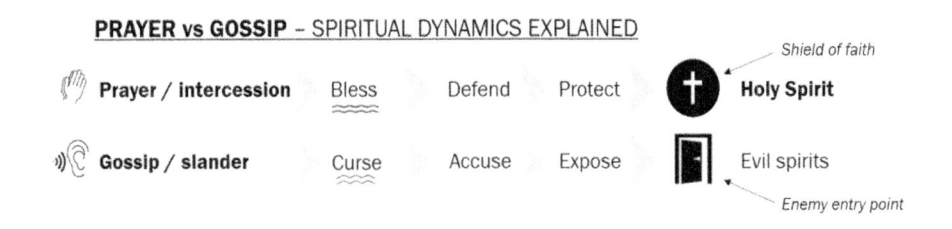

PRAYER vs GOSSIP – SPIRITUAL DYNAMICS EXPLAINED

Prayer / intercession	Bless	Defend	Protect	✝	**Holy Spirit** (Shield of faith)
Gossip / slander	Curse	Accuse	Expose	🚪	**Evil spirits** (Enemy entry point)

The illustration is further exemplified by the story about [88]Cain and Abel (see Gen. 4:1-17). Whether it's about gossip, jealousy or other sins, the key principle points to how sin opens a gateway for the devil into our thoughts and emotions. Conversely, walking in righteousness welcomes the Holy Spirit's good influence! A pre-emptive measure against sin is being filled with God's love. To begin with, control issues look pretty innocent and unintentional. Confidence in gifts, charisma or achievements may slowly morph into full-blown pride. If we don't glorify God, we risk nourishing a self-promoting and narcissistic attitude. If we battle insecurity, we can seek God for peace and security to avoid self-righteousness and immodesty. Whenever these things creep in, transparency and accountability will take the back seat by allowing control to escalate. Countless thriving churches have been split by wolves in sheep's clothing. We must constantly be on our guard and not provide the devil with any entry points (see Matt. 7:15, Acts 20:28-31). John mentions the crafty Diotrephes in 3 John 9-11, who sought pre-eminence at his church. He was a staunch opponent

---

[88] **My comment:** The Bible describes history' first murder, a tragic event that was caused by jealousy and a legalistic religious spirit. The same dynamic was at play in the stoning of Stephen (see Act 7:42-8:3). God warned Cain before the premeditated attack happened, with these telling words: *"sin is crouching at your door; it desires to have you, but you must rule over it."* (Gen. 4:7). The word for sin is חַטָּאת *chattat*, but the word for crouching is רֹבֵץ *robes* and is connected to the Akkadian word for an evil spirit - rabisu. It means the "lurker" or the "seizer". This spirit was lying in wait at the door of the soul, to seize the opportunity through Cain's sin, in order to gain control and cause death. Cain had the opportunity to resist it, by using his free will to do good. Sadly, he chose the path of destruction. Selfish pride is poison for the soul, and is the source of all kinds of evil (see James 3:13-16). **See also:** https://en.wikipedia.org/wiki/Rabisu

of John and others, who did God's work by unjustly accusing them. Insecure leaders feel threatened if they encounter people more competent or gifted than themselves. They will react carnally by trying to discredit or oust them. In doing so, leaders can come against God. In cases where control is involved and the Holy Spirit convicts of sin, we should offer help in the loving spirit of reconciliation (see Gal. 6:1-10).

Saul of Tarsus, the Pharisee, was livid with anger while fiercely persecuting the Way, adamant that he did the Almighty's work (see Acts 22:4, Gal. 1:13). His memorable deliverance from a religious spirit is a powerful testimony (see Acts 9:1-22, 26:9-18). The converted and changed Saul, now called Paul, repeatedly denounced the same religious spirit. In his important letter to the Galatians, he warned about its danger because it takes our focus away from the foundation of salvation by grace and faith in Christ Jesus. If you carry God's heart for people to be empowered and released into ministry, strong opposition will come from those who dislike the function of ministry gifts. The apostolic and prophetic anointing gives rise to much distress and discomfort in people who exert unwarranted control in our churches. The apostolic ministry, with its recognisable authority, is a felt threat to jittery control freaks. With a clear mandate to establish God's kingdom, genuine apostles carry a governmental anointing. Issues will surface if a church isn't accurately founded on Christ through the apostolic and prophetic ministry (see Eph. 2:19-20). Wrong foundations will still remain if the reality of the gospel isn't sufficiently bolstered (see 1 Tim. 3:15). Immature leaders—who base their positions on their own merits instead of relying on the function of their callings and gifts—oppose ministers who depend on God's anointing. Without a doubt, ministry anointing should be accompanied by godly behaviour. Allowing conflicting foundations to co-exist in a church is no option. Repentance and embracing God's agenda help us to remove flawed foundations. Sometimes we need a friendly reminder that ministry is actually about *helping* each other. We serve the Almighty and *his* people. Preachers sometimes try to build their self-serving empires by gathering similar-minded people. Our heavenly Father wants us to build *his* Kingdom, not cult-like and counterproductive empires. Kingdom builders are responsible leaders whose goal is to equip the House of God. Their holy ambition is to inspire and hire other leaders. They trust these beloved companions to steward the spiritual DNA of their fellowships. Leaders of this calibre strive to empower and equip fellow believers to serve, love and bless their surroundings.

Empowering preaching

When we preach and teach, our goal with the fivefold gifts is to equip and empower. Here are some tips and hints I have found helpful. Making truth applicable is vital if we want to strengthen and inspire people. Some preachers regularly read passages from the Bible. They mistakenly assume they are preaching God's message, but the Word has to be understood to be received and achieve its purpose in the believers (see Isa. 55:10-11). If the students of a baking class are handed the complete list of ingredients for a scrumptious cake, it still isn't enough. They will demand specific guidelines for the components, like how to blend them together, the correct baking temperature and estimated cooking time. The teacher must then explain the recipe so the students can understand it. I think you get the gist of it. For teaching to be worthwhile, preachers should present some practical tools when analysing spiritual truths, which is essential for discipleship. The *what* and the *why* aren't enough because people want to know *how*. The how is best conveyed when rightly explained and aptly modelled. We arouse hope and build motivation when we demonstrate what we preach. Jesus and Paul referred to themselves as relevant role models:

"I am the way and the truth and the life. No one comes to the Father except through me." (John 14:6 NIV).

"And my message and my preaching were very plain. Rather than using clever and persuasive speeches, I relied only on the power of the Holy Spirit. I did this so you would trust not in human wisdom but in the power of God." (1 Cor. 2:4-5 NLT).

"What you have learned and received and heard and seen in me—practice these things, and the God of peace will be with you." (Phil. 4:9 ESV).

Focusing on expository preaching helps us to examine what the Scripture teaches us without putting forward erratic beliefs. Still, if I talked about forgiveness, it would be mistaken if I just quoted verses and issued the strict command: "You have to forgive!" How to forgive and move on is, of course, relevant. That is challenging if you teach listeners inflicted with debilitating pain and long-term effects of trauma. Forgiveness may be a long journey, particularly for victims of calamities or abuse.

E -	Educating
M -	Mentoring
P -	Provoking
O -	Observing
W -	Word-focused
E -	Enthusiastic
R -	Repetitive & relational

NB: Preachers and worship leaders stand on holy ground and must revere the sacred space when they speak. Feel free to glean insights from the acrostic model below and utilise the tips relevant to your particular style and communication method.

Educating

Educate your audience with some engaging facts regarding your exposition. If, for instance, you are discussing a word like *grace,* explain its roots, its common usage and its application. Describe what it's *not*. Be concise! Amusing comments and brief social interactions with your audience will likely create lasting memories!

Mentoring

Mentor others by focusing on the practical implementation of a concept, for instance: How a believer can learn to operate diverse gifts of healing. Respond to questions, such as: How to proceed when nothing noticeable happens? Do we pray once more? To help people to better relate, use personal experiences, statements and illustrations. In any case, live or recorded testimonies are powerful.

Provoking

Provoke positively, especially if some expressions have become too hackneyed or casual. Be fun and creative! Never shy away from little twists and tweaks to challenge whoever is listening. Make use of fables and facts, ask relevant questions and share other perspectives. Awaken curiosity, and if necessary, shake up your audience a bit. Be wise and consider your strategy while prayerfully preparing the message.

Observing

Observe when you minister; read your audience well. How does it respond or react?

Does everyone get your message? Do you need to clarify it further or emphasise it somewhat differently? Is the Holy Spirit revealing things during your talk that you need to address later, during ministry time? Or is it better to bring it up right away? If you get words of knowledge or wisdom while preaching, share them.

Word-focused

As we live in a modern world, it's possible to preach with hardly any content derived from Christ's basic teaching or the Bible. To make it worse, some preachers concoct untruthful conclusions or present heresies. It's sad but true. Always try to connect Bible stories to everyday settings. Inspire your listeners to read, study and memorise the Scripture, especially the very words of Jesus Christ. Try to find suitable verses or passages to illustrate the topic and build faith based on the written promises.

Enthusiastic

Share your message with passion coming from your preparation in prayer and study. Excitement is infectious, especially when the Holy Spirit has stirred a zeal inside you. Enthusiasm is a familiar key driver for change and achievement. Try to inspire your listeners and increase hope by sharing fresh revelations.

Repetitive & relational

It can prove helpful to repeat the key points of your presentation when you deliver a message at least twice. According to science, repeated information accumulates in the listener's long-term memory. Combining teaching with a few practical exercises, like getting the audience to repeat some truths aloud or raising their hands, is clever. Participation is impactful.

If possible, keep your preaching short and sweet. Remember that people's attention span is limited. During the preaching, abandon your manuscript if necessary. Do it to prophesy or ad-lib as you feel led by the Spirit if you have the time. Rather than delivering a perfect speech, communicating the Father's heart to release his presence and glory is better. Let us be devoted vessels of God's love while *"rightly dividing the word of truth"* (see 2 Tim. 2:15). Fivefold fellowships with a fondness for the Word, with an emphasis on empowerment and discipleship, are extremely efficient. Apostolic Kingdom centres inspire and energise through visionary leadership and authentic relationships. Slowly but surely, these loving communities will turn into sumptuous surroundings of the Lord's light and life, lighthouses and greenhouses that enable growth. In the next chapter, we will focus on the spiritual gifts and how the Holy Spirit distributes these to equip and empower believers for service.

Receiving love & courage to soar

EMPOWER!

CHAPTER 9 - PROPHETIC POWERTOOLS

The spiritual gifts

To build the Church locally and globally, we need the spiritual gifts; they strengthen individuals as well as our congregations. Interestingly, Paul writes: *"Now concerning spiritual gifts, brothers, I do not want you to be uninformed."* (1 Cor. 12:1 ESV). *"Concerning the spiritual (gifts)*—in Greek πνευματικῶν *pneumatikon—I do not want you to be ignorant."* The word gift wasn't originally a part of the verse. It was added to explain the previous word. Since Paul wanted to teach about the gifts, he thought of the believers exercising them—describing them as spiritually inclined brothers. *"And we impart this in words not taught by human wisdom but taught by the Spirit, interpreting spiritual truths to those who are spiritual."* (1 Cor. 2:14 ESV). The second verse demonstrates the significance of treating revelation in a spiritually-minded way. Paul wanted to explain how spiritual truths and concepts are shared through spiritually equipped persons.

Why do I emphasise these expressions? In both the Greek and Hebrew languages, we find a clear linkage between word, person and spirit. Sometimes these represent the same thing. Words were associated with the people who uttered them and the spirit they emitted. Words affect us in good or bad ways: *"Death and life are in the power of the tongue, and those who love it will eat its fruits."* (Prov. 18:21 ESV). It's necessary to discern the spirit behind spoken words. We should test it and check if its content correlates with the biblical narrative. I wish to be like the Berean Jews, by comparing teaching and preaching with all God's counsel—his holy Word (see Acts 17:11). See also John 7:16-17, 1 Cor. 12:10, 1 Thess. 5:20-22, 1 John 4:1-6.

There is an ancient place in Israel called [89]Nebaioth—as נָבִיא *navi* means prophet. The prophet Samuel ministered at this specific location. It implies a flow of words or, to be more precise, prophetic words. When Samuel prophesied, it released a thick prophetic anointing resting upon the place. This presence impacted all who entered the geographical area, which had become a heavenly embassy (see 1 Sam. 19:18-23). The gifts and the vessels are intertwined. When we study the Scripture, we clearly notice that the Lord is concerned with the *message* and also how people respond to his appointed *messengers*. Spiritual persons are usually people of stature, seasoned in the things of God. Let us show them honour. Behind the gifts is the generous Giver, God, the Father. The gifts represent different attributes of his divine characteristics. Sin goes against the moral laws associated with his creation. To use God-given gifts selfishly—outside the intimate relationship with him—is possible. Anyway, it's incompatible with *who* he is. Jesus put forward this tragic reality when he spoke of ministers who didn't have integrity while prophesying and healing in his name. He would later say: *"I never knew you. Away from me, you evildoers!"* (Matt. 7:21-23).

In his letter to the Corinthians, Paul teaches about the spiritual gifts in chapter 12. To operate them with love, in chapter 13. To use them orderly when the church gathers, in chapter 14. We find that spiritual gifts can be imparted by the laying on of hands and by prophecy: *"Do not neglect your gift, which was given you through prophecy when the body of elders laid their hands on you."* (1 Tim. 4:14 NLT). What we spiritually carry is released or activated by prayer, proclamation and prophecy. Paul passed on the apostolic anointing at a corporate level, deeply invested in the edification and equipping of all the saints, as he understood the purpose of how ministry gifts function: *"For I long to see you, that I may impart to you some spiritual gift to strengthen you—that is, that we may be mutually encouraged by each other's faith, both yours and mine."* (Rom. 1:11-12 ESV). There are lovely *presents* in God's presence—waiting to be explored! Paul expected spiritual transactions to take place when he fellowshipped. Gifts flourish, and anointing overflows when we encounter the Lord. Let us seek God to get anointing directly from him so we may bless others!

---

[89] **My comment:** The name occurs as נְבָיוֹת *Nebaioth* in Isaiah 60:7 (Strong's Hebrew 5032). Other places use נָיוֹת *Naioth*, like in 1 Sam. 19:23

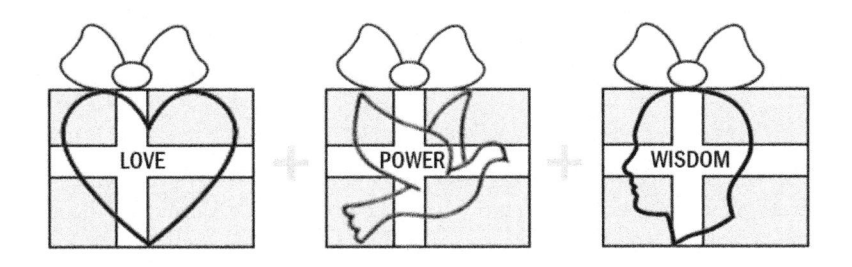

If we have unfulfilled needs but enough vessels to receive, God willingly pours out his anointing oil in *abundance*. He has no shortage of supplies, which the legendary story about the widow with the oil shows (2 Kings 4:1-7). Placing a demand on the anointing can't be done by complacent believers. Still, the spiritually hungry ones will draw out whatever you carry in the Holy Ghost! As a tool, *God-hunger* is very powerful. I have frequently experienced it first hand in meetings when preaching or teaching—it's the most beautiful thing. Cooperating with the anointing resting on individuals increases the expectancy drastically in services, and miracles sometimes happen. On sharing the Word in Lystra, Paul distinctly discerned faith. He shouted to a man in the crowd and asked him to stand up. The guy was instantly healed (see Acts 14:9-10). The opposite happened in Nazareth because they didn't treat Jesus with honour. Due to the villagers' unbelief, he couldn't perform any great miracles there. Except, by the laying on of hands, he healed a few people (see Mark 6:5).

In the New Testament, three passages list the gifts: Rom. 12, 1 Cor. 12 and Eph. 4. In Romans chapter 12, we find an overview of [90]the motivational gifts, these total seven: Prophecy, serving, teaching, exhortation, giving, leadership and compassion (see Rom. 12:6-8). Each of us usually carries a mixture of gifts.

These motivational gifts represent the main types of personalities we have:

1. Observer - a prophetically inclined person with a strong sense of justice.
2. Servant - a person having great energy and capacity for work.
3. Encourager - a person who constantly supports others with a desire to create growth and development.

---

[90] **Motivational gifts:** For further study on these seven gifts, I recommend **Discover Your God-Given Gifts Revised and Expanded** by Don & Katie Fortune ISBN: 9780800794675.

4. **Teacher** - a person having the ability to digest and disseminate information.
5. **Giver** - a frugal person with the ability to obtain and share resources in order to meet needs.
6. **Leader/administrator** - a person with organising skills, with the ability to lead.
7. **Mercy-giver** - an intuitive person with the compassionate ability to recognise and share the feelings of others. *Empath* is another word for the same gift.

Let us take a closer look at the [91]spiritual gifts, which totals nine. These God-given abilities are listed in 1 Cor. 12:

1. **Word of wisdom** - divine ability to solve a difficult matter.
2. **Word of knowledge** - divine access to information you naturally don't know.
3. **Faith** - extraordinary faith facilitating instant changes in difficult situations.
4. **Gifts of healing** - power to heal different diseases and weaknesses.
5. **Miracles** - casting out evil spirits, instant healings or grace to defy the laws of nature.
6. **Prophecy** – to share God's heart and talk inspired words by his Spirit, or from time to time, predict future events.
7. **Testing or discernment of spirits** - to detect, feel or smell different spirits.
8. **Tongues** - to speak languages unfamiliar to the speaker.
9. **Interpretation of tongues** - to understand and [92]explain messages uttered in an unknown language.

The spiritual gifts can further be divided into three groups:

1. **Revelation gifts** - wisdom, knowledge, discernment.
2. **Power gifts** - faith, miracles and healing.
3. **Vocal or inspirational gifts** - prophecy, tongues, interpretation of tongues.

---

[91] **Gifts:** In Greek singular χάρισμα *charism* - a divinely conferred gift or power. Both the Greek words *chara* - joy, and *charis* - grace, are connected to *the gifts* of grace. God's gifts χαρίσματα *charismata* (plural) come with joy and flow by grace.

[92] **My comment:** If the message in tongues is shorter than the interpretation, it might indicate that it was a prayer and, therefore, the answer comes as a prophetic message.

With revelatory gifts, bear in mind that the interpretation of dreams usually includes the operation of both words of knowledge and words of wisdom (see Gen. 41 and Dan. 2). Regarding the power gifts, instantaneous healings and casting out demons can be considered as the gift of miracles (see Matt. 8:3, Mark 9:38-40). Surely, a gift of miracles is in operation when someone manages to complete work in 30 minutes, which would usually require at least 3–4 hours of serious effort. When individuals are translocated by the Spirit or travel faster than usual, I consider these phenomena to be miracles as well (see John 6:21, Acts 8:39). Due to their supernatural origin, we cannot logically explain these conundrums of time and space.

Healings, in the plural, is a word indicating a cluster of healing gifts. Medical science lists 39 major categories of diseases. Jesus suffered 39 lashes of the Roman scourge before his crucifixion. By his stripes, we were healed! We can legitimately include grace to heal wounds of the soul as gifts of healing. Some believers carry healing just by the sound of their voices, which is truly remarkable. When they pray or speak in soothing and comforting ways, they bring healing to the soul. As for trauma, we routinely need to cast out the spirit of trauma or fear through deliverance. Listen carefully to the Holy Spirit when you are ministering. Another very impactful gift is *tongues.* It's the ability to speak heavenly or earthly languages. Spiritual gifts are abilities, expressions or manifestations given by Holy Spirit. When we exercise the gifts, we can expect the Presence to manifest! (See 1 Cor. 12:8-10, 28–30, 13:1). The last list holds a combination of ministry gifts, motivational gifts and spiritual gifts. Verse 11 reveals the origin and purpose of the gifts: *"All these are the work of one and the same Spirit, and he distributes them to each one, just as he determines."* The Holy Spirit gives spiritual gifts to those he hand-picks for vocations in the Kingdom.

The Spirit also confers gifts to those who *desire* them: *"<u>Pursue</u> love, and earnestly <u>desire</u> the spiritual gifts, especially that you may prophesy."* (1 Cor. 14:1 ESV). Words like *pursue* and *desire* are powerful expressions. Some believers may surmise that: 'If the Lord wants me to have a certain gift, it will drop into my lap'. Such a laid-back attitude is totally incoherent with the New Testament. God loathes complacency. He *can* mightily possess us by surprise, but that is not the norm. The Father loves to give to those who keenly *ask of* him. He has prepared an abundance—waiting to be explored by us—as he wants to *"show the incomparable riches of his grace"* in Christ Jesus (see Eph. 2:7). In my teens, I had a newfound and insistent hunger for the things of God. I still recall how God's Spirit trained me to be aware of the prophetic realm. The Spirit often notified me moments before a person spoke with tongues or prophesied in my local Methodist church. Due to this instinctive foresight, I sensed which person God would use. This was how God prepared me for ministry.

The Lord also gave me a prophetic dream where I saw myself from a bird's-eye view. I was strolling around, talking about the end times. I spoke words from Isa. 43:19-21. It's about how God will raise up a holy people that glorifies his name. Two years later, I prophesied for the first time. I could also interpret tongues and began to get prophetic words and pictures. Complacency is very dangerous. We constantly have to whet our appetite for heavenly realities by fixing our minds on the things above. We should devour his Word and seek revelation day and night. Take heed, spiritual hunger can be lost or replaced with other desires if we don't regularly tend to it.

Being spiritual is intentionally posturing ourselves to receive from God through our interaction with him. Are you persistently longing for God? Are you poised before him? Some of us may be unaware that our heart's attitude has already become our inner posture! Leaning into God is a habit we can develop through exercise. David, the great king, prophet and psalmist, trained himself to detect God's presence and wrote so beautifully: *"I have set the Lord always before me; because he is at my right hand, I shall not be shaken."* (Psalm 16:8 ESV). We position ourselves to receive and release, but it requires a heightened awareness of the Holy Spirit. The Father doesn't seek perfect vessels but perfect attitudes (see Matt. 5:48). He delights in humble and accessible hearts. He loves deeply, passionately and generously and has called us to reflect his heart at all times. In Galatians chapter 3:2-5 we see how grace connects everything. When you read the passage, observe how closely the Spirit is associated with grace instead of human achievements:

1. When we hear the gospel and are being born-again, it's all by grace.
2. When we receive the baptism of the Holy Spirit and fire, it's all by grace.
3. When we experience spiritual gifts and miracles, it's all by grace.

Whenever we exercise a gift—prompted by the Spirit—God releases his presence through that gift. Not having the gifts in operation in a church is missing out on the variety of Kingdom blessings they represent. At times, gifts powerfully supercharge the spiritual atmosphere the same way vocal intercession does. Some individuals are prayer warriors and break open the heavens within a few minutes. Others usher in God's presence through an edifying testimony, a song or the gift of prophecy.

Fruit versus gifts
To emphasise the fruit of the Spirit more than the gifts of the Spirit is quite logical. Character is indisputably more important than anointing or gifts. At the same time, we should ponder that fruit and gifts tend to go hand in hand. Please forgive my simplified explanation: Fruit relates to God's presence and gifts to his power. Let us disprove hasty conclusions about how gifts could make believers overly confident and stop them from living in sanctification. It all depends on the condition of our hearts. If we wish to please the Lord, we will use the gifts to glorify him and not brag about it. Learning how to flow in the gifts of the Spirit will potentially compel us to be more consistent in our walk with the Lord, not the other way round. The Holy Spirit carries with him a variety of the spiritual gifts and the ninefold fruit as well. If we remain filled with him, we can expect him to manifest the fruit together with the gifts. The development of Christian character and maturity is about fruit. To bear more fruit, God regularly prunes us (see John 15:1-17). Let me add that Paul spoke excessively in tongues in order to be filled with God's love and then manifested the rest of the gifts. He understood the incredible dynamics between flowing in divine love and flowing in the gifts (see 1 Cor. 14). We should always allow the Lord to express himself in and through us as he deems fit, as his grace is sufficient every time.

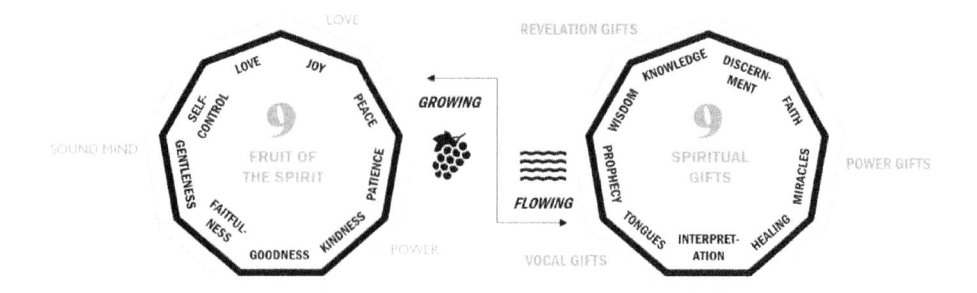

Some preachers have argued: How can powerless churches by any means bring glory to God? That conclusion misses the point entirely because truth has built-in power. When we get convicted by the *truth* of the gospel, we repent and surrender to Christ as our Lord and Saviour. Our focus can never be power displayed through miracles. We desperately need the power of God's Word and holiness. Holiness pulls us into the very presence of Jesus Christ, our sole source of spiritual strength. How can we be equipped with genuine power? By immersing ourselves in the Bible and pursuing Jesus alone! Revival history records periods when miracles were frequent. On other occasions, salvation and holiness were more apparent. God moved through the ages as a response to faith. Increased love for the Word and ceaseless prayer authenticated each revival. We should glorify God in the ways Jesus did when he walked the earth. Because he was merciful, he preached the gospel and healed and delivered people. In Messiah's ministry, operations of gifts and fruit were intertwined and inseparable. Where he came, he functioned in the power and authority of the Spirit.

We notice patterns for soul winning, the miraculous, and the grace to suffer for the gospel when studying Jesus and the first believers. Do we follow in their footsteps with a corresponding and otherworldly lifestyle? Jesus, the Living Word, fulfils all the blueprints for supernatural ministry. These patterns are easily confirmed by the four gospels, but not limited to these. Additionally, the biblical record comprises different types and shadows of Christ in the Old Testament. We see a wide array of his attributes, including pain and suffering, exemplified by men like Job and Joseph. Ministers who shy away from topics like healing and deliverance because they fear controversy lack revelation of the Father's compelling love and what the full gospel represents. Besides, cowardice in addressing other pressing matters—at the expense of biblical truth—proves disregard for God's expressed will. Refusing to preach repentance and sanctification to appease the crowd is demonstrably wrong. Jesus, as well as the apostle Paul, left patterns and templates for the believers to imitate. Paul said: *"Follow my example, as I follow the example of Christ."* (1 Cor. 11:1 NLT). *"Follow the pattern of the sound words that you have heard from me, in the faith and love that are in Christ Jesus."* (2 Tim. 1:13 ESV).

Concerning the gifts, these three approaches are determining factors:

1. Discover your gift. *Find it.*
2. Deploy your gift. *Use it.*
3. Develop your gift. *Perfect it.*

Study the Bible and research which gifts you have. You will experience joy and peace in the Holy Spirit by using any gift. And remember, your gift is invariably where your *passion* lies. When we let God guide us and we step out in faith, we develop our gifts further. Make sure to stay connected to Spirit-filled believers, people who are familiar with identical gifts. As vessels, we sometimes fail to manifest our gifts with maturity. Let us start where we are—transfixed on Jesus. What really matters is to go with the flow. We also *grow* as we *flow*! We should encourage each other by receiving ministry with an open heart. More seasoned believers have an opportunity to supervise and tutor by providing support and mentorship with a gentle spirit. The gifts will flourish as we learn to listen closely to the Holy Spirit and cooperate with him. Some believers access revelation gifts and see into the spiritual dimension, but others efficiently minister when they speak. In his first epistle, Peter encourages the believers to serve within their capacity:

"As each one has received a special gift, employ it in serving one another as good stewards of the manifold grace of God. Whoever speaks, is to do so as one who is speaking the utterances of God; whoever serves is to do so as one who is serving by the strength which God supplies; so that in all things God may be glorified through Jesus Christ, to whom belongs the glory and dominion forever and ever. Amen." (1 Pet. 4:10-12 NASB).

Using our gifts should be self-evident, as well as the necessity of holiness. Holy living *amplifies* the functions of these gifts by making them more powerful when in use.

Let us be diligent stewards and faithful with the gifts God so graciously provided. To see God's power released in a service and waves of the Holy Spirit surge through spiritual gifts is awesome! An attentive minister can successfully ride a wave and increase its impact through preaching or by other methods as the Holy Spirit leads. Discernment in our meetings is the absolute key to partnering with heaven. First, we need to know the 'reason for the season', what God focuses on. As I started writing this book, a season of empowerment and release began (2018). We live in an era with the *"times of restoration of all things"* (see Acts 3:21 and Amos 9:11). Year 5779 (2019), in the Jewish calendar, points to a period of 'Ayin' (eye), representing 70, and 9 representing the goodness of God and the birth of new things. The last decade was a lesson in prophetically discerning and seeing what God is doing.

As I write this book, we enter the biblical calendar and the years 5780-83 (2020-23), with 80 representing 'Pey' (mouth). I believe the next decade to be a period of fiery prophetic evangelism. We are getting ready for the end-time harvest! Although dark and trying times are approaching, I don't think that preaching 'doom and gloom' and the decline of society is what God has currently ordained.

We live in unprecedented times. We can move forward in bold faith, investigate our potential, and not shrink back when the best of times lie ahead of us. None of us knows with certainty how big our window of opportunity for *world evangelism* is. Jesus warned us: *"The night is coming when no one can work"* (John 9:4). In his book, 'A Tale of Two Cities', we find the famous Charles Dickens' iconic opening words: 'It was the best of times. It was the worst of times.' Persecution and outpouring will probably go hand in hand: Disruption and revival are running mates! The Church's glory days are likely to be times of trials entwined with triumphs.

Not long ago, my wife, Jane, had a lucid vision concerning revival fire—a prophetic spoiler of what God soon will do. She noticed Christians talking and witnessing to a group of people. As they did, some form of grey mist came out of their mouths. While some of the bystanders gave thought to the mist, most listeners remained apathetic. So far, the message didn't challenge them. Then, out of the blue, it rained down fireballs from the sky, igniting the mist. Celestial orbs of fire pierced their eyes—without hurting them—cleansing their vision. The fire also entered the lungs and the bellies of these believers. It was twisting and turning and purified them from the inside. This fire deftly devoured the internal strongholds and burnt them into smithereens. More reluctant strongholds melted and leaked onto the ground. After this intense but holy purging, the fire within the bellies surged more vigorously than before and had a powerful impact when discharged. The Lord's ambassadors were suddenly breathing pure fire! This amazing event triggered a different response from the crowd. The move of God rapidly gained momentum, and the audience seemed attentive and genuinely interested in the preaching. The realness of this major event led to more than a revival—it transitioned into a great awakening. The Holy Spirit reminded Jane of Jesus' words: *"I came to cast fire on the earth, and would that it were already kindled!"* (Luke 12:49 ESV). We will witness a significant and dramatic shift in how to evangelise. The gospel will attract non-believers as never before.

Only an immersion of holy fire can prepare us for the coming outpouring (see Luke 3:16). Jesus said that *"everyone will be salted with fire"*. The fiery love of God should consume us daily as living sacrifices (see Mark 9:49, Rom. 12:1). We all desperately need the Holy Spirit as our *Helper*. The Scripture encourages us to seek the gift of prophecy. What makes prophecy spectacular? Why is it instrumental in building God's kingdom? In 1 Cor. 14, we see how the *impact* of this gift makes it definitively indispensable for the Church. We often judge others and mislabel them because we assume they will not change for the better. The Father, in his merciful foresight, has a different approach: He observes everything from the throne perspective—not as us—dimly, through earthly glasses (see 1 Cor. 13:12). To fully guarantee a radical change of our identity, he sent Christ and then released the Spirit of prophecy.

An astounding aspect of prophecy is how God *redefines* and *renames* us! Prophecy and blessing pair up. Jesus called Simon bar-Jonah by the name Peter, or Cephas. Simon means 'reed', but Peter and Cephas mean 'rock'! The important renaming implied a transformation and change from one identity to another. Prophecy makes visible on the outside what has been hidden inside of us because it awakens God's calling and abilities. Jacob means deceiver. Esau's brother schemed his way through life until the deciding and defining moment at Penuel (see Gen. 32:22-32). 'Penuel' translates facing God. Close encounters with the Lord never leave us unaffected. His new title was 'Israel', wrestling with God, or the prince of God. As for Jabez, the Lord *redeemed* his name and *removed* traumatic pain by bestowing grace on him. The huge outpouring of the Holy Spirit, as predicted by Joel, is distinctly marked by prophecy: Sons and daughters will prophesy, the old men have dreams, and the young men have visions. Being filled with the Spirit, we prophesy. With our minds preoccupied with the heavenly realities, the Word percolates inside, and our mouths flow over (see Luke 6:45, Col. 3:1-2). Believers on fire preach about Jesus twenty-four-seven and passionately abide in their first love for him (Acts 4:18-20, Rev. 2:4). Prophecy fundamentally relates to the Spirit and the new epoch in the Messiah. Joel chapter 2 also hints at a second and worldwide Pentecost—the fulfilment of this great prediction—an outpouring larger than the first church experienced. I firmly believe that a prophesying tribe of believers will release the coming move of God!

God's sons are destined to manifest in great glory because they share in his nature (see Rom. 8:19). I believe that activation of gifts and ministries happens through an unbroken partnership with the prophetic Spirit. As we briefly discussed earlier, the word 'prophecy', referred to in Rev. 19:10, means *prophecies*. Testimonies contain the prophesying nature of God because they carry a built-in potential that can be replicated. Amos 9:13 predicts a convergence of events when prophecies are fulfilled at breakneck speed. One season will merge with another since *"the ploughman will overtake the reaper and the treader of grapes, the sower of seed."* Kairos-moments of the Lord will suddenly come together with an immense impact. We will experience breakthrough, increase and acceleration—all at once. My wife received these three keywords for 2017, based on Isaiah, chapter 54. Other preachers later reiterated the exact same words. To help his people better grasp it, did God prolong the invitation for his divine intervention? The Greek has two words for time; we find both in the New Testament: *chronos* and *kairos*. **Κρόνος** *chronos* is measured time, αιρός *kairos* is a season, an appointed time, the favourable and advantageous hour. They translate as *"times and seasons"* (Acts 1:7). *Kairos* is God's dimension, where he breaks into the present historic time with his eternal plans and purposes. It equals the Hebrew word מוֹעֲדִים *moʿēdim* - feasts or ordained appointments. We occupy the kairos realm by God's power when we prophesy and call it forth! A prophetic generation *will say to the captives, "Come out," and to those in darkness, "Be free!"* (Isa. 49:9 NIV). By his blood, Jesus released all the hostages of sin, shame, sickness and death! When Jesus shouted for Lazarus to come out of the grave, his dear friend was raised to life again. Immediately, Jesus asked for the strips of linen to be removed from his body because they restricted movement and resembled death (see John 11:43-44). This amazing miracle and sign may symbolise the spiritual resurrection of Israel as a nation but also the end-time generation where multitudes will be raised to new life in Christ.

Restoring and purifying the prophetic

Spiritual gifts may lie dormant or unused for a while. God wants to revive them! We have the ability and authority to rekindle the gifts again: *"For this reason I remind you to fan into flame the gift of God, which is in you through the laying on of my hands."* Quite often, we ask God to do what he instructed us to do. The next verse mentions how we stir up the gifts again: Through *"the Spirit of power and love and self-discipline"* (see 2 Tim. 1:6-7 NIV). It's one passage of Scripture that sheds some light on this truth. I appreciate the Books of Kings, originally written in Hebrew as one scroll. These incredible stories are useful when we try to illustrate biblical truths. The accounts of the prophets Elijah and Elisha are certainly worth further study.

One day the group of prophets came to Elisha and told him, "As you can see, this place where we meet with you is too small. Let's go down to the Jordan River, where there are plenty of logs. There we can build a new place for us to meet."
"All right," he told them, "go ahead." "Please come with us," someone suggested.
"I will," he said. So he went with them. When they arrived at the Jordan, they began cutting down trees. But as one of them was cutting a tree, his axe head fell into the river. "Oh, sir!" he cried. "It was a borrowed axe!"
"Where did it fall?" the man of God asked. When he showed him the place, Elisha cut a stick and threw it into the water at that spot. Then the axe head floated to the surface. "Grab it," Elisha said. And the man reached out and grabbed it. (2 Kings 6:1-7 NLT).

We must enlarge our corporate Kingdom vision to allow the Lord to raise up more prophets. As for Elisha, his house was too small, and the other prophets on his team wanted to expand it. The apostolic and prophetic anointing is an expanding force and stimulates a dynamic desire to build or occupy new territory. When one of the prophets cut down a tree, the axe head fell off and into the river. At once, the fellow went to Elisha. With great sorrow, he bemoaned that this axe was borrowed. The word for an axe is simply a piece of iron. By studying the Hebrew word בַּרְזֶל *barzel*, we see how it connects to what we carry in our hearts. *"The purposes of a person's heart are deep waters, but one who has insight draws them out."* (Prov. 20:5 NIV).

Barzel - iron, in Hebrew - reading from right to left: Beit-Resh-Zayin-Lamed
Beit - 2nd letter, represents the house of God, as well as the Son of God. The letter value is 2.
Resh - 20th letter, represents headship and authority, being first, to endure, shaking and moving. The letter value is 200.
Zayin - 7th letter, represents food, weapon, divide, remember, crowned male, or the Messiah. It is the sceptre to rule. The letter value is 7.
Lamed - 12th letter, represents the heart and teaching, the tallest letter touching both heaven and earth. The letter value is 30.

Lamed represents the throne of glory and the King of Kings. Lamed contains the letters *vav* and *kaf*, with a numeric value of 26—equal to the Tetragrammaton, YHWH, which is God's name—pronounced Yehovah. The [93]numeric value of the word barzel totals 239. God's Holy Name, [94]Yehovah, or LORD, is found 6,827

---

[93] **Numerics:** For further studies related to biblical gematria I recommend the book *Number in Scripture*, by E. W. Bullinger, or John Nuyten's websites.
[94] **YEHOVAH.** It appears with the full vowels יְהֹוָה - found at least 53 places in the Leningrad Codex. Today, we have more than 1,000 manuscripts with the full vowels. Yehovah is composed of 'Yeh' (from Yehi), 'ov' (from hove) and 'ah' (from hahyah). Yehovah means, "I was, I am, I will be." Semitic scribes developed systems of written vocalisation points to better record vowel sounds. Yehovah is also depicted in the top centre, the front page of the 1611 version of the King James Bible. I recommend Nehemia Gordon's well-researched book: *Shattering the Conspiracy of Silence*. The oral tradition forbade the Jews to say Yehovah, but most rabbis knew how to say it. Every 7th year they had a secret ceremony, going back centuries, where they passed on the Name to their own disciples. See my illustration with the names of the vowels. The incorrect Yahweh is from the Latinised Jove (Jupiter). Source: www.nehemiaswall.com › nehemia-gordon-name-god & www.escapeallthesethings.com/yahweh/

times in the Old Testament. Isn't it an offence to remove God's literal name from the Holy Bible? How does he feel about it? Sadly, the rabbis have a long-standing claim that one is not allowed to utter the Name, which is demonstrably false.

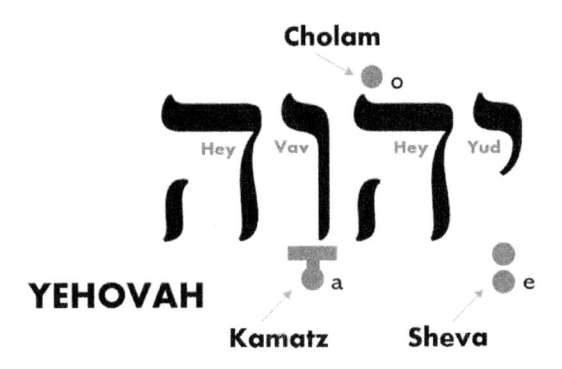

Cholam

יְהֹוָה

Hey — Vav — Hey — Yud

YEHOVAH — Kamatz — Sheva

1. The prophetic tool is like an axe. It's cutting through the darkness, revealing the truth and exposing lies. It's sharp and effective as it cuts through opposition and supplies us with ample building materials for the Kingdom. Revelation uncovers and builds (see Matt. 16:14-18, Eph. 2:20-22). Revelatory wisdom allows us to *build in the Spirit realm*. The revelation about God's Son, the Living Word, is a bedrock we firmly build on, central to faith and identity. Our works in Christ are lasting and eternal, like gold, silver and precious stones (see 1 Cor. 3:11-15).

2. The axe was borrowed. Gifts and anointings are spiritual tools 'borrowed' and entrusted to us. We must never forget this. We are just stewards of God's provisional grace and cannot take prophetic gifts or anointing for granted (see Gen. 22:13-14). On occasion, I have heard several Christians use the expression: 'My ministry'. Let me emphasise that none of us can insist on a ministry apart from Christ because we partake in *his* ministry. *"For just as each of us has one body with many members, and these members do not all have the same function, so in Christ we, though many, form one body, and each member belongs to all the others."* (Rom. 12:4-5 NIV).

We belong to Christ and his family, to the community of believers. *"But to each one of us grace was given according to the measure of Christ's gift."* (Eph. 4.7 NASB). The

---

Vowels. Please check out Dr Nick Posegay's book: *Points of Contact: The Shared Intellectual History of Vocalisation in Syriac, Arabic, and Hebrew.*

fullness of Christ was distributed to his earthly Body—his representatives on earth. Because we are servants, humility is required. To think that we are entitled to have a ministry is wrong. By grace, we access gifts and ministries to glorify our Creator.

MINISTRY BY GRACE - EPH. 4

Christ's gift | v 7 〉 Fivefold gifts | v 11 〉 Equipping | v 12 〉 Establishing | v 13 〉 Edifying | v 15 〉

3. "Where did the axe fall?" Elisha had to ask this. Sometimes we lose our sharpness or edge due to negligence or sin. Be candid and confess *when* and *where* you flunked and lost momentum. If we let him, the Holy Spirit will gently assist us and reveal the specifics. *"But I have this against you, that you have left your first love. Therefore remember from where you have fallen, and repent and do the deeds you did at first; or else I am coming to you and will and will remove your lampstand out of its place - unless you repent."* (Rev. 2:4-5 NASB). The subsequent step after recalling *where* we have fallen from is to take ownership of our mistakes. Repentance is always the right approach—turning to the Lord for a solution—recognising him as our help. Let me give you a brief example: If you open Google Maps on your phone and want to use Directions, you first need to know your current location in order to get to your final destination. If not, it's pointless to seek help from this online feature. Our destiny is likewise determined by our destination. When we choose to be truthful about where we stand, God directs us forward according to his good plans. In this Bible story, the streams of water, or the river, represent time and the busyness of life.

4. Throwing in the stick. Elisha fashioned a piece of wood and threw it in the river at the exact spot the disciple pointed out. Supernaturally, the wooden stick caused the axe head to float and come to the surface. Elisha's prophetic action alludes to the Tree, or the cross, and the finished work at Golgotha. The Father prepared the cross for his Son; its ultimate goal was to restore lost property. He did so to bring us back to him. The effective remedy for resurrecting our lost hopes and dreams is the cross. If we ask him for assistance, God will make gifts *resurface* and *reactivate* them. The word used for a stick is עץ *ets* - tree. In Hebrew, the two-letter word is Ayin-Tsade. It literally means seeing righteousness. For all the world to see, God publicly revealed his Righteousness at the cross, where Christ hung for our sake (see Rom. 3:25).

5. "Grab it!" Elisha immediately told the man to grab the floating axe head. Swift obedience is crucial. We risk losing the blessing if we procrastinate in the *moment* of divine intervention. Healing might also be lost if not rapidly seized by faith. *"Look carefully then how you walk, not as unwise but as wise, making the best use of the time, because the days are evil."* (Eph. 5:15-16 ESV). Do we meet the prophetic conditions given by the Holy Spirit? Can we expect him to move if we don't heed his voice or listen to his promptings? The following quote says it well: 'When we pray, God listens. When we obey, God acts.' Those who pay close attention to the Lord and develop a hunger for him will be the game-changers in the years to come. We should, therefore, only prophesy *if* God has spoken—out of an intimate relationship with his heart. *"For the Lord God does nothing without revealing his secret to his servants the prophets. The lion has roared; who will not fear? The Lord God has spoken; who can but prophesy?"* (Amos 3:7-8 ESV).

A caution to preachers with prophetic ministry:
At the moment, it looks like the Lord is chastising the prophetic community. God detests unbalanced prophetic utterances based on unloving and biased attitudes. He also loathes unchecked ambition and the craving for attention. We have to scrap our selfish aspirations if we want to represent the Father's heart. In fact, prophets should be the most courteous and endearing people on the face of the earth. Knowing the Father's redemptive thoughts is an inseparable part of the prophetic ministry. The humble and tender-hearted prophet Jeremiah wept out of deep compassion for the people of Israel because he was gutted: *"If only my head were a pool of water and my eyes a fountain of tears, I would weep day and night for all my people who have been slaughtered."* (Jer. 9:1 NLT). Holy tears are liquid prayers and heartfelt compassion intercession. Why, then, do weeping prophets seem so scarce today?

Has much of the so-called prophetic ministry become too detached from ordinary people's struggles and brokenness? I reckon that the prophets will be unable to reach our generation if they remove themselves from real-life scenarios. We can efficiently determine if a prophetic perspective is healthy by proving that we understand God's heart and the culture he called us to minister to. If we harmonise with the Father's heart and intentions, our mission will become plain as day. Many of today's famous prophetic ministries hook impressionable believers with teachings about spiritual warfare by focusing on demonic threats. Instead, they could have directed their attention to the mighty power of the Holy Spirit but rather choose to foment fear in unhealthy and irresponsible ways. Christians need discipleship, not imbalanced preaching, to make them co-dependent on prophetic pundits and their publications of dubious nature. The foundation of real empowerment and maturity is based on God's love through his Word and his Spirit. At this juncture, [95]Abba is unwavering in his goal to restore the prophetic ministry with a sharpened edge and clarity. He is redirecting us to his true purposes and plans. That will result in a way of life where his House can be built as he pleases.

Holy tears are liquid prayers and heartfelt compassion intercession.

---

[95] **Abba:** the Aramaic word for Father. Jesus and his disciples used this word, and it's commonly used by Messianic Jews, like אַבָּא שֶׁבַּשָּׁמַיִם *Abba Shebashamayim* - Our Father in Heaven. The title Abba sometimes refers to sages or rabbis. See this article: himpublications.com/blog/meaning-abba/

CHAPTER 10 - PROPHETIC PATHFINDERS

Fivefold ministry gifts
Today, there is a lot of confusion in the Body of Christ regarding ministry gifts. By nature, the fivefold offices may stir up controversy, which is often the case with the apostolic ministry because of its inherent authority. Other contributing factors to dissent in this area are misuse and misunderstanding of these gifts. How to identify the five offices Jesus gave to his Church? Research is vital, particularly into the New Testament. By reading through the four gospels, we soon discover how Jesus carried all the five offices and effortlessly flowed in all the spiritual gifts. The few exceptions seem to be tongues and interpretation of tongues, which appeared after The Day of Pentecost (see Acts 2). It's also worthwhile to study the Book of Acts and the epistles to take a closer look at the ministries of Peter, Paul and John and other believers in the early Church. Revival history is another gold mine for further studies.

I consider prophetic pathfinders pilots who discover the path and lead the way for others to follow. To my understanding, the fivefold offices were meant to spearhead the move of God by setting the pace for the race in the ongoing equipping of the saints. I think it's unfortunate that we have developed second-class church concepts, failing to correspond with the biblical prototypes. We have hindered people from being released into their God-given destinies by applying disempowering structures. With a pronounced focus on tradition, theology and social programs, we have often been remiss in manifesting the Father's purposes. Our arch-enemy utterly despises the authentic Church for being a carrier of Christ's presence in the world. If he can distort what a church should look like with counterfeits, he will not hesitate.

Through many centuries, the Church was deprived of much of its origin and Jewish roots, despite first being built on a foundation of the apostles and the prophets. God is now restoring his Church into greatness to be a functioning and powerful Body of believers. However, this divine restoration process is costly—it comes with steep price tags: Spiritual warfare, fiery trials and fierce opposition from agents within the Church. History shows that not everybody wants the new move of God, as it feels unsafe and threatens our conventional spiritual boundaries. Today, we notice an ongoing separation process between God's [96]true Church and large portions of mainstream Christianity. Our choice is to evolve or devolve spiritually; there is no middle ground. Will we become sanctified or secularised?

TRIALS — **OPPOSITION** — **REVIVAL RESTORATION REFORMATION** — **WARFARE**

Many are clueless in terms of what a prophet or an apostle is. Some think the apostles are like the dinosaurs—extinct. The cryptic apostles supposedly evaporated shortly after the first century, a viewpoint called [97]Cessationism. Along with doctrines like [98]replacement theology, this one has done a lot of damage and even held sway over some charismatic churches. A quite common view regarding apostolic ministry goes like this: Jesus' inner circle, with his twelve chosen apostles, established Christianity and became expendable after completing the biblical canon. This opinion is not as far-fetched as one should think because many still agree with it. For some scholars, the alleged absence of apostles naturally becomes a suitable excuse to promote and justify hierarchical and less organic church structures. Yet any proficient student of the New Testament will discover that several other apostles lived at the same time as the Lamb's apostles but also in the duration after their departure (see Rev. 18:20, 21:14). If that is the case, the Apostolic Age never ceased.

---

[96] **My comment:** The concept of God's people as a remnant of faithful believers is very prominent throughout the Old Testament, but also visible in the New Testament. (See: Gen. 7:23; 45:5-7, 1 Kings 19:18, Matt. 7:13-14, Rom. 11:2-5, Jude 1:3, Rev. 12:10-11, 17).

[97] **Cessationism** versus continuationism involves a Christian theological dispute whether spiritual gifts remain available to the church, or whether their operation ceased with the Apostolic Age of the church. Source: Wikipedia - en.wikipedia.org

[98] **Replacement theology:** An attack on biblical feasts and twisting of New Testament texts and claim that the Gentile Church has superseded the Jews as God's people. To defend their pagan traditions, The Catholic Church tried to purge so-called heretics from their midst in Europe, particularly those who celebrated Passover. They titled the Gentile Church the New Israel. These bogus claims are easily refuted by reviewing the New Testament record.

An ability to recognise the functions of fivefold ministry—the five offices given by Christ himself—is essential if we want to explore the true nature of the Church. Can a church even exist without apostles and prophets? Christ bequeathed these gifts to his Church (see 1 Cor 12:28, Eph. 4:11 NIV). The noted passages point to functions that should be integrated elements of what we think of as commonplace church life. To view these functions as outmoded or superfluous is unsupported by Scripture. According to Paul's revelation, the Lord placed these gifts within his Body. End of discussion. Nowhere do we find that God decided on a whim to remove or replace them with other gifts, like pastors, evangelists and teachers. These gifts are necessary but not all-sufficient because of their natural inhibitions. Besides, we don't need the fivefold if a ticket to Heaven is our only end goal. Assassins and evangelists will work perfectly well, and, of course, in reverse order! Some fanciful scholars conclude that the apostles and prophets were phased out or became redundant. Do we recognise that God placed apostles first, secondly prophets and thirdly teachers? Evangelists and pastors are listed in the last fivefold category: *"And God has appointed in the church, first apostles, second prophets, third teachers, then miracles, then gifts of healing, helps, administrations, various kinds of tongues."* (1 Cor. 12:28 NASB). In this verse, we observe how Paul ranks these gifts based on their essential functions.

Having a background in the Scandinavian Pentecostal movement, I am acquainted with some of the standard practices within charismatic churches—or at least how it was some decades back. I was issued a public written recommendation at the get-go of my preaching ministry. After this letter of approval, brand-new preachers set out as evangelists, then become youth pastors and, finally, senior pastors. Through years of faithful service, some ministers turn into revered and seasoned Bible teachers. To be validated like this, or asked to speak at conferences or on Christian television, is regarded as the greatest honour one can get. If you are a preacher, it proves that you are at the peak of your spiritual career. What about the office of an apostle? To imply that you have an apostolic ministry may not be acknowledged. Still, if you make this claim, you must show that you have planted churches in the capacity of a missionary or a pastor. I find that all church planters are definitely not apostles, although some genuinely are. Starting a new church can be achieved with leadership skills, force of personality and talented staff. Stylish church buildings, sound and light and social programs can be achieved with proper funding and the right business models.

WORK - PRACTICAL	MINISTRY - SPIRITUAL
Evangelist - preacher	Evangelist – grace to win souls
Pastor – leader/preacher	Pastor – grace to care for believers: shepherd
Teacher – experienced preacher	Teacher – grace to explain the truth: teacher/prophet
Missionary – preacher doing missions & help projects	Missionary – a sent one with grace to spread the gospel: apostle or evangelist

CHURCH · KINGDOM

At the risk of sounding like a broken record, in my view, the apostolic and prophetic function is key in the process of maturing the Body of believers into Christlikeness and a further release of the ministry gift. I base my findings on the New Testament, which I have examined for decades. Wouldn't it be wise to focus on the significance of these vital functions because of the life and anointing they impart to the Body of Christ? Paul mentioned the intent behind the gifts: The full equipping of all God's children to service in the Kingdom (see Eph. 4:12). Some conservative churches are big on teaching basic biblical doctrines but not that proficient in training believers to use spiritual gifts and ministry gifts. Sadly, when believers stay unchallenged or are not serving within their capacities, they remain immature.

When churches experience a glaring lack of organic growth, they compensate for it through various organisational structures. To my mind, it's healthier to invest time and effort to achieve personal development. This could fulfil some ministers' goal for their churches: higher levels of accountability and stability. Relationships and practical discipleship bring maturity. For some ministers, the structures set in place stop them from doing what their hearts long for, which is a paradox! Instead of going with their curiosity and hunger for genuineness, they allow irksome church politics and the fear of man to halt progression. Churches and denominations often prioritise church attendance, programs, volunteer work and financial contributions over focused discipleship. I want to see leaders on all levels being empowered and equipped through the fivefold ministry, as I firmly believe in [99]the priesthood of all believers. Not everyone carries fivefold gifts, but all are ministers of reconciliation. All born-again believers are leaders, chosen witnesses and ambassadors of God's

---

[99] **The priesthood of all believers:** A doctrine of the Protestant Christian Church: every individual has direct access to God without ecclesiastical mediation, and each individual shares the responsibility of ministering to the other members of the community of believers. Source: meriam-webster.com **My comment:** in the Church we are all priests through our High priest and mediator, Jesus (see Heb. 10:19, 12:24 and 1 Pet. 2:9, Rev. 1:4-6).

kingdom. To lead is taking on responsibility—leading by example among friends, family, colleagues and neighbours. We should powerfully demonstrate a Christian lifestyle through the gospel with wisdom, excellence and generosity.

To think that just a selected group carries ministry gifts is a misapprehension. Some preachers think that they—along with a few others—are the only ones capable of gathering the great end time harvest of souls. They concur that the rest of the Body of Christ must support their large ministries in order to serve the greater purpose. At best, it simply shows their ignorance because they don't recognise ministry gifts in the main. But consider this: If fivefold gifts really are sparse, why do the world's underground churches give rise to countless new leaders when their own leaders get imprisoned or executed? At worst, these ministries disregard fellow believers. Their hypothesis implies a nit-picking God who only uses professional evangelists and teachers—proven successful by their international ministries. My persuasion is that God, in his merciful foresight, made sure that no gift would be lacking in an effort to fulfil his perfect plans (see 1 Cor. 1:7). My concern is a dearth of *mature* ministry gifts in the Church, as an empowering Kingdom culture has been absent. It might also explain why some ministers wrongly presume that fivefold offices are rare. God will change the present situation by drastically *catapulting* believers into powerful fivefold ministry like never before. If we are *capitulating* to him through prayer and consecration, the Lord will accelerate this process (see Jos. 3:5, 2 Chron. 7:14, Acts 6:1-9; 13:1, 5). A key to unleashing the prophetic voice with apostolic authority is making room for this dynamic to unfold. Apostolically gifted leaders have to take charge as role models and mentors before this transition can take place.

My next comment is not meant as a snide remark: Some pastors compare churches to functioning hospitals—sanctuaries caring for people in need. The initial thought behind the idea seems selfless and biblical. The famous story of the good Samaritan illustrates this principle of mercy (see Luke 10:25-37). Here is why I find the hospital analogy a bit troubling and incomplete: At the moment, many of today's churches are damaged and have become unfit as safe environments for distressed individuals. These churches are suffering loss because of the ongoing spiritual war. Inasmuch as I care deeply for the Church, as a shepherd myself, I believe that pastoring ought to lead somewhere. Apostolic oversight aims to confront and remove abusive leaders, as this, in turn, will allow genuine pastors to bring much-needed healing.

⬅——— Go higher

1. CAPITULATING
through prayer and consecration

Go lower ———➡

2. CATAPULTING
through purpose-driven dicipleship

I confidently believe that God wants churches to function more like military bases, to successfully train believers for war. An army demonstrates a tight-knitted and high-functioning family where all its members are willing to die for each other. How else do we imagine overcoming the gates of Hades? The apostles are ideal candidates for taking on that brave task. Apostolic ministry is about discipling nations—which involves the equipping of God's beloved ones, whatever their background. Upon revisiting Jesus' words, I consider the Great Commission to be doable. That begs the question: Is this assignment feasible without the apostles taking the lead? If believers generally were called to disciple others, at some stage, it would require discipleship of themselves. That inevitably brings us back to fivefold ministry. Joel 2:28-32 tells us how the great harvest will be gathered: Sons and daughters will prophesy, and old men have dreams. Preaching of the gospel, prophetic visions and angelic visitations will be common, and people will call out to Jesus for salvation as a result. Previously, I likened God's people to a forceful army mobilised for combat, seamlessly working together as one man ([100]see Joel 2:1-11). These two passages from Joel's well-known chapter complete each other. As an analogy, to blow the trumpet before the battle is not very different from prophecy (see Judg. 7:20, 1 Cor. 14:6-8). God mobilises the warriors, servants who heed the apostolic roar of his voice to move forward in battle. Simultaneously, he releases labourers for the harvest—another aspect of how the Lord beckons his children. *And he said to them, "The harvest is plentiful, but the labourers are few. Therefore pray earnestly to the Lord of the harvest to send out labourers."* (Luke 10:2 ESV). A full-scale invasion of prophesying harvest workers will soon intimidate the enemy. They will effectively preach the gospel and call the nations to repentance. These equipped believers are genuine world-changers.

---

[100] **My comment:** I don't claim that this passage literally refers to Christians but use it as a prophetic application to illustrate my point.

Building the fivefold with a pure heart

It's time for a wake-up call for the believers who are passionate about being a part of a new wineskin. Here is what the Lord showed me: God creates a new wineskin out of people who are hungry for change because they represent the Father's heart for their families, communities and nations. I see the new wineskin as hearts connected in commitment to Jesus and each other. Together we will carry God's anointing. To usher in a greater move of God, we must put aside our own agendas. I view the new wineskin as a conceptual description of an apostolic pattern. It's a timeless picture: It reveals how we can reflect the Father's heart as his House (see Mark 2:18-22).

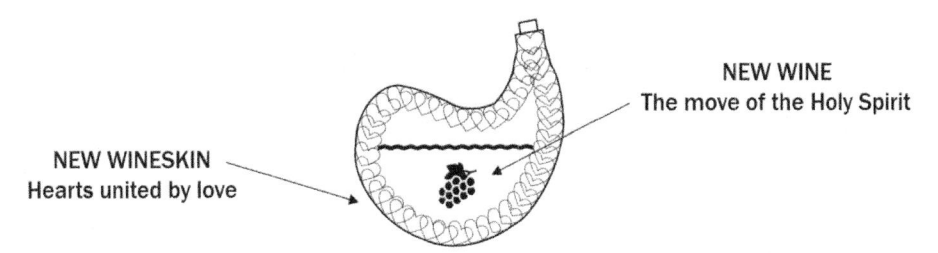

NEW WINE
The move of the Holy Spirit

NEW WINESKIN
Hearts united by love

God calls his children to transition into a vessel carrying his glory in this world. The revelation of the wineskin is easily grasped, but the practical ramifications are much more demanding. It necessitates an organic structure with a vision-driven approach to support the fellowship's life and increase. After we have determined our mission, vision, and core values, the natural outcome is to rethink our structures. A church without functional organic systems will wind up as programme-driven, process-led, or politically-led rather than *mission-led*. Organic structures, good decision-making and governance processes help to sustain growth—with resources being maximised and used wisely. The mission-led approach gives us enough leverage to adapt to the challenges and changes we face in the seasons and years ahead.

As with all good friendships, there is a price to pay for a God-given relationship. Let us listen to the Lord's heartbeat. This season, he picks the team he wants us to join. We are building the House of the Lord in vain when we don't let God form us or if we forget to nurture relationships within the Body of Christ (see Psalm 127:1). God calls us to build with his presence, led by his Spirit. Pride and self-serving ambitions are typical stumbling blocks within Christian ministry. There are two paths to take: We either become stepping-stones or stumbling blocks. God prefers stepping-stones because they elevate people and make them successful. Stumbling blocks will make others trip over and cause offence. Lord, grant me the grace to be that stepping-stone! The Lord calls leaders to lay down their lives for others. *"Greater love has no man than this, that a man lay down his life for his friends"* (John 15:13 ESV). Our lesson is learned when we habitually choose to love and trust God's family, despite shortcomings and weaknesses. Some believers abscond churches in periods of great transition and shaking, as these events are grossly uncomfortable. Discontented, we disconnect from one church and then try to transfer our commitment to a dissimilar church—hoping for things to improve. Staying, praying and obeying is usually the better solution. Don't leave your church unless God gives you clear instructions. He wants us to be planted without the risk of damaging our roots by moving from pot to pot—if you get the picture. Faithfully sticking with our community will help us to stay blessed and nurtured, even in dry seasons (see Psalm 92:13, Jer. 17:7-8).

The devil has often succeeded in sowing discord and division among ministry gifts because of fear, envy and hurt. A vital part of the joining process in God's House is humility and healing. When we open up to God and each other, he can reconcile and rebuild us. Living stones are versatile and pliable, and the Lord puts them in the perfect spot for a seamless fit in his House. He restores those who are contrite and poor in spirit: the humble, whose shame, disappointment and pain he can access (see Isa. 57:15, Matt. 5:3). These unassuming people are the smooth building blocks he prefers because they allow him to chip away their rough edges. Being human, even pastors and preachers compensate for feelings of insecurity or abandonment. The solution to emotional deficit is to receive the Father's unconditional love for us until we regain our health. Let us, therefore, come to Christ, the Living Stone, and surrender to all his glorious purposes for our lives (see 1 Pet. 2:4-8). Transparency and accountability between true friends are powerful tools to heal us and make us whole. Friends who pray and stay with us in the process are extremely valuable.

The correlation between callings and gifts is conspicuous. Our bridal calling is to fellowship with God's Son and abide in him and his words (see John 15:4-7, 1 Cor 1:9, 1 John 2:28). Whether we are flowing in gifts—or bearing fruit—it should always be the by-product of loving and knowing him. Fivefold ministry has nothing to do with personal ambition in the church or recognition based on a powerful anointing. If you desire to be 'the man of the hour' or 'the man of power', you let your puffed-up ego side-track and manipulate you. Women may also fall prey to the same temptation, but men are more susceptible to it. The sad result is that people will see you, not Christ. But it's all about Christ, the chief apostle, who prophesied: *"I will build my Church"* (Matt. 16:18, Heb. 3:1). Understanding the fivefold and God's father heart will not infallibly prevent us from screwing things up even as established believers. At critical stages of the building process, plans sometimes go awry because people slip back into their old behavioural patterns. Christians usually succumb to pressure when the adversary pushes trigger buttons of pride or pain. To stay consistently loving and humble, without a boastful focus on personal ministry at the expense of the empowerment of fellow believers, is a path to success.

Let us have a little heart check-up: Is our main reason for belonging to a church to love, serve and bless other believers? If these preferences don't match our priorities, we won't participate in a fivefold wineskin. Another question is this: Are we willing to submit to other leaders in love and honour their callings and gifts in spite of their mistakes? I think we could all benefit from Joseph's anointing to help us stay the course. By the way, I am not thinking about the version most frequently referred to—the business or prophetic anointing. In the face of deep betrayal, Joseph forgave his brothers and restored his relationship with them! The most godly and anointed believers forgive their brothers, and even their worst enemies like Stephen did. Let us follow in the footsteps of Joseph and Stephen (see Gen. 50:15-21, Acts 7:60).

Other leaders' imperfections will typically expose our proneness to faultfinding and cockiness. It's quite painless to point out others' flaws and mistakes. Are we ready to love fellow leaders in their unlovable mess? Do we help peers if they struggle with marriage, sexuality, anger, addictions or other problems? We all have disadvantages; God isn't concerned with these impediments. They were all dealt with by Christ on the cross. Despite our issues, his response is loving us and showing us our rightful identity. We shouldn't shy away from healthy confrontations when we deal with things that need to be resolved at leadership level but rather speak the truth in love. What we say doesn't necessarily guarantee a merciful approach from our side, like: 'I say this in love'. Are we able to explore the cause without criticising the actions? Zig Ziglar puts it very well: 'It's not the situation, but whether we react (negatively) or respond (positively) to the situation that is important.' At the crossroads in our lives, it is imperative to extend grace to those who really need it.

"Dear children, let us not love with words or speech but with actions and in truth." (1 John 3:18 NIV). *"Brothers, if anyone is caught in any transgression, you who are spiritual should restore him in a spirit of gentleness. Keep watch on yourself, lest you too be tempted. Bear one another's burdens, and so fulfil the law of Christ. For if anyone thinks he is something, when he is nothing, he deceives himself. But let each one test his own work, and then his reason to boast will be in himself alone and not in his neighbour. For each will have to bear his own load."* (Gal. 6:1-5 ESV).

On a related note, we shouldn't be surprised but saddened in cases where Christian leaders fall. Whatever the scenario may be, we should grieve and not gossip. I will leave out the broader discussion but emphasise that the true goal of reaching out to a disgraced leader is the spiritual rescue of that individual's *character*. Are there true signs of repentance? A restoration process doesn't imply an easy transition back to pulpit ministry. It surely depends on the gravity of the committed offences. All *victims* must be prioritised and well taken care of in the process. Each case is sensitive and is to be handled wisely and prayerfully by paying attention to all parties involved. Leaders who frequently exploit fellow believers must step down. That said, the Lord is driven by his mercy, and his nature is redemptive. When confronted with sin or shortcomings, our response should, without fail, be honest and compassionate. Don't forget that the devil is an accuser. Who do we swear allegiance to: God or the accuser? *Alignment with the assignment* provides us with unfeigned purpose, purity and power. Obedient love demonstrates these qualities. By the way, spiritual power and authority come from three sources: Assignment, doctrine and intimacy.

1) Assignment/mission: *"And he called the twelve and began to send them out two by two, and gave them authority over the unclean spirits."* (Mark 6:7 ESV). *Jesus came and told his disciples, "I have been given all authority in heaven and on earth. Therefore, go and make disciples of all the nations, baptizing them in the name of the Father and the Son and the Holy Spirit. Teach these new disciples to obey all the commands I have given you. And be sure of this: I am with you always, even to the end of the age."* (Matt. 28:18-20 NLT).

2) Doctrine/truth: *"The people were amazed at his teaching, for he taught with real authority—quite unlike the teachers of religious law."* (Mark 1:22 NLT). *And they were all amazed, so that they questioned among themselves, saying, "What is this? A new teaching with authority! He commands even the unclean spirits, and they obey him."* Mark 1:27 ESV).

3) Intimacy/fellowship: *Jesus said to her, "Did I not tell you that if you believed you would see the glory of God?" So they took away the stone. And Jesus lifted up his eyes and said, "Father, I thank you that you have heard me. I knew that you always hear me, but I said this on account of the people standing around, that they may believe that you sent me." When he had said these things, he cried out with a loud voice, "Lazarus, come out." The man who had died came out, his hands and feet bound with linen strips, and his face wrapped with a cloth. Jesus said to them, "Unbind him, and let him go."* (John 11:40-44 ESV). Due to Jesus' sacrificial love, he could say: *"For you granted him authority over all people that he might give eternal life to all those you have given him."* (John 17:2 NIV). *"And being found in appearance as a man, he humbled himself by becoming obedient to death— even death on a cross! Therefore God exalted him to the highest place and gave him the name that is above every name, that at the name of Jesus every knee should bow, in heaven and on earth and under the earth, and every tongue acknowledge that Jesus Christ is Lord, to the glory of God the Father."* (Phil. 2:8-11 NIV).

God wants us to linger in the local church through the storms of warfare and firmly withstand the devil's attempt to detach us from the dear people he introduced to us. They are God's beloved ones, and we belong together as a family. The ugliness and nastiness that could emerge if some ministry gifts don't get the expected recognition will only cause destruction. At times, we have run-ins with power-hungry people who insist on being served instead of being servants themselves. Jesus became the most prominent servant of us all and explicitly instructed his disciples to follow his humble example (see Matt. 20:27-28). Paul certainly didn't get any VIP treatment, and said this: *"For I think that God has exhibited us apostles as last of all, like men sentenced to death, because we have become a spectacle to the world, to angels, and to men."* (1 Cor. 4:9 ESV). The first apostles were hated and brought low but endured it. Why are some preachers today so easily affronted? Is it because of pride and self-preservation? Jesus came to lay down his life for the sheep—he never tried to build a famous ministry (see John 10:1-30). The biblical expression 'shepherd' is a factual description of a leader. The Lord will judge the self-seeking shepherds because they misrepresent his nature (see Ezek. 34:1-24). In chapter eight, we saw how deceitful leaders usually manipulate Christian church culture through exploitation. We show ourselves unworthy to be entrusted with God's people if we fail to demonstrate the same selfless love as Christ. *"I will seek the lost, and I will bring back the strayed, and I will bind up the injured, and I will strengthen the weak, and the fat and the strong I will destroy. I will feed them in justice."* (Ezek. 34:16). Loving ministers pursue purpose over promotion and protection over a position. Our pastoral mission is to 'serve and protect' the sheep of his pasture. God will, in time, recompense shepherds who faithfully serve him because they love his people. *"Humble yourselves, therefore, under God's mighty hand, that he may lift you up in due time."* (1 Pet. 5:6 NLT).

Today, the Lord raises up teams of apostles and prophets. We must be on our guard and diligently protect and consolidate these relationships. Covenant relationships are the high ground we should occupy and retain. Satan will strike to divide us unless we resist him. Before Jesus returns, I envision how dynamic fivefold ministry teams will carry breakthrough anointing and open heavens over cities, regions and nations. The raging powers of hell will try their utmost to prevent this scenario—viciously plotting and campaigning against it. But God will use the fivefold to foil the enemy's plans. Leaders' care and concern must involve the future of the Body of Christ. Are we capable of seeing the bigger picture? When we love our brothers and sisters in other denominations and churches, we build God's House together—in sincere unity. Of course, as different tribes of Kingdom people, we have our own peculiar traits. The Father shapes the new wineskin out of the remnant of overcomers. He is preparing the nets for his harvest, making them robust, resilient and unbreakable. The secret that ties together these nets of relationships is God's love, tested through fire. These nets will hold the harvest of souls coming into the Kingdom.

The Lord is raising up teams of apostles and prophets. We must be on our guard and diligently protect and consolidate these relationships.

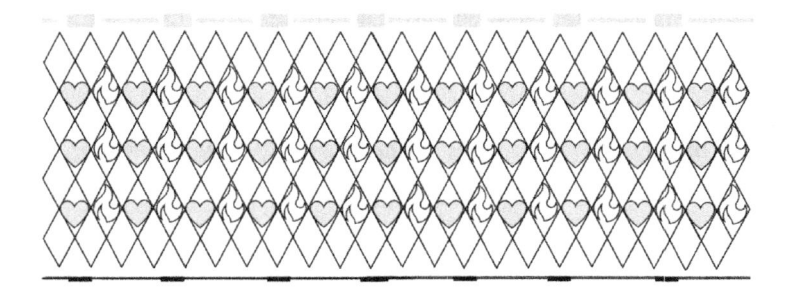

Let us look at the five offices, or the fivefold ministry gifts, as outlined in Ephesians chapter 4. As I see it, God distributed these gifts to men and women equally. I base my opinion on a scriptural view free from social agendas. Revival history provides us with many examples of great men and women of God with mature ministry gifts, both in recent and ancient times. Ministry gifts are various anointings and functions of the Spirit given to chosen individuals. When these anointings are imparted to the Church—through supernatural ministry—believers will get sudden breakthroughs, hear clearly from God, confidently proclaim his message, lavishly love on people and efficiently educate them in the things of God. The New Testament defined fivefold leaders as πρεσβύτερος *presbyteros*, overseers ἐπίσκοπος *episkopos,* and shepherds, or watchmen, ποιμήν *poimen*. These Greek words describe the function of an elder, or spiritual leadership, in different but complementary ways. Is an *elder* a ministry gift in itself? No, it's a role description of a fellow leader or another ministry gift.

In Acts, we find apostles and elders. The apostle Peter described himself as a fellow elder, implying that elders are fivefold ministers (see Acts 15:4, 1 Pet. 5:1). An elder is typically a seasoned ministry gift. Fivefold leaders should model the behaviour for the community culture they want to establish. Such a church culture should always encourage truth, love and honour. It challenges leaders to stress Christian identity more than issues within wholesome boundaries defined by devotion and discipline. Experienced leaders won't deride you if you fail or feel weak. They will show you who you truly are in Christ. God tends to use humble apostolic leaders to [101]break and mould us, an essential process in building character. Our part is to nurture

---

[101] **Break-in:** The process of crushing a horse's wild spirit in order to calm it and make it safe to ride. Dead-broken horses are perfectly serene and well-trained. They don't startle easily and are reliable. The analogy works well to explain how we die from selfish ambitions. Afterwards, God can entrust us with the responsibility to shepherd and support his people. Are we willing to pay this price?

growth through partnership, knowing that when we succeed, our leaders succeed and vice versa. In my brief treatise, I will look at varying aspects of fivefold ministry. God wants us to comprehend, together with all his holy people, the full magnitude of his glory: the breadth, length, depth and height of his love (see Eph. 3:16-19). I believe the entirety of ministry gifts illustrates these dimensions of Christ's sacred love. Keep this in mind while you are unpacking the five offices with me.

1) APOSTLE - ἀπόστολος *apostolos* means a sent one, a delegate, a messenger, or one sent forth with orders, a person commissioned with authority.

Characteristics: In ancient times, Greek apostles were fleet admirals. They were military strategists who bravely conquered new territories and colonised them. The Romans followed a similar pattern and sent delegations of citizens to influence the people groups within their frontier territories. The chosen delegates mirror the New Testament ἐκκλησία *ecclesia*—a chosen congregation or assembly. As we have seen, the most common translation of the word is 'church'. The invaders sought to assimilate other ethnic groups with their ethos and mindset—culturally, politically and religiously. This process was seen as vastly successful when the conquered nation adopted the languages and customs of the occupying force by blending into a new social-cultural system. In a similar yet uncoerced fashion, Heaven establishes an earthly embassy, God's House, stately representing the King of Kings. His House is indwelt by his Holy Spirit and becomes a demonstration of the Father's love—the transforming power that declares: *"As in heaven, so on earth"* (see Matt. 6:10 ASV).

Function: God made the apostles the first line defence and did so deliberately. As servants and builders of communities, Jesus commissioned his apostles to disciple nations. They were called to be world changers, chief builders and influencers of cultures. The apostolic office brought a renewed mandate to subdue the earth and to have dominion over it (see Gen. 1:28, Matt. 28:18-19, Rom. 8:19). The leading four apostolic functions are 1) building Christ into the believers, 2) training them in righteousness, 3) demonstrating a holy lifestyle, and 4) breaking open the heavens by releasing God's glory. It's a breakthrough ministry. The apostle Paul did the same when he planted new churches in cities and regions: He broke spiritual opposition and laid Christ as the foundation in the believers' hearts (see Col. 1:25). You may ask: Are all church planters apostles? No, but the apostolic ministry definitely breaks the ground open for God's kingdom to be established against all odds. Along with the prophets, apostles are facilitators and stewards of the new moves of God. These two offices have a special grace to carry God's glory and sustain revivals. Some have compared the apostle with the thumb on the hand. It freely reaches the other four fingers and supports them. If the fingers represent the rest of the fivefold, we notice how the apostle can easily adapt to prophesy, evangelise, pastor and teach whenever necessary. That ability lies within the apostolic grace. However, it doesn't negate the necessity of other ministry gifts. Mature apostles will labour hard to cooperate with other fivefold ministers without claiming resources in a self-centred manner.

Application: An apostle sharply envisions the purpose of the Church and holds the blueprint to relationally build teams and activate believers in their callings and gifts. To exemplify how an apostle identifies the vision and can translate it from fiction to fact, Paul compared the function to a master builder or an architect. In ancient times architects could instruct the local builders to move pillars on-site because they were hands-on in the building process (see 1 Cor. 3:9-10). In the New Testament, the apostles appointed elders, or fivefold leaders, in the local churches (see Acts 14:23, Tit. 1:5). In tandem with the prophet, they affirm God-given identity in believers through divine encouragement and revelation. Apostles often discern the resources 'within the House' and are capable of uniting members through visionary leadership skills, empowering teaching and loving relationships. Apostolic oversight is a huge blessing. The apostle helps fivefold ministries and other gifts to work harmoniously together. It collides with the traditional view where one expects the pastor to do all the ministry, including much-anticipated church growth and keeping the wealthy donors happy. Naturally, some pastors become exhausted or leave the ministry. Such pressure is inhuman and unbiblical. The whole body of believers needs help to be empowered; fully equipped for ministry. Apostles are efficient not only by speaking to thousands, but they manage to have meaningful one-on-one interactions. The same duality was seen in Jesus' life when he spoke to droves of people or met them face to face (see the Gospel of John). The greatest apostle of all is our beloved Lord and Master: *"Therefore, holy brothers, you who share in a heavenly calling, consider Jesus, the apostle and high priest of our confession"* (see Heb. 3:1 ESV).

Conclusion: Regardless of age, apostles predominantly display Christlike attributes and humble authority. More evolved apostles underline and accentuate function while actively serving the Body of Christ locally, regionally or globally. They don't misuse the anointing for position or stardom and dislike attention. Apostles seem to access an extraordinary grace to endure suffering and hardships, a supernatural resilience. They are divinely called to stand on the front line, ready to pay the price and exemplify a Kingdom lifestyle others can imitate (see Acts 9:15-16, 1 Cor 4:13). Unique for the apostle is the great ability to build in the spirit realm and create space, opportunities and freedom to support other believers to function and fulfil their calling. *"In my Father's house are many mansions; if it were not so, I would have told you; for I go to prepare a place for you."* (John 14:2 ASV).

Apostles pioneer ground-breaking models and systems to benefit God's creation and advance his Kingdom. We will see more and more churches and businesses emerge that are founded on Kingdom principles. Apostles long to see Christ fully developed in the believers and travail in prayer as intercessors. These spiritual fathers and mothers have the capacity to birth revival through persevering prayer. They pass on their legacy to new revivalists by fostering and mentoring the next generation! The apostle resembles the breadth of the love of God by declaring his whole counsel (see Acts 20:27). The apostolic gift is combined with other fivefold ministry gifts. The pioneering itinerant-apostle is most known, but there are also church-apostles. Some are pastors; others are members but still carriers of renewal and revival as firm spiritual pillars in their local churches.

2) PROPHET - προφήτης *prophetes* is a mouthpiece, an announcer, or a spokesman, it's an individual who flows with revelation or words from God.

Characteristics: In the Bible, we find the phrase חֹזֶה *chozeh* - 'seer' (Amos 7:12). The prophetic ministry is also about seeing into the spiritual realm, having pictures, dreams and visions. A prophet has a zeal for righteousness and clearly discerns the will of God but is also well aware of the demonic dimension. Prophets see beyond the obvious. With intuitive insight into people's thoughts and hidden motives, they quickly put together the jigsaw puzzle of the soul. Jesus constantly flowed in revelation: *"But Jesus would not entrust himself to them, for he knew all people. He did not need any testimony about mankind, for he knew what was in each person."* (John 2:24-25 NIV). *Jesus knew what they were thinking, so he asked them, "Why do you have such evil thoughts in your hearts?* (Matt. 9:4 NLT). Prophets are passionate and radical because they often see the world in a black-or-white fashion. A prophet keeps it real and categorically hates falsehood and compromise (see Psalm 45:7). God seems to balance prophetic ministry with a gift of compassion. Prophets are sensitive to the movement of the Holy Spirit. The Lord shows his servants, the prophets, his plans for the next season or the years to come (see Amos 3:7-8).

Function: Seasoned prophets stand in the counsel of the Lord and cooperate with Heaven's vision. They are cautious not to exalt what they sense above God's written Word (see 2 Tim. 3:16-17, Heb. 1:1-2, 2 Pet. 1:19-21). The prophetic realm is often associated with foreknowledge of future events and giving out personal prophecies. Still, predicting future events is only a peripheral part of the prophetic dimension. True prophets exert godly influence today that impacts tomorrow. The *future* is up for grabs for those who are determined to *seize* it. Historic timelines can be corrected by prophetic voices to prevent future possibilities from being snatched from God's children and to establish the Fathers' plans for coming generations. By listening to prophetic warnings, we may actively avert disasters through repentance and fervent intercession. A process set in motion by a spoken prophetic word is significant. The purpose of a prophetic message is our edification, exhortation and consolation. To exhort means to warn, admonish and rebuke (see 1 Cor. 14:3). Most people want to get cushy prophetic words, but are we willing to listen to the voice of the Lord when he hands out words of tough love? Why are prophets always persecuted? They aren't exactly crowd-pleasers! Truth often stirs up controversy. Prophecy brings division between spirit and soul when God's Word challenges our foolish and selfish agendas. Powerful catalysts for change can be when a prophet releases *a word* from the Spirit or even *an inspired dance*. It shifts the atmosphere and blesses those who receive it.

Application: We need to recognise the spiritual seasons and the vessels God is using. The prophets understand the times and the seasons (see 1 Chron. 12:32, 1 Pet. 1:10-12). As his mouthpieces, prophets are an indispensable part of the instrument we call God's will. When the wind of the Holy Spirit blows through the reed of the cross, a sound of grace reverberates for a desperate and longing world to hear it. So far, we have seen how pictures and visions carry the prophetic word and should not be despised.

The instant the Spirit descended on Jesus and manifested as a dove, John the Baptist managed to discern the Holy Spirit in his physical form. He identified the Messiah by seeing into the spiritual dimension (see John 1:32). John proclaimed what he *saw*. The prophets and teachers in the church at Antioch could clearly distinguish the apostolic anointing resting over Paul and Barnabas (see Acts 13:1-3). When the Lord reveals his secrets to the prophets, he usually assigns prophetic revelation to several of his servants. To corroborate prophetic revelation, God confirms the same message to various prophets. Sometimes God reveals his secrets to some people but withholds them from others. No single prophet is supposed to know or analyse all things, which calls for great humility within the prophetic community. All prophets should belong to local churches and stay well-connected to the apostolic ministry because God doesn't want satellites. It's problematic if evangelists and prophets go rogue and also refuse to submit to leaders in a local church. If we isolate ourselves, we lose out on the safety net God provides us through accountability and unity.

Conclusion: The foundation of the Church is the apostles and prophets. Together they carry revelation and breakthrough power. They discern and pray together and create and release together—well able to navigate the moves of God through the firestorms of opposition. Like Nehemiah, they restore the foundations and the walls of protection with their builder and warrior anointing. Undaunted, they continue to build until the walls are complete, each with their trowels and swords in hand (see Neh. 4:13-21). The Father promised to pour out his Holy Spirit on all flesh in these last days. The exact same Spirit who causes sons and daughters to prophesy is raising up a whole new *generation of prophets*. Visitations, visions, dreams and prophetic revelation will unleash God's presence. Unsaved people will be invaded by a realm of glory, prompting them to call upon Jesus' name! Prophets shaped ancient history, and the prophets will once again shape the worldview of our generation and the coming generations. Visionary leadership is unachievable if we don't properly align with the prophetic. The authentic Church is inherently prophetic because the Spirit of prophecy inhabits all genuine believers. All prophets are intercessors, praying for

God's plans to unfold. Samuel led, taught and prophesied. He also interceded for the nation of Israel (see 1 Sam. 12:23). A generation without prophetic revelation will stray from the Lord's ways and cast off moral restraints. They end up spiritually destitute—bereft of Kingdom values (see Prov. 29:18). The fear of the Lord closely relates to our view of him, which is determined by levels of prophetic discernment. The prophetic dimension represents the length of the love of God through a keen ability to recognise spiritual *patterns* and look into the future.

3) EVANGELIST - εὐαγγελιστής *euangelistēs* means a bringer of good news, sharing the gospel—the good news about Jesus, the Messiah.

Characteristics: Despite being an important ministry, it's the least represented in the Bible. It will perhaps come as a surprise to many. Philip, the evangelist, is listed, and Timothy (see Acts 21:8, 2 Tim. 4:5). Some denominations and churches use evangelist as their umbrella term for travelling ministers and not as a description of the ministry gift evangelist. Revivalists sometimes apply evangelist as a fitting title, but these ministers could be apostles or prophets who preach and teach a message of biblical repentance. An evangelist is passionate about reaching people through witnessing, gospel preaching and outreaches. Sharing the message of salvation is an evangelist's absolute pleasure and joy. The evangelists specialise in the field of soul-winning. They usually have a bold motivation kindled by the fire inside, a zeal that inspires them to proclaim Christ everywhere. Some evangelists thrive on opposition from reluctant non-believers and are qualified to declare and defend the faith. The brilliant authors who uphold the Christian faith and write compelling tomes about Apologetics may be evangelists with profound teaching ministries. Their objective is reaching the *unchurched* and educating believers to become effective witnesses. Like the apostles, some evangelists may carry gifts of healing and perform signs and wonders to point to the saving grace of our Lord Jesus Christ (see Acts 8:5-8).

Function: 1) God gave evangelists to enable us to reach out to our communities and bring the lost into his everlasting Kingdom. 2) The evangelistic ministry trains and equips everyday believers. It unleashes the true power of the gospel and is essential. Elaborate evangelistic crusades or so-called seeker-sensitive services cannot fill this need. Trendy church experiences with succinct uplifting messages and appealing music might impress some lost souls, but can they create lasting encounters with the living God? The fire of evangelism must become a blazing part of the local churches' DNA because it makes the gospel contagious—leaving nobody untouched. Beyond question, we should all know how to testify about our personal encounters and tell others about Jesus, the cross, the resurrection and his return to earth. That way, we can lead them to Jesus and connect them to the family of local believers.

Application: Evangelists have an unrivalled understanding of the finished work on the cross, sin, forgiveness and reconciliation. Whilst approaching strangers on the street might be daunting to most of us, an evangelist relishes the challenge! They are thrilled by bringing the gospel into new territories, compelled by Christ's amazing love. Exploring new avenues and methods to evangelise is a suspenseful kingdom adventure for the evangelists, and they also love media communication.

Conclusion: Currently, God significantly restores the evangelistic ministry. He will soon unleash innumerable evangelists to gather a great harvest of souls. By the way, pioneers usually combine the gift of the apostle and the evangelist because they are risk-takers! For them, the ultimate adrenaline kick is the excitement of introducing outsiders to our heavenly Father's amazing love. Evangelists represent the height of God's love as they thoroughly understand the splendour and majesty of Christ's redemptive work.

4) PASTOR - ποιμήν *poimén* means shepherd, carer, one who feeds the flock and protects the least, the last and the lost. A guide and an overseer, able to see others' needs.

Characteristics: The biblical title 'shepherd' is associated with elder: *presbyteros*, overseer: *episkopos* and leader: *proistemi*. As a result, some conclude that an elder and a pastor account for the same ministry. I have to disagree, based on what I find in the New Testament. As mentioned earlier, these words point to ministers within local churches and leaders with fivefold ministry. Churches have paid pastors on staff to look after their members. It includes administration, preaching and teaching, conducting services and individual counselling. The term 'pastor' ascribes to a leading role. It's indiscriminate in relation to the ministry gift itself. Hopefully, any church pastor does carry one or more of the ministry gifts. Pastors are sometimes associated with teachers, and some will even insist that these gifts represent one ministry—which gives a final tally of four ministry gifts. I beg to differ. Arguably, there are some pastors who are exceptional counsellors. They are great with people and full of compassion but cannot expound on a subject as well as a gifted Bible teacher does.

Function: Let us examine how the gift to care for people relates to the ministry gift pastor. Multiple pastors are present in a congregation with a hundred members or more. They are oftentimes seasoned believers with a gentle and loving spirit. People naturally gravitate towards pastors as they radiate genuine love, compassion and reliability. The levels of trust skilled pastors can build within a short stretch of time are astonishing. Pastors are truly trust magnets! They have an exceptional capacity for love and showcase character and integrity. These believers are dependable and faithful persons who build long-term relationships within the church. A pastor can listen and properly relate to people's issues and infuse hope and wisdom to support them. Pastors indeed take after the apostles in being wise mentors, role models and showing parental care. Apostles and pastors vigorously defend the flock. These two ministry gifts have a marked emphasis on discipleship. When Jesus claimed to be the door to the sheep, his Jewish audience accurately understood what he implied. The sheepfolds were stone-built with somewhat circular walls. The enclosed pen had one tiny opening. By now, you may have riddled out where the shepherd on duty slept during night-time. In the wall! In his job as a gatekeeper, he became the physical door of protection and could fight off wild animals with his rod and staff. Psalm 23 and the Gospel of John suddenly come to life (see Psalm 23:1-6, John 10:1-16).

Application: Sometimes pastors join a ministry team or prayer team at church to get to exercise their gift. Caring for other people's needs brings immense satisfaction to a genuine pastor. The opposite may also have a negative consequence. On the one hand, being hindered from helping—when wanting to do so—might give rise to depression or anxiety. On the other hand, losing ourselves to others' problems could potentially drain us emotionally. This common issue applies to all gifts from God. We will get filled with joy, peace and energy if we use them the way we should.

Conclusion: Pastors know their sheep, and the sheep know and trust their pastors (see John 10:14). The Lord connects us to *teams* in the Body of Christ. He does it to inspire us, grow us, hold us accountable and protect us. Jesus remarked that some Jewish listeners didn't belong to his sheep. He stated the plain fact that they refused to submit to his leadership. The Lord will always connect you and me to secure yet stimulating environments to strengthen our faith. Do we recognise the shepherds God appointed to watch over us and to support us in our walk? Pastors represent the depth of the love of God, as they, together with the teachers, help us to become established and rooted in the faith. An apostolic gift may gradually develop in some pastors. It will enable them to build the local church stronger or maybe get involved in church planting or networking with ministries or churches within a larger region.

5) TEACHER - διδάσκαλος *didaskalos* means teacher, instructor or scholar. It referred to individuals known for mastery in their field of learning. To some degree, it would have involved research.

Function: Pastors like to apply a few practical angles to their talks, whereas teachers delve into specific aspects and provide a more complete understanding of biblical truths. Several churches and movements were originally founded as direct results of outstanding teaching ministries. When the Lord restored indispensable truths to the Body of Christ, new churches branched out around the globe. The teachings often focused on revived truths or a broader application of those truths. In the UK, God endowed epic preachers like John Wesley and C.H. Spurgeon with brilliant teaching gifts. They were highly influential and significant in their lifetime in how they led thousands of believers into a deeper life in God, which also attested to their gifted apostleship. Their ministries had a lasting impact long after their departure.

The Bible is chock-full of concepts, principles and precepts, what we usually define as theology or teaching about God. Church history shows how faith was developed and conveyed by different traditions and practices. Baptism evolved into an excess of rituals. As I see it, sound doctrinal focus requires a finetuned balance emerging from revelation and relationship with the Holy Spirit as we examine God's Word. Shouldn't we expect teaching to induce a change of heart and not merely increase our head knowledge?

Application: Deception is bound to come—we must stay watchful because of false teachers. Jesus and the apostles warned about these charlatans, and all the more as the end times events unfold. The Bible unequivocally warns against false teachers and lying prophets (See Matt. 7:15-20; 2 Pet. 2:1-21). We find many false doctrines and practices today, even within popular charismatic churches. In an ill-mannered style, they promise miracles or breakthroughs if you 'sow a seed' to these ministries. Scripture is often twisted to exploit people's needs. When leaders assert that God isn't limited by the revelation of his Word, it opens up a Pandora's box of fallacy and deceit. By exalting tradition above the Bible, the Catholic Church could justify its adoption of pagan customs. To further support their countless heresies, the Vatican added non-canonical writings to their Bible version, the Vulgate. Together with the sale of indulgences, these appalling practices contributed to the ensuing protestant Reformation. Martin Luther legitimately condemned the Papacy for its blighted system when he boldly stated: 'A simple layman armed with Scripture is greater than the mightiest pope without it'. Luther's tagline was *sola Scriptura*—by Scripture alone: The Holy Bible is the sole infallible source of authority in Christian faith and tradition. No genuine Christian will argue otherwise. Despite Luther's impressive achievements, he didn't denounce the detrimental anti-Semitism committed by the church fathers before his time. He continued to spout the same hatred and vitriol, mainly because the Jewish community didn't side with him in his uprising against the infamous Church of Rome. Centuries later, Adolf Hitler justified [102]the Shoah, or Holocaust, by building his inflamed rhetoric upon some of Luther's literature.

Having said this, notice how God's Spirit always points you to the Scripture and the teachings of our Lord. [103]Smith Wigglesworth said: 'I understand God by his Word. I cannot understand God by impressions or feelings. I cannot get to know God by sentiment. I can only know him by his Word.' He said: 'It is a dangerous practice to be governed by feelings. We are saved not by feelings but by the Word of God.' The *plumbline* for testing the veracity of theology or prophecy is the foolproof Old Book. Let us devour God's Word and ponder it day and night. To elevate reason, or

---

[102] **The Shoah:** שואה *Shoah* is the Jewish term for the Holocaust, used since the 1940s. en.wikipedia.org/wiki/Shoah_(disambiguation)
[103] **Source:** Smith Wigglesworth: The Secret of His Power (Living Classics), by Albert Hibbert ISBN: 9781577949770

subjective feelings, above the authority of the Scripture is a slippery slope leading to spiritual decline. The saying 'You are what you eat' refers to bodily consumption; the same idea relates to what our minds feed on. Don't be fearful, but be prayerful when you seek out TV shows, videos, podcasts and music labelled as Christian. Ask the Holy Spirit for discernment. All that glitters is not gold or from God!

Conclusion: Jesus' extensive knowledge of the Scriptures astonished the scholars of his day, as he hadn't undergone traditional rabbinical training. The Master taught them how to validate revelation correctly. *Jesus answered them, "My teaching is not mine, but his who sent me. If anyone's will is to do God's will, he will know whether the teaching is from God or whether I am speaking on my own authority."* (John 17:16-17 ESV). The litmus test wasn't their ability to grasp spiritual concepts but whether the holy fear of the Lord possessed them. God wants open ears and swift obedience! Jesus was a recognised rabbi because of his deep insight and the countless signs that followed him (see John 3:2). Shouldn't we, too, expect signs and wonders to occur when ministers operate with revelation? Don't forget that burning hearts are as crucial as the burning sensation of God's healing presence (see Luke 24:32).

A passion for God's Word and a flow of wisdom and revelation mark the ministry gift teacher. Astute thinkers and researchers match naturally gifted teachers. Some of them are capable of defining complex ideas in an easily understood phraseology. Brilliant teachers generally have exceptional memory because of a gift to store vast amounts of information. A few may later become Bible teachers. The Berean Jews probably had many teachers among them. They lovingly received the message and daily examined the Scriptures to investigate for themselves (see Acts 17:11). The teaching gift often merges with other ministry gifts, like apostle and teacher, prophet and teacher, etc. God diligently watches over all his promises, and he never takes doctrine lightly (see Jer. 1:12). *"Not many of you should become teachers, my brothers, for you know that we who teach will be judged with greater strictness."* (James 3:1 ESV). God tends to place prophets and teachers in the local church as a safeguarding measure to make sure that we tout sensible doctrine. *"Two or three prophets should speak, and the others should weigh carefully what is said. And if a revelation comes to someone who is sitting down, the first speaker should stop. For you can all prophesy in turn so that everyone may be instructed and encouraged."* (1 Cor. 14:29 NIV).

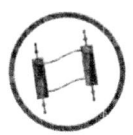

Apostolic covering, spiritual authority & submission

Albeit disputed, I want to include 'apostolic covering' in my discourse. Within the charismatic community, quite a few people are enamoured with this relatively new phenomenon. It is said to be [104]"the mechanism of spiritually shielding, protecting and providing true fathering and mentorship to individuals, leaders, churches, ministries or groups of people within the Body of Christ'. Some Christians find this concept biblical, while others disregard it. However, apostolic covering is no excuse to justify power abuse. We cannot assume headship apart from Jesus Christ, who is the Head of the Church, and we should humbly submit to the Holy Spirit. Genuine apostleship is about calling, not about rank or position. The same principle is, in part, foreshadowed in Moses. He was in charge of the nation of Israel and resided over seventy elders and the priesthood. His assignment and intimacy with the Lord qualified him as their *servant leader* (see Num. 12:6-7). God thoroughly examined Moses and found him to be faithful in all of his House. He was appointed based on credibility and responsibility. Moses greatly resembles Jesus, the Apostle and High Priest of our confession (see Heb. 3:1-2). How God dealt with Israel shows a pattern of apostolic authority, with clear parallels to the New Covenant. We receive wisdom and counsel from trusted advisors who have proven their love for us in laid-down lives of service. Most ministers who espouse apostolic covering seem to honour the concept of accountability by staying connected to leaders they respect.

We have three areas where accountability to other leaders proves valuable:
1) **Relationship.** We should respond to our spiritual leaders in love. Mentors will not insist on having authority over us but gently invite us to fellowship and mutual friendship. They demonstrate their maturity through great humility. We appreciate their loving discipline, even though we may not always enjoy it. The most quoted verse regarding biblical submission is Heb. 13:17. It has inconsistencies because of the English King James' politicised tampering with Tyndale's translation of the New

---

[104] **Source:** Citation by John A. Tetsola.

Testament. In the text, the words *obey* and *submit* do not correlate with the Greek definitions, which mean t*o be persuaded by* and to *give room and pre-eminence.* We don't submit blindly to leadership—whether they are pastors, elders, deacons, etc. Spiritual authority has its given place in our relationships with Christlike shepherds, who lead by example and teach the pristine Word of God. These are true leaders, tried and tested. We look to our leaders in the Lord as trusted guides (see Heb. 13: 7, 9). Our spiritual parents, or partners, direct us and hold us accountable. They edify and support us when we have healthy relationships with them. In Matt. 16:16-24 we find an interesting wordplay, only evident if we examine the Greek text: *"You are Peter* Πέτρος *petros, and on this rock* πέτρα *petra, I will build my church."* Peter means little rock or a piece of rock, while petra represents the bedrock. *"Listen to me, you who pursue righteousness, you who seek the Lord: look to the Rock from which you were hewn, and to the quarry from which you were dug."* (Isa. 51:1 NASB). Jesus called himself the Rock – petra, and Peter - petros. He shared his nature with Peter. Our Lord chiselled and sculpted his friend into a man of God (see 1 Cor. 3:11, 10:4). A picture of such a relational approach is more like [105]the pyramid in reverse, where leaders respectfully choose to get behind or beneath others to help them. Serving and leading as an apostle or a prophet loses its lustre once people realise the severity of the calling and responsibility involved. The same servant principle works in the marketplace: Skilful entrepreneurs often cooperate with the partners they mentor to develop character and scale their businesses. Apostolic ministry works through spiritual parents, who disciple people while displaying the persona of Christ.

2) **Releasing.** Thriving sons and daughters usually develop into competent fathers and mothers. Being trained in righteousness is a process where we learn to grow and develop. It's wonderful when experienced preachers entrust the pulpit to ministers they mentor. Paul had Timothy as his son in the faith. Elijah had Elisha, and Moses had Joshua etc. Numerous churches have structures where the senior pastor leaves the leadership to his son, much like an inherited responsibility. Fair enough. It might be proper to do so if their gifts are truly *apostolic*. But, at times, God raises up other

---

[105] **Top or bottom:** Contrary to the misperceived notion where apostles are at the top of a hierarchical structure, true apostles carry weight by serving others. No coercion is involved. A foundational edifice upholds the heavy load of a building. By divine design, apostles can cope with colossal pressure through responsibility in prayer and pastoral oversight.

leaders who carry the same spiritual DNA as the movement they belong to. Perhaps these leaders will be more successful and influential if they get the chance to lead. In my view, appointing others to leading positions in the ministry shouldn't be done out of family ties or favouritism but after much thought and prayer. Sadly, some churches are strictly run as business empires with a lot of profit and prestige. I find the biblical models to be more empowering because they build on relationships and not on a rigid set of principles. We entrust the keys of the Kingdom to faithful and hungry people. They are the ones that God will equip to continue our legacy. Some of them will do greater things than us (see 2 Kings 2:9, John 14:12). Did Elisha pray for a double portion because he felt he would be needing it? Jesus prophesied about greater works: Peter was the first in line to enter into this realm of greater glory. All who touched Jesus' clothes were healed (see Mark 6:56). In the Book of Acts, Peter moved in signs, wonders and healings. Nobody touched Peter physically, but the moment his shadow fell on the sick, they were all instantly healed (see Acts 5:15-16).

3) Restraining. Shortly after Jesus had announced his death and resurrection, Peter strongly criticised him. The possibility of losing his Master terrified him (see Mark 8:31-34). Jesus immediately rebuked Peter for lending his voice to human reasoning and the devil. Peter didn't see why the Messiah had to suffer; God's thoughts were foreign to him. Leaders who provide a spiritual safety net, who watch over us, know if we are out of line and are not afraid of chastising us. On one occasion, the disciples tried to turn away the women who wanted Jesus to bless their children. Jesus got very upset and reprimanded them (see Mark 10:13-14). He even rebuked John and James. He named them Boanerges, *"the sons of thunder"* because they wanted to call down fire on an unrepentant Samaritan village (see Luke 9:55). Jesus made it clear that their harsh attitude wasn't appreciated by him. But did he boot them out of his school of ministry? By no means! Spiritual mentors will not sugar-coat the facts for us but provide the much-required salty remarks to wake us up! Some are of the opinion that only men can provide spiritual covering. I think they are mistaken. The husband is designated, by God, as the head of the family because he carries a natural mantle of protection. Honouring his function is a huge blessing for the family (Eph. 5:22-33). However, spiritual authority is not about gender, as we are all children of God and, thereby, sons of God. If men can be the Bride of Christ, then women can be sons of God! During the time of the judges, we find that the prophetess Deborah was instructing a man, Barak, the military leader of Israel. He listened to her godly advice and successfully fulfilled his mission. Interestingly, Deborah dubbed herself *"a mother in Israel"* (see Judges 5:7). She understood that her role was important. Alongside the fathers of the Church, we need the mothers. Calling and maturity can establish authority. The Body of Christ is not based on a hierarchically organised system. Firstly, we have to connect with Christ, the Head, and secondly, with each other. Multi-headed monsters will emerge once inferior or heavy structures replace biblical authority, like the dreaded scarlet beast with seven heads and ten horns (see Rev. 17:3). Individuals or institutions demanding your compliance risk standing between you and Christ. Resist corrosive leaders who insist on your subservience in exchange for their so-called covering. To lord over people is not God's way because greatness is shown through servant leadership (see Matt. 20:25-28 and 1 Pet. 5:3). We are warned: *"... be not entangled again in a yoke of bondage."* (see Gal. 5:1 ASV).

A mature apostolic elder supports your calling and the overall vision for the Church (see 1 Pet. 5:1-4). Spiritual supervision keeps you safe and helps you to grow in your calling and your gifts. In order to rightly value *headship*, we have to understand the principle of *sonship*. Sons learn and grow when they submit to spiritual authority because cooperation requires trust. In life and ministry, none of us is exempt from challenges. Belonging to a community benefits us, but a rebellious and independent mentality hurts us. I am convinced that preachers and pastors will benefit from long-term relationships with other upright and seasoned servants of the Lord. The accountability bit brings out the best in every leader. It makes us fly much higher in our momentums and prevents us from plummeting into a hellscape of despair if we crash. Being members of the Body of Christ, we profit from each other by mutually submitting to our brothers and sisters in the fear of the Lord (see Eph. 5:21).

The Almighty God wants his servants to stay pure, to keep us uncontaminated from sin. Preachers with a marked ministry anointing might be tempted to think that they don't need to submit to leaders they regard as less anointed. They are misinformed. Unfortunately, ministry anointing doesn't reveal maturity or a sanctified lifestyle. We currently access by grace what Jesus received by obedience, by fulfilling the Law for us (see Matt. 5:17, Rom. 10:4). Knowing this, Peter, after healing the lame man, said that his *godliness* didn't cause the miracle to manifest (see Acts 3:12). Ability to respect other ministers is a precautionary measure. If we carry the anointing, it will not exempt us from temptation or battling sin—the opposite is true. Regardless of how anointed you think you are, please consider that anointing never rules out basic biblical principles. This is a non-negotiable fact: All ministers need accountability, spiritually and practically. Jesus, after his baptism, before the launch of his official ministry, was *"full of the Spirit"* (Luke 4:1). After staying in solitude, in a desolate wasteland where he resisted the devil for forty days, he returned to Galilee *"in the power of the Spirit"* (Luke 4:14). Unlike Peter, Jesus' increased anointing didn't come from ministry. The Son of God got it through consistency and integrity because he withstood temptation, obeyed and pleased the Father. God's one and only Messiah showed a character beyond reproach. The Son met all the Father's strict conditions. When he left the Judean wilderness, it was apparent that he had passed the test with flying colours. Shortly after, Jesus began to minister with great power and authority when he entered the public sphere.

Some believers seem to have an anointing over their character due to faithful service and consistent living for years. They have the Father's approval stamped on them. These disciples may lack a long track record of signs and wonders, but people around them are stunned by their righteous living. They can testify how these pillars of faith lived through painful ordeals like sickness, personal loss, and gut-wrenching church splits. Despite traumatising circumstances, with tremendous stamina, they manage to maintain a high standard. The love and faith they radiate are undisputable signs, making people around them wonder. Anointed ministry can take you to a place of prominence, but consistent integrity allows you to exert a lasting influence. Stand your ground and stay well-connected. Success can pose a distraction and side-track even the strongest Christian. We want to model a coherent lifestyle where we glorify the Father. Sagacious leaders consistently and consciously surround themselves with a clever crew, not to make them look good but to make them better.

Apostolic structures

Apostles and prophets are the foundation of the Church, together with Christ, the Chief Cornerstone (see Eph. 2:20). How to best build on this firm foundation? We cannot see in the New Testament that the offices of the apostles and prophets were eliminated or removed. With the Body of Christ still residing on the planet, that is not likely to happen. I believe these to be logical arguments. It's unthinkable to have functioning churches without the fivefold. All ministry gifts and spiritual gifts will be operational until Jesus comes back for his bride. In my view, the facts speak for themselves. Kingdom ministry should be about how we represent Jesus, with no attention to titles or positions. Men and women of faith aspire to leave behind godly and good legacies. They focus on function, with no need for personal recognition.

Paul defined a future timeline where ministry gifts will operate within the Church (see Eph. 4:11-15). Don't forget that the early disciples of Christ didn't have the theology and traditions we have today. The Jewish Christians embraced a Hebrew mindset. They were well-acquainted with the [106]Tanakh and the teaching of Jesus and the apostles. Their perception of faith was *relational* since they still had notable apostolic leaders among them. Ministry gifts have elements of structure, direction and other inherent attributes. I am not referring to church structures, but spiritual DNA and its great importance. Let me illustrate: In a household, we have the loving authority of the parents. Their fundamental presence constitutes the environment and atmosphere we call home. Guidelines are good, but can never substitute father and mother, only add to or reinforce what they represent at home. Comparatively, attempting to replace apostolic authority and prophetic revelation with religious regulations or institutional structures is foolish and absurd. Ministry gifts define the nature of the Church in how they manifest Christ, biblical principles and prophetic patterns. I am convinced that flourishing churches prove the apostolic function to be present, whether acknowledged or not. Revival history shows that the apostles and prophets facilitated and sustained what the Holy Spirit so graciously brought. Many of these visionaries were also great teachers, evangelists and pastors. Evan Roberts was one of the trailblazers in The Welsh Revival, who carried great glory

---

[106] TANAKH תָּנָ״ךְ an acronym derived from the names of the three divisions of the Hebrew Bible: Torah (Instruction, or Law, also called the Pentateuch), Nevi'im (Prophets), and Ketuvim (Writings). **Source:** https://www.britannica.com/topic/Tanakh

and blessing in this mighty move of God. When critics attacked him for being at the forefront, he withdrew from his prominent place in the meetings. Roberts' decision was devastating because God's presence dissipated, and the revival ceased. Revival always comes with new faces, as visibility and responsibility go hand in hand. When a person spearheads a move of God, who are we to question the Holy Spirit? Instead, we should support leaders the Father uses as his vessels and vigorously shield them from demonic attacks through our constant prayers and respectful comments.

God gave me revelation about the new wineskin; I want to explain it. Jesus used it as a metaphor in Matt. 9:14-17 and Mark 2:22). We find two words for new in both texts. They describe new wine; in Greek *neos,* and new wineskins; in Greek *kainos*. Our Bible translations show no distinction between these, but they are keys to what Jesus communicated. The scribes claimed they rigorously adhered to the traditions received by Moses and accused Jesus of breaking them. On one occasion, they asked him why his disciples did not fast. He responded by relating to a wedding feast, the opposite of a fast! Did Jesus question fasting in general? No, but he did discuss its *application* and said it was a time of celebration, not mourning. In this scenario, he described himself as the Bridegroom, at the very centre of the party! Jesus continued by saying that one pours new wine into *new* wineskins. He compared it to mending clothes. Using unshrunk patches of fabric damages the garment, whilst an inexact application of God's Word wounds people since *"the letter kills, but the Spirit gives life"* (see 2 Cor. 3:6). Jesus reinterpreted the Scriptures in light of the prophetic and addressed the necessity for a renewed understanding of these. *The principle of God's Word is defined by the presence of the Spirit.* God's Spirit confirms his Word and vice versa. Israel moved with the pillar of cloud and fire. It illustrates how we can follow the prophetic Spirit. We navigate the various seasons ahead with his help (see Exod. 40:34-38). The new wineskin represents inherent structure and is connected to our hearts. New wine, however, points to the glory we are supposed to carry. Wineskins of leather required tender love and care, or else they would dry out and become old, hard and brittle. In lack of flexibility, the old wineskins would burst due to the new wine's expanding force. Jesus said that newly formed wine, in Greek νέος *neos*, has to be poured into renewed wineskins. The Greek καινός *kainos* means renewed. For basic pliability, the preferred treatment was soaking the wineskin first in seawater and then rubbing it with olive oil. Thus, the skin regained its capacity and softness.

Salty tears of remorse and the Holy Spirit's anointing oil bring renewal inside. Salt also refers to the irreplaceable and preserving power of God's Word (see Mark 9:49-50, Col. 4:6). Before a great movement of the Spirit, believers will travail in prayer, convicted of sin and how it pains the Lord. In the humbling process of confession and repentance, our hearts are being purified and softened—made ready for the new wine, the emerging move of his Spirit. The King will come in his majesty within an existing Kingdom culture. Churches that trust worldly systems yet insist on wanting the flow of the Spirit are defying his plans. Paying lip service is easy. The Most High never tolerates idolatry and leaves no stone unturned in his strides to align us with Heaven's norm for life and godliness. The everlasting and unshakeable kingdom will defeat every noxious entity that comes against it: *"Wherefore, receiving a kingdom that cannot be shaken, let us have grace, whereby we may offer service well-pleasing to God with reverence and awe: for our God is a consuming fire."* (Heb. 12:28-29 ASV).

The principle of God's Word is defined by the presence of the Spirit.

Apostolic expansion
Isaiah heralds the apostolic model:

> *"Sing, O barren woman, you who never bore a child; burst into song, shout for joy, you who were never in labour; because more are the children of the desolate woman than of her who has a husband," says the LORD. Enlarge the place of your tent, stretch your tent curtains wide, do not hold back; lengthen your cords, strengthen your stakes. For you will spread out to the right and to the left; your descendants will dispossess nations and settle in their desolate cities."* (Isa. 54:1-3 NIV).

The Jewish nation was designated to possess the vast landmass between the Nile and Euphrates, the land of Canaan, as their God-given inheritance. In this passage, the tent is the dwelling place and represents Israel's people. Prophetically, it points to the Church and how God instructed us to expand our allotted spiritual territory. *"See, I will make you into a threshing sledge, new and sharp, with many teeth. You will thresh the mountains and crush them, and reduce the hills to chaff."* (Isa. 41:15 BSB). We are to *occupy* until Jesus returns (see Luke 19:13). *Expansion* is natural; our destiny by faith is to *conquer* new areas of influence and regain lost territory. This concept foreshadows an apostolic blueprint and a biblical mindset. Another basic Kingdom principle is this idea: To become loving, we first need to release love by practising love. The next logical phase is to let release spiritual children into ministry because they are a natural continuation of the family. Previously, we looked at how to be trained in righteousness. We start to model and exemplify what we gain in our journey with the exalted Lord. It means that spiritual parenthood is not limited to imparting knowledge but also character-building: It disciples and disciplines. Paul instructed Timothy to entrust his ways in the Lord to reliable people, so *they* could teach others. Invest and release! His apostolic legacy could potentially impact four generations of believers (see 2 Tim. 2:2). History shows that a *continuation* rarely occurred, although there were [107]exceptions to the rule. The Church seems to have failed in passing on revival culture through spiritual fathers. Ancient Israel reflects the same depressing pattern. The nation served the Lord as a whole until the elders who had outlived Joshua withered away, those who *"had known the works of the Lord"*. (See Joshua 24:31). Three generations were impacted, except for the fourth. Sad to say, the next generation did not know the Lord (see Judges 2:10).

4 GENERATIONS OF BELIEVERS

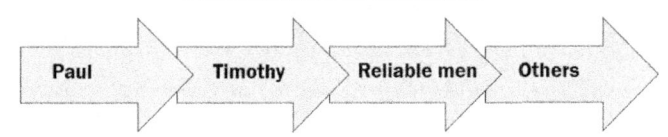

Paul → Timothy → Reliable men → Others

Invest to release: Teach the teachable who can teach others 2 Tim. 2:2

A steady declaration of his acts sustains an atmosphere where God continues to do miracles. *"One generation shall praise Your works to another And shall declare Your mighty acts."* (Psalm 145:4 NASB). By commemorating the Lord's majestic acts, we faithfully keep his testimonies. Declaring his testimonies while living consecrated lives, what can beat that? If we proclaim the fulfilled promises and believe that the Lord is still the same, he will continue to perform his mighty works. Stories about divine interventions are powerful, and the adversary fears our voices. If we forget to speak the truth Heaven revealed to us, we waste our boldness. Civil rights legend

---

[107] **The Moravian Community in Herrnhut**, Germany, had a prayer watch that lasted for 100 years. It started in 1727, and by 1765 this small group had sent our 300 missionaries to the ends of the earth. Ceaseless prayer sustained the constant fire of evangelism. Source: https://christianhistoryinstitute.org/magazine/article/one-hundred-year-prayer-meeting

Martin Luther King, Jr once said: 'Our lives begin to end the day we become silent about things that matter.' The eventful stories and chronicles from the Bible must echo through the nations; therein lies the future for our children.

Forgive my brief deviation: Today, some Christian movements emphasise the need for credible scriptural doctrine but fail to teach on the fivefold. Other movements concentrate on revelation knowledge, as well as the ministry gifts, yet lack a proper underpinning of solid theological truths. Professing believers frequently suffer from confirmation bias due to a rather poor discernment. Against better judgement, we tend to stand up for our favourite preachers or churches, often without researching the biblical basis of their held beliefs. It's silly how we let them escape our scrutiny because we are fond of them. Do we take doctrine lightly as long as these churches and ministries make us *feel* good? Feelings can be so misleading.

Many Christians stumble as they fail to do a proper exegesis of the Bible passages. Conversely, they misinterpret the meaning behind the words (see 2 Pet. 1:19-21). Is one of the results of this error that God's people perish for lack of understanding? (See Hos. 4:4-6). *"For a time is coming when people will no longer listen to sound and wholesome teaching. They will follow their own desires and will look for teachers who will tell them whatever their itching ears want to hear. They will reject the truth and chase after myths."* (2 Tim. 4:3-4 NLT). Teachers of God's Word will be judged more harshly than others (see James 3:1). All ministers ought to conduct themselves worthily regardless of age. If we please God by persevering in godliness, it will lead to tangible outcomes. Sanctified lives and holding fast to good doctrine results in eternal salvation for ourselves and those who hear us. On our journey with the Lord, let us zero in on progress, not human perfection. A little progress is far better than being stuck in the same rut as last week, month or year: *"Don't let anyone look down on you because you are young, but set an example for the believers in speech, in conduct, in love, in faith and in purity. Until I come, devote yourself to the public reading of Scripture, to preaching and to teaching. Do not neglect your gift, which was given you through prophecy when the body of elders laid their hands on you. Be diligent in these matters; give yourself wholly to them, so that everyone may see your progress. Watch your life and doctrine closely. Persevere in them because if you do, you will save both yourself and your hearers."* (1 Tim. 4:12-15 NIV).

PROGRESS

PERFECTION

Let us revisit Isaiah 54. Who will do the stretching of the Tent? It is the *children* of the promise, not the parents! They are competent, as they have been educated in the things of the Lord. *"All your children will be taught by the Lord, and great will be their peace."* (Isa. 54:13 NLT). A fivefold vision will thrive in an authentic apostolic climate. Empowerment results in prosperity and development. Gone is the curse of spiritual barrenness. However, if we fail to care for people and don't give them room to function in their callings and gifts, they will usually choose to vacate the Tent, or the House, which causes a decrease rather than an increase. *"My tent is destroyed, and all my cords are broken; my children have gone from me, and they are not; there is no one to spread my tent again and to set up my curtains. For the shepherds are stupid and do not inquire of the Lord; therefore they have not prospered, and all their flock is scattered"* (Jer. 10:20-21 ESV). Every generation desperately seeks validation, to be seen, heard and respected. Those who pursue love and affirmation will journey wherever they find nurturing leaders. Feeling significant is biblically related to both sonship and royalty. Wise shepherds manage to pastor churches while infusing hope and purpose. Their behaviour preserves loving and lasting relationships within the community as they earnestly seek God's counsel and invest in their congregations. Stupid shepherds are aloof and unconcerned, but skilful pastors listen to the flock. They *include* and *empower* those they serve. Avoiding an attitude of 'us and them' demonstrates a model where leaders serve with humility. However, leaders who shut down the prophetic voice or fail to provide pastoral care cause members to get hurt and leave the fellowship.

Stupid shepherds are aloof and unconcerned, but skilful pastors listen to the flock. They include and empower those they serve.

If members have no say in important matters, it creates discontent. It's not wise for leaders to run a church by executive decisions. A better approach is a partnership, where leaders include members in the decision-making processes. After consulting within their fellowship, the Jewish leaders of the Jerusalem church could advise the growing churches of the Gentiles, saying: *"For it seemed good to the Holy Spirit and to us to lay no greater burden on you ..."* (Acts 15:28 NLT). The 'us' or 'we' spoke for the majority of the members. They were in absolute harmony with their leaders and had no dissent. The believers were gathered in one accord and united through the Holy Spirit. Such unity can only manifest when we concentrate on a love for God's Word, his presence and the people created in his image (see Acts 2:42). Risks are always involved when starting a new church. It usually takes time to establish and grow it, despite thoughtfulness, genuine passion and a precise apostolic perspective. Some members will stay, and others will move on. Some leaders will leave, but others will join the community. When planting a church, we must be careful not to treat it as our pet project, as our brothers and sisters should share ownership of the vision. It's easy to become emotionally attached but harder to let go of control. However, we can surrender our plans to the Lord through prayer. He will help to protect what he birthed through us. Still, it is wrong to see ourselves as unique and irreplaceable, unrivalled in our insight on the fivefold. The Father cares more for his Church than we—he will pick whomever he approves of to bless our fellowship to complete it. God typically invades our comfort zone. Leaders need to get their rough edges filed away and learn to trust others and be less suspicious. It's much better to maintain meaningful relationships with faithful friends who challenge us and not prefer those who try to impress us. *"Wounds from a sincere friend are better than many kisses from an enemy."* (Prov. 27:6 NLT).

Healthy fivefold churches, stripped of a controlling leadership, can be difficult to find. Right now, these kinds of churches are enormously scarce. God needs to raise them up as an answer to focused prayer. Churches with defined apostolic structures adequately empower their members and reproduce new leaders all the time. How these churches view leadership is irrespective of family ties, academic background or ordination but based on humility, maturity and calling. Quintessential factors that make these congregations trustworthy and relevant are transparency, accountability and team consciousness. They work because they treat men and women equally and celebrate cultural and racial diversity. It often results in multi-ethnic leadership, at least in larger cities. Simeon, called Niger, was most likely black and a prominent leader in the church at Antioch (see Acts 13:1-2). This rare breed of fivefold leaders encourages fellow Christians to serve the Lord in their capacities by giving them room to bloom and thrive.

A picture of how fivefold leadership is supposed to function is a large tree with deep roots. The foundation of the apostles and the prophets—together with the other fivefold offices—is the vast root system, as they stabilise and nurture the tree. All the ministry gifts are essential to the church's inner life but seem more subtle at times. Within a fivefold church, its leaders can be hard to pinpoint because they like to stay low-key. Being unpretentious and likeable, they aren't vying for attention or craving special treatment. Nor do they cover up private insecurity by jockeying for positions or flashing neat, showy business cards with eye-catching titles. Their top priority is equipping and maturing the church. The flock recognises these shepherds through the relaxed and loving authority they radiate. Undoubtedly, hierarchical top-down structures regularly get pummelled by organic frameworks that better represent the Kingdom of God. A flat leadership structure relies on mutual respect and humility, where all five ministry gifts work together as a team.

Wise and visionary leaders try to draw attention away from themselves. They want to help believers to flow with the Holy Spirit the way they do. If leaders encourage a model of servanthood and partnership, it allows for the local church to be united and strengthened. I like the following quote: 'If serving is beneath you, leadership is beyond you.' We rebuff self-centred ambition when we foster a wholesome culture of honour, impartial love and generosity. Because selfishness discourages growth, church leaders should be mindful not to put themselves forward at the expense of others. Sensible leaders happily lead from behind, not visibly at times, knowing they inspire confidence by helping others. They come alongside friends who need input and assistance. A fivefold leadership culture requires sacrifice and dying to self. That might be unappealing to people who love the limelight but dislike the hard work.

In Christ, we become to let others become. By faith, through God's grace and love, we constantly seek to empower others. We model to reproduce, build to expand and create to inspire. Churches with an apostolic mindset bravely demonstrate all these attributes.

CHAPTER 11 - PROPHETIC PARTNERS

Women in ministry

The topic of women in ministry is so important that I would be remiss if I failed to mention it in this book. I don't present an in-depth study, but my brief contribution to the subject. I believe in apostles, prophets and even female pastors; hence I risk being labelled by some as a heretic, despite my solid Pentecostal background. Those who disagree are free to refute me without presenting their preconceived notions.

Before I begin to teach about women in ministry, let me underline some points:

A) My objective is not about women's or human rights issues, although these are vastly important.
B) Neither will I discuss so-called equality nor inclusion or the need to being culturally relevant in today's society.
C) The overall focus is a biblical approach to how women can serve the Lord and fulfil their calling.

I don't want you to misread the title of this chapter. It doesn't at all suggest women are inferior. *Partner* means that women have the same value, significance and access to ministry gifts as men. But not all churches share my view. When looking at today's situation, I feel compelled to address this situation further. In general, Christianity has some female preachers and pastors, but women aren't always treated fairly or unbiased. Many women doubt their entitlement to preach, teach or prophesy in the churches they belong to. Do we have a Scriptural basis for women ministering in the Church on equal terms with men? We will soon answer this question. Several churches, especially some of the *conservative* evangelical ones, deny women the right to preach, teach or be ordained for ministry. I find the very nature of this dilemma heart-rending because most of the churches' members are women. Are there logical reasons to deprive these gems of the opportunity to edify the Body of Christ? Some pastors excuse themselves by saying that women get permission to share some Bible verses or sing. Would it be impertinent of me to ask where the fine line goes between testifying and teaching dogma? Besides, the gospel itself is filled with teaching about the virgin birth, the death and the resurrection of Christ and other biblical truths.

If women quote Bible verses systematically and consistently, it might be regarded as teaching—even if it's just testimonies.

I also take issue with churches that shut out women from the leadership team. Some church movements will not ordain women as ministers, let alone give them a leading role. They prefer an enclave of male clergy because they are adamant that the Bible strictly supports men as leaders. Do we understand that the early Christians didn't build biblical leadership models overnight? Some believers think they can pick and choose from the Book of Acts, as they reckon it contains a blueprint for authentic Christianity. Yet they refuse to examine its content in a timewise or cultural context. Christians who applaud the Jerusalem church's handling of poverty by distributing goods to those in need but think of the apostolic ministry as a relic is a case in point. The leaders who dismiss female leadership tend to reinterpret and reinvent passages in the New Testament to justify their own bigoted views. Nevertheless, we should consider that new leadership structures evolved over time. It's wise to ponder how some of the held views are not set in stone and thus could be debated and revised.

Please forgive my little rant: If we don't want to reconsider our stance, it proves that we regard personal opinions more than genuine respect for God's Word. Not being properly grounded in truth may easily backfire at us, despite all our good intentions. It's pivotal to think through *what* we believe and *why* we believe it. [108]*Reductionism* will jumble our beliefs because we forget to think through the more complex issues. As for contested topics, we may end up oversimplifying, parodying and distorting relevant facts. It also explains why Christian hecklers revile and ridicule those they disagree with because of their intolerance. Such arrogant bullying is inexcusable, as every human has an intrinsic and eternal value in God's eyes. If a debate is heating up, it's tactful to disagree without being disagreeable. I vouch for a deep clean of the house of God, a detox cleanse of the Body of Christ due to the confusion we face! We need a healthy relationship with God because of notable worldwide challenges.

---

[108] **Reductionism:** Theological reductionism in Christian Theology is cutting down the Christian revelation to suit one's own theory. According to M.A. Smith, Marcarion, whose heretic sect exhibited traits of Gnosticism, was an early example of a reductionist in this respect.
Source: www.conservapedia.com/Reductionism

Some believers mix faith with heresy, politics or patriotism. Recently, we could see how many [109] prophetic ministries got carried away by a deluded sense of superiority and faulty judgement. A majority of these refused to humble themselves and repent of their apparent mistakes (see Rev. 2:20-22). Shouldn't their demonstrable lack of accountability be a big red flag to us? The Bible says that *"judgement begins with the house of God"* (1 Pet. 4:17). *"But when we are judged by the Lord, we are disciplined so that we may not be condemned along with the world."* (1 Cor. 11:32 NIV). True repentance helps us to rethink, re-evaluate and readjust our attitudes. Unwillingness to change, or lack of modesty, shows that we don't fear the Lord (see Psalm 55:19).

We should consider that new leadership structures developed over time.

THINK OUTSIDE THE SQUARE & THINK INSIDE GOD'S GRACE

Profound thinking is rare—the same goes for Christianity. We usually parrot what we have already been taught rather than exploring truth at a more fundamental level, and we are certainly not the first ones behaving this way. *So Jesus said to the Jews who had believed him, "If you abide in my word, you are truly my disciples, and you will know the truth, and the truth will set you free."* (John 8:31-32 ESV). Quite a few Jews were convinced that Jesus was the Messiah, but their mindset was trapped because they resisted the truth that could liberate them. For our mindset to change, we must daily cleanse our souls by redirecting our attention to God and his Word:

"This book of the law shall not depart from your mouth, but you shall meditate on it day and night, so that you may be careful to do according to all that is written in it; for then you will make your way prosperous, and then you will have success." (Jos. 1:8 NASB).

---

[109] **Source:** https://religionunplugged.com/news/2021/4/28/charismatics-issue-prophetic-standards-to-address-false-trump-prophecies

"Therefore put away all filthiness and rampant wickedness and receive with meekness the implanted word, which is able to save your souls." (James 1:21 ESV).

Success is proclaiming, pondering and practising God's Word. Healthy habits build our faith and make us catalysts for change. The Israelites connected [110]truth to God's Word and the importance of knowing the completeness of it, both the content and the context. *"The sum of your word is truth"* (Psalm 119:160). Where, when and how Hebrew letters and terms appear in the original texts are clues to consistent patterns of revelatory theology. The Scripture has marvellous secrets enshrined: Layer upon layer, truth upon truth and concept upon concept (see Isa. 28:10). The Jewish sages and scribes were sticklers for detail and meticulously counted every letter, dot and dash to preserve the biblical manuscripts with accuracy. As skilful craftsmen, curates and custodians of truth, they were mandated by God to make a stellar effort. We are indebted to their sacrifices. Jesus confirmed the Law and the Prophets down to each pen stroke and symbol and made a point of this sacred tradition (see Matt. 5:17-18).

The heroes and heroines of faith encountered God's presence and sought personal growth while meditating on God's majesty: *"I will reflect on all You have done and ponder Your mighty deeds."* (Psalm 77:12 BSB). With our new and upgraded status as Kingdom citizens comes wisdom, knowledge and clever thinking—inspired by the Holy Spirit and his immeasurable mind (see 1 Cor. 2:9, 16). To distil spiritual revelation into more understandable truths is never wrong. Thinking godly and creatively reflects Christlike virtues and is something we should pursue. A number of the early church fathers and Christian mystics were brilliant thinkers. These

---

[110] **Tav.** "Tav is the last letter of the Hebrew word emet, which means 'truth'. The midrash explains that emet is made up of the first, middle, and last letters of the Hebrew alphabet (aleph, mem, and tav: **אמת**). ... Thus, truth is all-encompassing, while falsehood is narrow and deceiving." Source: en.wikipedia.org › Taw ›.

luminaries glorified God with their thoughts, commonly expressed through their impressive dissertations. In his excellent book, 'The Divine conquest', A. W. Tozer cites a passage from a beautiful masterpiece called [111]The Athanasian Creed. It really captured my attention the first time I read the portion because it is an amazing feat! The creed reveals staggering insight with its ability to explain complex theological truths in just a few words:

"There is one Person of the Father, another of the Son: and another of the Holy Ghost."

"But the Godhead of the Father, of the Son, and of the Holy Ghost, is all one: the Glory equal, the Majesty co-eternal."

"And in this Trinity, none is afore, or after other: none is greater, or less than another; But the whole three Persons are co-eternal together: and co-equal."

"So that in all things, as is aforesaid: the Unity in Trinity, and Trinity in Unity is to be worshipped."

Women in ministry: The Old Testament on the subject

Well, let us move on with our argumentation regarding women in ministry. The Lord created the man, Adam, and then fashioned Eve, the woman, as a good partner and companion to him. Did he create an inferior helper? No, he made an *equal* and a *friend*. Due to sin, the woman became subject to the man's rule. That was a curse not intended by God. Male domination became a part of the same curse. In Christ, God restored the order of creation. Now, the woman is redeemed back to a pre-fall state. (See 1 Cor. 11:10-13, Gal. 3:26-28, Eph. 5:21-33). Deborah, the prophet and judge, was chosen by God along with other leading women (see Judges chapter 4-5).

---

[111] **Comment:** The creed was probably first written in the fifth century. Some propose the seventh century, since there is no historical record of the creed until 633 at the fourth council of Toledo. Originally it was written in Latin and not in Greek. Several possible authors from the fifth century come to mind—these persons were influential thinkers of their time, including Ambrose of Milan and Augustine of Hippo. Its author was most likely the French saint, Vincent of Lérins. **Source:** www.ligonier.org/learn/articles/athanasian-creed/

> The late apostle-prophet [112]Jill Austin wrote this:
> *"What did Deborah do? She moved in government. She is what you call a fivefold minister. The Lord is raising up women as apostles, prophets, teachers, evangelists, and pastors. Yes, there is a corporate apostolic anointing that is starting to move, and we will all move in it like Christianity 101. This is a realm where the government and weight of God comes, and people get saved, healed and delivered. That is part of what is moving now, but God is also moving people into office."*

Let the Deborahs of our time arise! Joel's prediction pointed to a time when women would prophesy and preach. It foretold the woman's elevated status under the New Covenant (see Joel 2:28). Christ removed the curse from the Garden and *reinstated* the woman as an equal to the man. It didn't translate into visible reality all at once but implied an *ongoing restoration* process. Christian men practically assume their God-given responsibility by reassuring that gifted women are loved, acknowledged and included in ministry. Encouragement should lead to hands-on and productive results. More men need a conscious ability to take a step back, so women can flourish in their capacities. To exercise these gifts more frequently and with confidence, even some pastors' wives could need an extra push from their spouses.

Women in ministry: The New Testament on the subject

Mary, the sister of Martha and Lazarus, sat down at Jesus' feet and received teaching. To be tutored was usually a privilege accessible to men since women were precluded. At a very young age, Paul sat at Gamaliel's feet and was supervised and educated by a renowned and revered rabbi (see Acts 22: 3). Jesus was a recognised rabbi as well, although he lacked the traditional background. He commended Mary's teachability and changed the social and spiritual rules for rabbinic tradition in the society of his day (see Luke 10:38-42). When Jesus aptly remarked that Mary had chosen *"the best part"*, he praised how she valued God's Word with top priority. However, Martha was stressed out to no avail, as she too could have paused her busy serving and taken a breather while enjoying her Master's anointed teaching. The Lord loves when we rest and spend time in his presence.

---

[112] **Quote from August 8, 2006:** elijahlist.com/words/display_word/4364

שְׁמַע יִשְׂרָאֵל יְהוָה אֱלֹהֵינוּ יְהוָה אֶחָד

Hear, O Israel: The LORD our God, the LORD is one.

Jesus treated women with dignity and respect. The story about the woman caught in adultery illustrates this beautifully (see John 8:1-11). The section isn't included in the oldest Greek manuscripts but belongs to the New Testament majority text. By most scholars it is rated as genuine. Additional passages confirm Jesus' regard and respect for women (see Luke 7:36-50, John 4:1-42). Jesus validated women's status as reliable witnesses in society by first revealing himself as the resurrected Lord to the ladies. The famous disciple Mary Magdalene was one of them. Jesus had cast out seven demons from her (see Matt. 28:1-8, John 20:11-18). Following the Pentecost event, women gradually emerged as leaders within local churches. In Rom. 16:1-2, Phoebe presided over a congregation, or church, in her house and is described with *diakonos* and *prostatis*. Διάκονος *diakonos* is affiliated with serving as a minister or messenger and *prostatis* with leadership. The mistaken belief that women couldn't pastor coloured our modern translations, like the ESV. So, the translators preferred second-class wordings like helper, benefactor or patroness. Hence, Christian women shouldn't accept being patronised. Pun intended. Προστάτης *Prostatis / proistēmi / proistamenous* is 'to stand before or stand at the head of'. The second verse applies the feminine variation of the word (see also Rom. 12:8, 1 Thess. 5:12).

Another scenario further piqued my interest: Priscilla, and her spouse Aquila, took Apollos aside and *"explained to him the way of the Lord more accurately."* (Acts 18:26 ESV). Did Priscilla upskill a recognised male teacher? How outrageous! Or is it? Luke, the author of Acts, failed to mention why Priscilla taught, maybe because her ministry was very well-known and acknowledged. Junia and Andronicus were said to be *"outstanding among the apostles"* (see Rom. 16:7). Junia, from Joanna, was not masculine but a feminine name. I wonder if these two apostles were [113]a married power couple. We cannot know for sure, but Junia was definitely not a man!

---

[113] **My comment:** While some scholars think they were married, Andronicus may also have been a brother or another relative of Junia.

Some theologians find the mere proposal distasteful: [114]*Female apostles!* Countless preachers never bother to consider the thought, as the idea falls outside the scope of their imagination. Circular arguments are quite common among preachers stuck in a particular lane of reasoning. Far too often, we tend to ignore historical context or testimonies. It beats me. Albeit disputed, is it right to exclude women from apostolic ministry? [115]Photene, or St. Photina, was known as the Samaritan woman at the well (see John 4). Christian tradition details that she had an impactful apostolic ministry. She preached all around—including Carthage and Smyrna, in Asia Minor—where she finally was martyred. In Phil. 4:2, Paul discussed Euodia and Syntyche. He asked a brother for assistance to reconcile these sisters because they probably had a fallout. Perhaps they exercised leadership at some level in the church at Philippi? Their tasks could have included administration, preaching, prophesying or teaching.

Difficult scriptures explained

Let us look at 1 Cor. 14:34-35. We must relate to biblical texts within their context, and this passage discussed the need for order when the church convened. Strangely enough, some theologians use the text to entertain the idea that a woman can't be permitted to teach or preach at church. I guess they suffer from poor interpretation skills. The women and children were probably seated separately from the men in the Corinth church, not unlike the synagogues. That might explain why some women shouted to their husbands during the services, as they were eager to understand the meaning of some of the words or expressions used by the visiting preachers. To talk loudly was indecorous, as banter interfered with the meetings. Therefore, it makes sense that Paul addressed this noise issue.

Let us examine another passage, 1 Tim. 2:11-15. Because of its relation to Creation and its seemingly ecclesiastical character, many consider this scripture to be more complex. Ecclesiastical truths define major church doctrines in the New Testament context. Christian leaders have often used the quite bewildering passage to diminish women's central role in the Church. Some scholars conclude that Paul, in a highly

---

[114] **Healing evangelist Maria Woodworth-Etter** was clearly an apostle. She has been called the 'grandmother of the Pentecostal Movement'. She exercised tremendous spiritual authority. See: https://www.newlifepublishing.co.uk/articles/maria-woodworth-etter-the-mother-of-pentecost/

[115] **St. Photina.** Source: http://www.orthodox.net/questions/samaritan_woman_1.html

dogmatic way, prohibited women from any form of public ministry or teaching the Word of God. It seems to me that own biases and lack of basic skills to understand texts and interpret the New Testament revelation explain why they readily misapply these verses. Consider that in both his letters to Timothy, Paul addressed rampant heresies and their imminent threat to the house churches at Ephesus. Is this passage prescriptive in denying women the right to preach? Absolutely not, as Paul probably tried to rectify a specific situation where some women brought false teachings.

It's noteworthy that Paul referred to the order of Creation by saying that Adam was first formed, then Eve. Why is this significant? [116]Gnostic teachings, or Gnosticism, were widespread. Gnostic, from the Greek *gnosis*, means knowledge. Biblical stories were frequently circulated and taken out of context. One of these teachings was the beguiling [117]'Eve myth'. According to this myth, Eve animates Adam's passive body into a living soul and first emerges herself as the living embodiment of the Female principle. She then creates the life of the male and becomes both his daughter and his mother. The awful myth sustained the concept of Eve being superior to Adam. Paul had to battle heresies at the time of the first Church. Since Ephesus was the religious seat of the Artemis cult, with pagan priestesses and prostitutes, it's realistic that some women broadcast their Gnostic 'revelation' to the Christian community. New Age philosophies and political activism have usurped many Western churches. Today, we also encounter other epidemic falsehoods—like hyper-grace, hyper-love, Cessationism and replacement theology. In the passage, the word used for authority [118]αὐθεντέω *authenteó* literally means to domineer. Paul didn't allow women to treat men dismissively, all the while disseminating false doctrines. Viewing the passage within the context of heresy, rebellion, and witchcraft makes Paul's severe reaction more understandable. Allow me to add that a cherished preacher friend of mine made me aware of that these verses specifically concentrate on *married* women. The mention of childbearing in verse 15 corroborates his valid claim. In verse 12, the

---

[116] **Gnosticism** is a collection of religious ideas and systems that originated in the first century AD among early Christian and Jewish sects. Various groups emphasised personal spiritual knowledge over the orthodox teachings, traditions, and authority of the Church. Source: en.wikipedia.org
My comment: Gnosticism denied the deity of Christ and mixed Greek philosophies (e.g. Plato) with other pagan origins or Jewish myths.
[117] **The Eve Myth:** The source I had when I began writing this book is unfortunately lost.
[118] **Strong's Greek Concordance #831. Source:** biblehub.com/greek/831.htm

apostle says: *"I do not permit <u>a woman</u> to teach or to assume authority over a man ..."* Paul confirmed how the man is the head of the woman, tasked by God to be the leader of the marital relationship. To lecture one's husband is opposed to the divine order of Creation (see also 1 Pet 3:1-6). By graciously submitting to his authority, she permits Christ to correct her spouse in case the man is misinformed. After all, it's Christ who governs the man, but also the Church. In another passage, Paul talked about the use of head coverings in Corinth. It mostly related to decency and how the wife could show regard for her husband (see 1 Cor. 11:2-16). In compliance with Greek culture, she thereby paid respect to authority in general. This mentality also dictated how women prophesied or taught in the local churches. God is a God of order. Hence Paul appropriately instructed the congregations to show discretion by honouring marriage and respecting governing bodies. The crux of the matter wasn't whether a woman could or should preach or prophesy, but it was *how* she did it. Christians were key influencers of the culture, for Jews and Gentiles alike. As such, Paul advised redeemed men and women to conduct themselves in the best possible manner to wisely promote the gospel within the traditional cultural boundaries.

The apostle eloquently expressed the same principle: *"Finally, brethren, whatever is true, whatever is honourable, whatever is right, whatever is pure, whatever is lovely, whatever is of good repute, if there is any excellence and if anything worthy of praise, dwell on these things."* (Phil. 4:8 NASB). Revival culture typically integrates all these indispensable aspects. One of the contributing factors to Christianity's growth was a blameless lifestyle, what we usually associate with sanctification, but also miracles and providing for the marginalised and poor. These are good conservative values most cultures think highly of, like charity, love for family and decent behaviour. God displayed his glory through Christian communities full of integrity and power.

I reckon that preparation for revival and expansion should lead to a simplification of existing structures in the churches' charities. One example is help to financially destitute people, who most likely will suffer because of bureaucracy and prolonged handling of cases. Intricate structures tend to hamper ministry to our communities. Besides, budgets should demonstrate the heart of the church and be administrated by a few responsible members who can act swiftly on behalf of the congregation. It's worth mentioning the US revival that occurred through the Brownsville Assembly of God, in Pensacola, Florida, in 1994. Many of the city's bartenders and strippers within the sex industry were saved during this revival and therefore had to quit their demeaning jobs immediately. The hosting church collected vast sums of money to contribute financially to these and others who needed emergency help. In the Book of Acts, we find an organic and efficient model. How the Jewish mother church of Jerusalem dealt with the poverty-stricken had a monumental impact:

"They devoted themselves to the apostles' teaching and to fellowship, to the breaking of bread and to prayer. Everyone was filled with awe at the many wonders and signs performed by the apostles. All the believers were together and had everything in common. They sold property and possessions to give to anyone who had need. Every day they continued to meet together in the temple courts. They broke bread in their homes and ate together with glad and sincere hearts, praising God and enjoying the favour of all the people. And the Lord added to their number daily those who were being saved." (Acts 2:43-47 NIV).

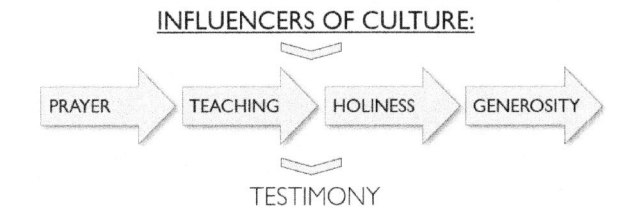

INFLUENCERS OF CULTURE:

PRAYER → TEACHING → HOLINESS → GENEROSITY

TESTIMONY

Concerning the New Testament text, how do we view the above passages about women in ministry? We interpret them by using several criteria:

1) Can other scriptures help us to interpret the more difficult ones?

We have seen how important it is not to take portions of the Bible out of their given context. One passage of Scripture will usually explain another because God's Word contains clues to knowledge. If we study a subject, there are passages of Scripture that shed light on the more difficult verses. We can only receive revelation through a close relationship because *"the fear of the Lord is the beginning of wisdom."* (Prov. 9:10, Psalm 25:14). God Almighty, in his great mercy, hides certain truths that could otherwise be unbearable for an unrepentant person. For this very reason, Jesus often made use of parables (see Matt. 13:11-15). Revelation and responsibility go hand in hand—God requires more of those who know more (see Luke 12:48, John 16:12). We shall find if we truly seek. However, the quest for knowledge cannot be our only goal. As beloved sons and daughters, we have embarked on a love adventure where personal encounters with the living God are within reach!

2) In which context was the content written or expressed?
When examining the Bible, this aspect is also crucial. Ministers and Christians who lack curiosity and passion for learning routinely forget to contextualise. On a broad range of topics, lethargy and a twisted approach could stop us from getting increased insight. At times, it's convenient to analyse sacred Scripture by resorting to personal speculations and stereotyped sentiments because we are settling for second-hand knowledge. Ignorance often leads to arrogance. If spiritual truths were that simple to grasp, we wouldn't have been instructed to ask for wisdom and revelation by:

A) *making our ears attentive,* B) *inclining our hearts,* C) *crying for discernment,* D) *pleading for insight,* E) *seeking it as silver* (Prov. 2:2-5). The Bible cleverly mentions that: *"It is the glory of God to conceal things, but the glory of kings is to search things out."* (Prov. 25:2 ESV).

Lack of discernment has led to unnecessary division in the Body of Christ because of misapplications of spiritual truths. Insecure leaders are guilty of these offences, being fixated on having right rather than doing right. Speculations about doctrines have superseded relationships and reduced churches to echo chambers for the like-minded. Division is the result when pride and misleading religious spirits dominate. Back in the '70s and the '80s, Scandinavian Pentecostal churches expected women to wear head coverings, like hats etc. One misappropriated Pauline texts in a bid to lecture women for no apparent reason. Believers were wronged, and non-believers got exasperated by it. These incidents cast a shadow on the Jesus movement and the radical overhaul the Lord desired for his Church. On hearing this, millennials would wag their heads in disbelief. By reading the four gospels, we find that some of Jesus' comments referring to traditions received from Moses—like the many observances connected to the temple—now are moot and irrelevant. Of course, they were all pertinent to the Jewish setting Jesus spoke into, and we can learn from them. To do some good research about the ancient cultural environment, represented within the framework of the Scripture, is wise. We should also pray for the Holy Spirit to guide us *"into all the truth"* (see John 16:13). Truth exceeds letters. We should worship both *"in Spirit and in truth"*. Prolific worship is to encounter and know God and the fullness of him (see John 4:24, 2 Cor 3:6). Jesus said: *"The words I have spoken to you—they are full of the Spirit and life."* (John 6:63 NIV).

Revelation and responsibility go hand in hand—God requires more of those who know more.

3) Can the conclusions we make when we review a particular text be confirmed by the overall teaching on the subject?
Some teachings, which deprive women of ministry and leadership, depend entirely on a single verse or maybe a few Bible verses. In lockstep with heretic tradition, some preachers refuse to include sentences before or after the passages they love to quote. Let alone do they compare these verses to the New Testament revelation as a whole. To me, the inability to decipher details creates distortions and shows contempt for biblical texts. When the Berean Jews listened to Paul's talks, they were wise enough to search the Scriptures daily (see Acts 17:11). Because of some renowned pastors' views, should we accept teachings based on shoddy guesswork? Why are some men unreservedly stuck in their ingrained prejudice against women? Go figure! Some of the Christians who oppose female preachers or pastors will do whatever they can to besmirch them by bringing up their past, if they are [119]divorced and remarried, etc. Sadly, they refuse to hold their male favourite preachers to the same strict standards. The following illustration explains hypocrisy, although in a simple and satirical way.

MISOGYNY IN MINISTRY

Preacher (Unloving): "She has had seven demons!"

Teacher (Judging): "She is a woman..."

---

[119] Recommended article: preachitteachit.org/ask-roger/detail/how-do-we-handle-divorce-and-remarriage-issues-in-our-church/

Prophetic discernment is more needed in the Church than ever. A hypothesis may sound polished, persuasive and spiritually correct but prove to be inaccurate. With today's technology, YouTube videos or PowerPoint presentations can be sleek and professionally put together yet deceiving and misleading. We should all the more evaluate the teaching but also test the spirit behind it. Testing the spirits is critical and not inferior to other revelation gifts. Our souls get drenched with the Spirit of Truth when we pray and read the Scripture consistently. That gives us a heightened awareness of the spiritual dimension. We then begin to sense what the Lord thinks.

4) When an explanation is shared, is it being received with peace and joy by the hearer?

Some may object and say: What do feelings have to do with God's Word? This isn't about subjective feelings or attitudes for or against biblical truths. Our focus should be responsiveness to the Holy Spirit and what he endorses. Traditions and practises contrary to God's heart should create a sense of uneasiness or dissatisfaction in us. God, the Father, created us to react to a wrong spirit or behaviour contrary to his presence. We have, as Christians, accepted mediocre standards and often ignored his promptings because of the pervasive tolerance for religious or political spirits. Some believers get vexed on hearing revelatory preaching, a fact that should concern us! The same people may sit and listen to tedious and repetitive religious entertainment for hours on end, but find it hard to endure five minutes of anointed speech. I have observed this inconsistency first hand. Maybe the Lord has to 'comfort the afflicted and afflict the comfortable?' In order to wake us up from a false sense of peace, God, in his mercy, sometimes shakes us to the core. He will try to warn us through our intuition, or inner radar, to prevent us from ending up in spiritual captivity. If we neglect our spiritual health, our internal faculty of attentiveness and sensitivity will malfunction. But the Holy Spirit testifies with life, joy and peace within us when we are aligned with his blessed Word (see Rom. 8:16). If we stay *fine-tuned* to his voice, we learn to value what he thinks of as spiritually palatable and to disregard the rest.

In light of the texts we have reviewed, I think it's safe to include women in the same kind of ministry in the Church that men currently access. To deprive women of that privilege and right must be considered unbiblical, as well as inhuman. It should, of course, be self-evident that we first thoroughly examine those we entrust with public speaking or leadership, man or woman. Biblical records, and historical sources, show that God, without any exceptions, equipped women for fivefold ministry.

Some Christian leaders still struggle with the concept of female ministers in our local churches. A related question is: Can women serve as senior pastors or as bishops and even apostolic overseers? Of course, our answer depends on what *lens* we interpret reality through. It's fascinating how God equipped women during revivals with mantles of leadership. History proves that every time the move of God cooled off, men almost always banished women from prominent positions. It indicates a battle since time immemorial and that the spirit of this age vehemently decries powerful Christian women. The accuser vividly recalls the prophecy from the Garden: *"... and I will put enmity between thee and the woman, and between thy seed and her seed: he shall bruise thy head, and thou shalt bruise his heel."* (Gen. 3:15 ASV). The global Antichrist spirit of the worldly networks fights all attempts to initiate and advance a further release of women into their identity or God-given destiny (see 1 John 4:3). A woman bore the promised Messiah, and throughout history, numerous women birthed revivals through their fervent prayers. When God poured out his Spirit, men and women ministered as equals, side by side. Sons and daughters were prophesying, an attested pattern. Do we long to see a sustained and prolonged movement of the Holy Spirit? That isn't likely to happen unless brave women exercise their gifts and influence. I encourage Christian men to demonstrate spiritual responsibility and stand shoulder to shoulder with women so they can broadly thrive and excel in all areas of Kingdom ministry. It all brings us back to Genesis, where God called the man and the woman to fulfil their mission together:

Then God said, "Let us make man in our image, after our likeness. And let them have dominion over the fish of the sea and over the birds of the heavens and over the livestock and over all the earth and over every creeping thing that creeps on the earth." (Gen. 1:26 ESV). *"There is neither Jew nor Gentile, neither slave nor free, nor is there male and female, for you are all one in Christ Jesus."* (Gal. 3:28 NIV).

The circle has finally been completed through Christ, our Saviour. Let us keep it unbroken and faithfully serve the Lord with one heart and one mind.

WOMEN EMPOWERMEN

CHAPTER 12 - PROPHETIC POWER PRAYERS

Inspirational prayers from the Bible

Personal edification through devotions is fundamental, and the Bible is full of great prayers. Every time we pray, we inspire faith and build a closer friendship with God. Ministry was supposed to flow out of intimacy. While you pray, ask the Holy Spirit to give you increased revelation and a deeper relationship with the Father. He longs to pour his love upon you and renew you from glory to glory. I have picked thirty-one prayers, one for each day of the month. You can use these selected prayers and blessings as they are, verbatim. If you wish to make them more relatable, you may also insert your own name. Praying God's Word is a powerful tool in building our faith! Many of these prayers I know by heart, and they have blessed me for years and still do. We set our hearts on pilgrimage to encounter the Holy One through prayer, praise and proclamation! God bless you as you pray and worship!

The Aaronic blessing

And Jehovah spake unto Moses, saying, Speak unto Aaron and unto his sons, saying, On this wise ye shall bless the children of Israel: ye shall say unto them, Jehovah bless thee, and keep thee: Jehovah make his face to shine upon thee, and be gracious unto thee: Jehovah lift up his countenance upon thee, and give thee peace. So shall they put my name upon the children of Israel; and I will bless them. (Num. 6:22-27 ASV).

The Aaronic blessing

יְבָרֶכְךָ יְהֹוָה , וְיִשְׁמְרֶךָ

Ye-va-re-che-cha YEHOVAH ve-yeesh-me-re-cha
The LORD bless you and keep you

יָאֵר יְהֹוָה פָּנָיו אֵלֶיךָ , וִיחֻנֶּךָּ

Ya-er YEHOVAH pa-nav e-le-cha vee-choo-ne-ka
The LORD make his face to shine upon you and be gracious to you

יִשָּׂא יְהֹוָה פָּנָיו אֵלֶיךָ , וְיָשֵׂם לְךָ שָׁלוֹם

Yee-sa YEHOVAH pa-nav e-le-cha ve-ya-sem le-cha sha-lom
The LORD lift up his countenance upon you and give you peace

I have cited the Aaronic blessing in Hebrew. The *ch* has a guttural sound—like the German *Bach* and Scots Gaelic *loch*. Also, I have replaced the traditional Adonai with God's literal name, Yehovah. As mentioned earlier, his name isn't ineffable. It appears thousands of times in the Old Testament. More about the Lord's name is in chapter 9. We discussed the prayer of Jabez in chapter 1 because of his significant testimony. It seems like Jabez wanted to extricate himself from pain and break the curse of feeling hopeless and stuck in the same place. This prayer is incredible!

1. Prayer for blessing and freedom from trauma
Jabez was more honourable than his brothers. His mother had named him Jabez, saying, "I gave birth to him in pain." Jabez cried out to the God of Israel, "Oh, that you would bless me and enlarge my territory! Let your hand be with me, and keep me from harm so that I will be free from pain." And God granted his request. (1 Chron. 4:9-10 NIV).

2. Prayer for protection
O LORD, how many are my foes! Many are rising against me; many are saying of my soul, "There is no salvation for him in God." Selah But you, O LORD, are a shield about me, my glory, and the lifter of my head. I cried aloud to the LORD, and he answered me from his holy hill. Selah I lay down and slept; I woke again, for the LORD sustained me. I will not be afraid of many thousands of people who have set themselves against me all around. Arise, O LORD! Save me, O my God! For you strike all my enemies on the cheek; you break the teeth of the wicked. Salvation belongs to the LORD; your blessing be on your people! Selah (Psalm 3 ESV).

3. Prayer in times of despair
How long, O LORD? Will You forget me forever? How long will You hide Your face from me? How long must I wrestle in my soul, with sorrow in my heart each day? How long will my enemy dominate me? Consider me and respond, O LORD my God. Give light to my eyes, lest I sleep in death, lest my enemy say, "I have overcome him," and my foes rejoice when I fall. But I have trusted in Your loving devotion; my heart will rejoice in Your salvation. I will sing to the LORD, for He has been good to me. (Psalm 13 BSB).

4. Prayer for God's presence
A miktam of David. Keep me safe, my God, for in you I take refuge. I say to the Lord, "You are my Lord; apart from you I have no good thing." I say of the holy people who are in the land. "They are the noble ones in whom is all my delight." Those who run after other gods will suffer more and more. I will not pour out libations of blood to such gods or take up their names on my lips. Lord, you alone are my portion and my cup; you make my lot secure. The boundary lines have fallen for me in pleasant places; surely I have a delightful inheritance. I will praise the Lord, who counsels me; even at night my heart instructs me. I keep my eyes always on the Lord. With him at my right hand, I will not be shaken. Therefore my heart is glad and my tongue rejoices; my body also will rest secure, because you will not abandon me to the realm of the dead, nor will you let your faithful one see decay. You make known to me the path of life; you will fill me with joy in your presence, with eternal pleasures at your right hand. (Psalm 16 NIV).

5. Prayer for integrity
"Who can discern his errors? Declare me innocent from hidden faults. Keep back your servant also from presumptuous sins; let them not have dominion over me! Then I shall be blameless, and innocent of great transgression Let the words of my mouth and the meditation of my heart be acceptable in Your sight, O LORD, my Rock and my Redeemer." (Psalm 19:12-14 ESV).

6. Prayer for guidance
"Show me your ways, LORD, teach me your paths. Guide me in your truth and teach me, for you are God my Saviour, and my hope is in you all day long. Remember, LORD, your great mercy and love, for they are from of old." (Psalm 25:4-6 NIV).

7. Prayer for forgiveness and cleansing
"Have mercy upon me, O God, according to thy lovingkindness: According to the multitude of thy tender mercies blot out my transgressions. Wash me thoroughly from mine iniquity, And cleanse me from my sin. For I know my transgressions; And my sin is ever before me. Against thee, thee only, have I sinned, And done that which is evil in thy sight; That thou mayest be justified when thou speakest, And be clear when thou judgest. Create in me a clean heart, O God; And renew a right spirit within me. Cast

me not away from thy presence; And take not thy holy Spirit from me. Restore unto me the joy of thy salvation; And uphold me with a willing spirit." (Psalm 51:1-4, 10-12 ASV).

8. Prayer for godly fear
"Teach me your way, O LORD, that I may walk in your truth; unite my heart to fear your name. I give thanks to you, O Lord my God, with my whole heart, and I will glorify your name forever." (Psalm 86:11-12 ESV).

9. Prayer for Zion
"But You, O LORD, sit enthroned forever; Your renown endures to all generations. You will rise up and have compassion on Zion, for it is time to show her favor—the appointed time has come." (Psalm 102:12-13 BSB).

10. Prayer for the peace of Jerusalem (Yerushalayim)
Pray for the peace of Jerusalem: "May they prosper who love you. May peace be within your walls, And prosperity within your palaces." For the sake of my brothers and my friends, I will now say, "May peace be within you." For the sake of the house of the LORD our God, I will seek your good. (Psalm 122:6-9 NASB).

11. Prayer for purity
"Search me, O God, and know my heart; test me and know my anxious thoughts. Point out anything in me that offends you, and lead me along the path of everlasting life." (Psalm 139:23-24 NLT).

12. Prayer for healing
"Heal me, LORD, and I will be healed; save me and I will be saved, for you are the one I praise." (Jer. 17:14 NIV).

13. Prayer for revival
"I have heard all about you, LORD. I am filled with awe by your amazing works. In this time of our deep need, help us again as you did in years gone by. And in your anger, remember your mercy." (Habakkuk 3:2 NLT).

14. The Lord's Prayer
"After this manner therefore pray ye. Our Father who art in heaven, Hallowed be thy name. Thy kingdom come. Thy will be done, as in heaven, so on earth. Give us this day our daily bread. And forgive us our debts, as we also have forgiven our debtors. And bring us not into temptation, but deliver us from the evil one." (Matt. 6:9-13 ASV).

15. Prayer for boldness and miracles
"Now, Lord, consider their threats and enable your servants to speak your word with great boldness. Stretch out your hand to heal and perform signs and wonders through the name of your holy servant Jesus." (Acts 4:29-30 NIV).

16. Doxology I
Oh, the depth of the riches of the wisdom and knowledge of God! How unsearchable his judgments, and his paths beyond tracing out! "Who has known the mind of the Lord? Or who has been his counsellor?" "Who has ever given to God, that God should repay them?" *For from him and through him and for him are all things. To him be the glory forever! Amen.* (Rom. 11:33-36 NIV).

17. Trinitarian blessing
"May the grace of the Lord Jesus Christ, and the love of God, and the fellowship of the Holy Spirit be with you all." (2 Cor. 13:14 NIV).

18. Prayer for spiritual wisdom
"Ever since I first heard of your strong faith in the Lord Jesus and your love for God's people everywhere, I have not stopped thanking God for you. I pray for you constantly, asking God, the glorious Father of our Lord Jesus Christ, to give you spiritual wisdom and insight so that you might grow in your knowledge of God. I pray that your hearts will be flooded with light so that you can understand the confident hope he has given to those he called—his holy people who are his rich and glorious inheritance. I also pray that you will understand the incredible greatness of God's power for us who believe him. This is the same mighty power that raised Christ from the dead and seated him in the place of honour at God's right hand in the heavenly realms. Now he is far above

any ruler or authority or power or leader or anything else—not only in this world but also in the [120]world to come. God has put all things under the authority of Christ and has made him head over all things for the benefit of the church. And the church is his body; it is made full and complete by Christ, who fills all things everywhere with himself." (Eph. 1:15-23 NLT).

19. Prayer for glory
"For this cause I bow my knees unto the Father, from whom every family in heaven and on earth is named, that he would grant you, according to the riches of his glory, that you may be strengthened with power through his Spirit in the inward man; that Christ may dwell in your hearts through faith; to the end that you, being rooted and grounded in love, may be strong to apprehend with all the saints what is the breadth and length and height and depth, and to know the love of Christ which passes knowledge, that you may be filled unto all the fullness of God. Now unto him that is able to do exceeding abundantly above all that we ask or think, according to the power that works in us, unto him be the glory in the church and in Christ Jesus unto all generations for ever and ever. Amen." (Eph. 3:14-21 ASV).

20. Prayer for perseverance and strength
"For this reason, since the day we heard about you, we have not stopped praying for you. We continually ask God to fill you with the knowledge of his will through all the wisdom and understanding that the Spirit gives, so that you may live a life worthy of the Lord and please him in every way: bearing fruit in every good work, growing in the knowledge of God, being strengthened with all power according to his glorious might so that you may have great endurance and patience ..." (Col. 1:9-11 NIV).

21. Prayer for love and discernment
"And this is my prayer: that your love may abound more and more in knowledge and depth of insight, so that you may be able to test and prove what is best and may be pure and blameless for the day of Christ, filled with the fruit of righteousness that comes through Jesus Christ, to the glory and praise of God." (Phil. 1:9-11 BSB).

---

[120] **My comment:** World, from the Greek αἰώνιος *aionos* means age, which some translations use.

22. Prayer for increased love

"Night and day we pray most earnestly that we may see you again and supply what is lacking in your faith. Now may our God and Father himself and our Lord Jesus clear the way for us to come to you. May the Lord make your love increase and overflow for each other and for everyone else, just as ours does for you. May he strengthen your hearts so that you will be blameless and holy in the presence of our God and Father when our Lord Jesus comes with all his holy ones." (1 Thess. 3:10-13 NIV).

23. Prayer for holiness and wholeness

"Now may the God of peace Himself sanctify you entirely; and may your spirit and soul and body be preserved complete, without blame at the coming of our Lord Jesus Christ. Faithful is He who calls you, and He also will bring it to pass." (1 Thess. 5:23-24 NASB).

24. Prayer for a godly lifestyle

"So we keep on praying for you, asking our God to enable you to live a life worthy of his call. May he give you the power to accomplish all the good things your faith prompts you to do. Then the name of our Lord Jesus will be honoured because of the way you live, and you will be honoured along with him. This is all made possible because of the grace of our God and Lord, Jesus Christ." (2 Thess. 1:11-12 NLT).

25. Prayer for increased love and faith

"I always thank my God, remembering you in my prayers, because I hear about your faith in the Lord Jesus and your love for all the saints. I pray that your partnership in the faith may become effective as you fully acknowledge every good thing that is ours in Christ." (Philemon 4-6 BSB).

26. Prayer for Covenant blessing

"Now may the God of peace, who through the blood of the eternal covenant brought back from the dead our Lord Jesus, that great Shepherd of the sheep, equip you with everything good for doing his will, and may he work in us what is pleasing to him, through Jesus Christ, to whom be glory for ever and ever. Amen." (Heb. 13:20-21 NIV).

27. Prayer for guidance
Instead, you ought to say, "If it is the Lord's will, we will live and do this or that." (James 4:15 NIV).

28. Blessing and assurance
"And the God of all grace, who called you to his eternal glory in Christ, after you have suffered a little while, will himself restore you and make you strong, firm and steadfast." (1 Pet. 5:10 NIV).

29. Doxology II
"Now to him who is able to keep you from stumbling and to present you blameless before the presence of his glory with great joy, to the only God, our Saviour, through Jesus Christ our Lord, be glory, majesty, dominion, and authority, before all time and now and forever. Amen." (Jude 1:24-25 ESV).

30. Blessing - Grace, mercy and peace
"Grace, mercy, and peace will be with us, from God the Father and from Jesus Christ the Father's Son, in truth and love." (2 John 1:3 ESV).

31. Prayer for Christ's return
He who testifies to these things says, "Yes, I am coming soon." Amen. Come, Lord Jesus. The grace of the Lord Jesus be with God's people. Amen. (Rev. 22:20-21 NIV).

Printed in Great Britain
by Amazon